Managerial Economics

BARRON'S BUSINESS LIBRARY

Managerial Economics

Holley H. Ulbrich
Mellie L. Warner
College of Commerce and Industry
Clemson University

New York • London • Toronto • Sydney

All inquiries should be addressed to:
Barron's Educational Series, Inc.
250 Wireless Boulevard
Hauppauge, New York 11788

Library of Congress Catalog Card Number 88-18390

International Standard Book Number 0-8120-4182-8

Library of Congress Cataloging-in-Publication Data

Ulbrich, Holley H.
  Managerial economics / Holley H. Ulbrich.
      p. cm. — (Barron's business library)
  ISBN 0-8120-4182-8
  1. Managerial economics. I. Title. II. Series.
HD30.22.U33 1990
338.5′024658—dc20   89-18390
                                          CIP

PRINTED IN ITALY

Preface

A book on microeconomics, or preferably managerial economics, belongs in the library of any business manager. Economics bears the same relationship to management that physics does to engineering, or psychology to education, or political science to public administration. It provides the basic theoretical tools and principles that appear, over and over again, in a thousand different situations and problems. To think like an economist is to weigh the costs and benefits of alternative courses of action, to choose the best, or optimum, cost, to follow a decision through its primary and secondary effects, and to be attuned to the self-interested motives and responses of customers and suppliers.

All business is built on an economic foundation. Thus, a broad knowledge of basic economic theory—demand and supply, elasticity, production costs, competition and monopoly—will enhance the value of the other books in this series. In addition, business managers need to know something about the workings of the labor market in which they buy as well as the international marketplace in which their firms buy, sell, and cope with international competition. As citizens, as well as taxpayers and representatives of firms subject to government regulation, managers need to know something about the economics of government, too.

Economics in its original incarnation was the study of household management, so the term *managerial economics* may sound a bit redundant. In the last century, however, the term *management* has become most frequently associated with running business firms of various sizes, and managerial economics has emerged as a specialized branch of economics that looks at the working of markets and the making of economic decisions from the particular perspective of the business firm. Virtually all other courses and textbooks in economics adopt the perspective of the household as worker, citizen, and consumer, so it is always a challenge for economists to abandon this usual viewpoint and shift to that of another group of very important participants in the market, managers of business firms. We found the opportunity to do so an interesting challenge and a rewarding experience.

This book is not "all you ever wanted to know about economics." It is, rather, a foundation on which to build your knowledge of economics and related business disciplines, with topics carefully selected for their relevance to business management. We encourage you to further your education both with the suggested readings in the final chapter and the other volumes in this series.

We would like to thank our husbands, Carl and John, for their patience and support during this project; Tom Friedlob, general editor of this series, for his support and encouragement; and Christine Ulbrich for assistance in preparing the numerous graphs that are the stuff of which economics is made.

HOLLEY ULBRICH, Ph.D.
MELLIE WARNER, Ph.D.

Contents

BARRON'S BUSINESS LIBRARY

Managerial Economics

Basic Concepts: Economic Content and Method

INTRODUCTION AND MAIN POINTS

In 1976, the science of economics shared with the United States of America a bicentennial anniversary. The book that marks the establishment of economics as a separate discipline, British economist Adam Smith's *Wealth of Nations*, was published in the same year as the U.S. Declaration of Independence.

Adam Smith was interested in economic growth, and he saw the use of markets as an effective way to accomplish that purpose. Thus, he advocated a public policy of minimum government in every sphere—*laissez-faire*, "let them be." Let the market work, he wrote, let the invisible hand of competition and self-interest make decisions. Economics began as a rationale for a public policy of letting business firms do their own thing, and do it well, with minimum government intervention.

In the two intervening centuries, economics has taken a much closer and more systematic look at how business operates. What began as a descriptive science in the 19th century has developed into a management tool. Economists not only observe how business firms maximize profits, they also develop methods that help business managers do a better job of controlling costs, analyzing markets, and increasing profits. Today, economics is a policy-oriented social science as well as an essential tool of business management.

After studying the material in this chapter:

■ You will be able to explain what economics is and how it is useful for business decisions.

■ You will be able to identify the basic components of an economic model and to understand how such models are used.

■ You will be able to interpret a simple economic graph.

■ You will be aware of the limitations of economic method.

■■ You will understand the basic principles of choice that govern economic decisions—opportunity cost, maximizing and minimizing, and deciding at the margin.

WHAT IS ECONOMICS?

Economics is the study of how decisions are made about the allocation of scarce resources among competing uses. Some of these decisions are made by individuals (or households) in deciding how to spend their income, how many members of the household should work and at what kind of job, whether to lend money or to buy stocks or bonds, and even how to allocate the scarce time of household members so as to make sure that the household chores get done. Governments, likewise, make many decisions about allocating resources. They decide what share of people's incomes to tax in order to pay for public goods and services, and what combination of military, welfare, education, and other services to provide.

Business firms decide what productive resources to purchase, how to combine them to produce output, and what mix of goods and services to produce. (While businesses come in all sizes and forms—including partnerships, proprietorships, corporations, branch plants, and franchises—economists refer to any particular business enterprise as a business firm or just a firm.) Obviously, business firms are guided in making their decisions by the availability of resources from households and by the preferences of households for different kinds and amounts of goods and services.

Economics is divided into two major subareas, microeconomics and macroeconomics. Microeconomics is concerned with the decision-making process of individual firms and households—how much labor to buy, how many hours to work, whether to buy cake or doughnuts, how far to live from work, where to locate a plant. Macroeconomics deals with the sum total of those individual decisions—total output, total employment and unemployment, the price level rather than individual prices. A rise in the price of butter is microeconomic; a rise in the price of the average market basket of goods bought by households is macroeconomic. Unemployment in the auto industry is microeconomic, while the fraction of the entire labor force that is not working but actively seeking work is a macroeconomic concern. Although macroeconomics gets most of the attention in the newspaper and on the evening news, microeconomics explains how day-to-day decisions are made that then add up to the aggregates that make the headlines. This book is only concerned with the microeconomics of individual decisions.

It is possible to view microeconomics from the perspective of either the consumer or the firm. Most introductory economics books are designed for college or high school students and look at the economy from the perspective of the consumer/worker, who is selling labor and purchasing goods and services in the marketplace. The consumer/worker must understand not only how the household decision process works, but also what is happening in the business firms on the other side of the market. Managerial economics, which looks at the economy from the perspective of the firm, covers many of the same topics in microeconomics as a book aimed at the consumer/worker, but with a difference in emphasis and in the kinds of examples used. This book is an introduction to managerial economics—microeconomics for the business owner or manager.

USING ECONOMICS FOR MANAGEMENT DECISIONS

The hard core of microeconomic theory is maximizing and minimizing. Getting the most output out of available resources, getting a given level of output at the lowest resource costs, maximizing profits, minimizing losses—all these decisions are the bread and butter of microeconomics. Households try to maximize satisfaction out of a given level of income, or they try to minimize the cost of buying the goods and services they want. A government that is responsive to citizens and voters will try to provide a given level of public services at a minimum tax cost or, alternatively, to try to get the most possible public services out of a given level of taxes.

Maximizing and minimizing are also the central problems facing the business firm. Should the firm hire another worker or put some of its present workers on overtime? Which choice will minimize the cost of producing the desired extra output? Should this firm expand its present plant size or build a second plant? If interest rates go up, how will that affect the optimal level of inventory? What if this firm does so well that competitors are attracted to the market—how can it protect its market share?

All of these questions are implicitly asking how to minimize costs or losses, or maximize output or profits. Although many of these are applied management questions, the foundation for the answer is always in microeconomic theory. As you learn some microeconomic theory, you will see that there are some fairly standard techniques for maximizing and minimizing that apply to all kinds of problems facing business firms, households, and government.

ECONOMIC THEORIES, MODELS, AND THE REAL WORLD

The real world in which households, business firms, and governments meet in order to engage in production and exchange is very cluttered with detail. If economists concentrated on including all the details, they would quickly lose sight of the forest for the trees. It would be impossible to see the patterns of similarity between one firm's decisions and another's, let alone the similarity between the decision-making practices of households and business firms. In order to focus on the essential features of individual economic behavior, economists develop models. An economic model is a simplified representation of reality, much like a scale model of a housing development or a simple model airplane.

The most famous microeconomic model is supply and demand. Demand expresses how much buyers (usually households) want to buy at various alternative prices, while supply shows how much producers will offer for sale at various prices. The analysis of market behavior with supply and demand makes certain assumptions about the behavior of households that underlie the demand curve,[1] and about how costs change as output expands or contracts on the supply side. Based on those assumptions, the simple supply-and-demand model can be used to predict what happens to prices and quantities if other conditions change. By the end of this book, you will be familiar with dozens of useful applications of this one simple model.

Economic models express theories about relationships between two or more variables in the form of graphs or equations. Theories can be very complex, such as the theory of relativity, or they can be very simple, such as the child's theory that if I pull the cat's tail, it will scratch me. The foundations of the supply-and-demand model are in theories about how households and firms make choices. In general, theories consist of assumptions and hypotheses, first, then the predictions or conclusions that follow from those assumptions, much like the proofs you learned in geometry class. A theory should be testable. That is, it should be possible to check it against the facts and see if it is an accurate predictor. If it is, then it is a good theory. If it isn't, back to the drawing boards!

HOW ECONOMISTS USE GRAPHS AND STATISTICS

Most people associate economics and economists with endless graphs and statistics. It is true that economists tend to approach almost every problem by drawing a graph, because graphs in economics are simple and convenient ways to represent theoretical models. The supply-and-demand model is very cumbersome in words and numbers and very intimidating in algebraic equations, but a supply-and-demand graph is a compact way to represent a very complex reality.

A simple supply-and-demand model is shown in Figure 1-1. The horizontal axis measures the quantities people wish to buy or sell at the various prices measured on the vertical axis. The demand curve, labeled D, slopes down from left to right, indicating that this buyer or group of buyers will purchase smaller quantities at higher prices and larger quantities at lower prices. For example, at a price of $4.00 Townville's citizens are willing to buy only 200 movie tickets a week, but at a price of $1.00 they will buy 1000 tickets a week. The supply curve (S) slopes upward from left to right, reflecting the fact that sellers will offer more at higher prices. Perhaps the movie theater will add extra showings if they can command a higher ticket price. We will be seeing this model often throughout this book.

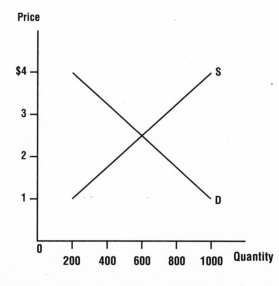

FIG. 1-1 *A Simple Supply and Demand Model*

Microeconomic theory is particularly full of simple graphs such as Figure 1-1. If you have forgotten how to draw graphs— something most people learn to do in high school algebra—you may want to review it. Generally you can pick up the knack with the first few graphs.

In microeconomic theory, you will see many hypothetical numbers—prices, output numbers, cost figures—for imaginary firms or households making their decisions. (Macroeconomics, in contrast, is more likely to use real numbers, such as the price level, the federal budget deficit, or the unemployment rate.) Figure 1-1 uses hypothetical numbers. You will need to substitute your own numbers in these examples in order to make your own microeconomic decisions.

HOW ECONOMISTS SOLVE PROBLEMS

The economist is an academic counterpart to the plumber or the auto mechanic. Faced with a problem, the economist carries a kit of analytical tools around and pulls out the one most likely to address the problem successfully. In microeconomics, that tool is most often a supply-and-demand model, although there are also a variety of other tools for special purposes.

Suppose, for example, you asked an economist to help you choose between two plant sites. This problem was chosen because we have not yet developed any models to use, and choosing a plant site lends itself to a tool or technique widely used by noneconomists as well—cost-benefit analysis. While we will not use cost-benefit analysis very much in this book, most people use it as a handy approximation for more sophisticated economic approaches to making choices among alternatives. Thus, it provides a useful illustration of an economic approach to problem-solving.

The economist would begin by asking your help in identifying all the costs and benefits that you find to be associated with each alternative site. These might include access to materials and transportation, property taxes, availability of water, size and quality of the local labor force, proximity to markets, and availability of additional land for expansion. Then the economist would attempt to measure all the costs and benefits in dollar terms. If one site involved a longer commuting distance for managers, for example, the economist would place a dollar value on the extra time and expense as a cost of that location.[2] When the inventory of the current dollar value of costs and benefits of each site is complete, the economist will be able to offer a comparison of the two alternatives for you to use in making your site decision.

LIMITATIONS OF ECONOMICS

Economics cannot, ultimately, make decisions for you. There are too many subjective, nonquantifiable factors that enter into business decisions. Economics can only help you evaluate the measurable part. For example, suppose that a household was trying to decide whether the wife, who has been caring for the couple's preschool children, should get a job outside the home. This is a very economic decision. The economist can estimate her potential present earnings after taxes as well as the increased future earnings that will come from additional work experience, balanced against the costs of day care, commuting, clothing, and even the cost of replacing some part of her time in household production. But no economist can compare the satisfactions and frustrations of working versus staying home to raise children, because that is highly subjective and varies greatly from individual to individual. Likewise, an economist can demonstrate to you that a Canadian vacation would be less costly in terms of time and money than a trip to Europe, but that may be irrelevant if you have an overpowering urge to stand in St. Peter's Square in Rome!

Such subjective elements exist in business as well as household decisions. Many firms are located where they are because of the owner's preference for a particular region or urban environment, or because of other conditions that cannot be expressed in quantifiable terms. The combination of products produced should reflect consumer preferences, but it may also reflect the owner's preference for what he or she thinks the firm should be making. Subjectivity plays a smaller role in most business decisions than in household decisions, however. A business firm that insists on "doing its own thing" rather than responding to consumer preferences will experience losses and ultimately go out of business. However, there are still subjective choices that can be made by firms, such as product names and colors, plant location, hiring graduates of certain colleges, and other considerations that are small enough in their impact on output, sales, and profits to persist over long periods of time.

Subjective preferences are the most important limitation on the usefulness of economics, but they are not the only limitation. Economists' models are simplified representations of reality. If they were not simplified, they would be too cluttered to be very useful for prediction and control. But the simplifications themselves can limit the predictive power of these models. The most important simplification in economics is called *ceteris paribus*, which is a Latin expression for "other things being equal."

Suppose that a cost-benefit analysis convinced you to locate your plant at Site B in State X. You did, and you lost your shirt. Your competitor chose the alternative site in State Y and prospered. What went wrong? The economist made some assumptions that certain factors would not change, and they did. Perhaps the markets that were close to your site evaporated as a major employer in the area decided to relocate. The tax breaks that were offered by State X may have been rescinded during a budget crunch. The analysis does not carry an implied warranty. Instead, like a pack of cigarettes, economists' predictions and recommendations should carry a warning: Failure to observe the ceteris paribus limitations of this model could be hazardous to your financial health!

Ceteris paribus conditions are particularly important in supply-and-demand models. A widely discussed and distressing prediction among college administrators in the 1980s was based on the declining number of high school graduates. The college population would decline, they thought; small colleges would be forced to close, and tuition would rise very slowly. This prediction was not fulfilled. Instead, with smaller families, a larger percentage of high school graduates could afford to go to college. Increased enrollment by nontraditional (older) students also helped to fill classrooms and keep up demand.

This latter example also illustrates another problem faced by economists; self-fulfilling and self-negating prophecies. When college administrators read these dire predictions, they took defensive actions. They developed aggressive recruiting strategies and packaged financing options that enabled students with lower incomes to attend college. They marketed their services to a nontraditional clientele through continuing education programs and by offering classes at times convenient for working adults. Thus, the prophecy was at least partly proved wrong because it provoked a defensive response on the part of colleges.

Economists' prophecies can also be self-fulfilling, particularly in the stock market and commodities markets. A predicted grain shortage and higher bread prices can immediately drive up the price of grain both now and in the future as grain users scramble to assure safe supplies. Comedian and talk show host Johnny

Carson once started a rumor about an impending shortage of toilet paper that sent buyers scrambling to the store shelves and, at least temporarily, created the predicted shortage!

As long as you are aware of such limitations, economics can be a very useful way of organizing information that you can use to help you make better (i.e., more profitable) business decisions. As we develop the tools of managerial economics, we will be careful to stress the limitations of our models as well.

INTRODUCTION TO CHOICE

Most of the material in this book is about choice—how to make profitable choices, how people and firms actually choose in practice, and how changes in the rules of the game affect the choices people make. We will therefore conclude this introductory chapter with a summary of some of the basic elements of consumer and producer choice.

Getting the Most/Spending the Least

One basic element of choice has already been introduced. The decision rule for both households and business firms (and even government) is a maximizing or minimizing rule. Consider the household first. Consumers (households) want to maximize the income they can earn out of their available stock of productive resources. Alternatively, the household may try to earn a given level of income with the minimum amount of productive effort. The first way of looking at the problem defines it as a maximizing problem; the second, a minimizing problem.

Once the household's income has been determined, the next goal is to use that income to obtain the maximum possible level of satisfaction through the consumption of goods and services. Any given shopping trip, however, can be viewed as a maximizing or a minimizing problem. You can go to the supermarket with the goal of getting the most value or satisfaction out of a $100 expenditure (maximizing) or with the goal of getting a satisfactory week's groceries for the minimum dollar outlay (minimizing).

Finally, the household makes several sets of choices simultaneously. Since one of the "goods" households normally want to consume is leisure time, a decision to earn more and spend (or save) more is a decision to enjoy less leisure. Furthermore, if some of the income is saved rather than spent, it can be used to acquire other earning assets. The savings of the households can be put into certificates of deposit or bonds, or invested in owner-ship rights (such as stock) in firms to earn a future income stream of interest and dividends. Maximizing and minimizing over time is a complicated process.

The same kinds of choices face business firms even though they are operating on the opposite side of the market. While households sell the services of productive resources (chiefly labor but also other resources), firms are buyers of the services of these resources. The household buys final goods and services. The firm sells goods and services to households. What are the maximizing/minimizing decisions facing the firm?

The firm wishes to acquire the necessary productive resources at minimum cost. Often the firm can use resources in different combinations. It may be possible to pick apples with many work-ers and very little capital equipment[3] (ladders and baskets) or with sophisticated picking equipment and few workers. If work-ers are cheap and capital is expensive, the firm will use more labor-intensive methods; if workers are relatively expensive, the firm will switch to methods using relatively more capital in order to economize on the high-priced labor.

The firm also has to make choices about how much to pro-duce and, if it produces several products, about the mix of output as well. Should the dairy produce more cheese and less butter, more skim milk and less yogurt? What level of output and what combination of products will maximize revenue?

Once again, the buying decisions (hiring workers and buying capital equipment and materials) and the selling decisions (how many units of output and in what combination) are not indepen-dent of each other. The level of output to be produced will determine how many productive resources (or inputs) are needed. The prices of productive resources relative to the price that can be received for their output will determine how many units the firm will produce. Maximizing and minimizing both take place in the firm on both sides of the market at once.

Money Costs and Opportunity Costs

For both households and firms, making wise decisions requires a clear understanding of the terms "cost" and "price." What does it cost a student to go to the movies the night before a final exam? It costs not only $4 for the movie ticket but also two hours of the time that could have been spent in studying. Thus, part of the movie's cost may be a letter grade in the course! The *opportunity cost* of anything is the value of the next best alternative forgone.

Suppose you start a small business producing craft items for sale. At first you run this business out of the spare bedroom of your home, using your time, some capital equipment and raw materials, and one helper. It's easy to measure income from sales. But how do you determine the cost in order to measure your profit? If you only measure the price of your helper's time, raw materials, and capital equipment, you are missing some important items. One is the value of your own time. If you were not investing this time in the business, you could have been earning money elsewhere. Those forgone earnings are an *opportunity cost* of this trade or business.

Another cost is the value of the next best alternative use of your spare bedroom. Perhaps it would not have generated a money income, but it could have been used as a study or a guest room or to provide one of your teenage children with a separate bedroom—all uses with a positive value. The one of those uses with the highest value represents the opportunity cost of using the room for business purposes. We will return to the problem of measuring costs in Chapters 6 through 8.

Deciding at the Margin

Most choices, economic or other, that are made by consumers, workers, or managers of firms are not of the all-or-nothing, once-in-a-lifetime variety. Occasionally there is such a momentous decision—whether to change jobs, get married, relocate, buy a house, enter a new business, or build a new plant. The plant site example in this chapter was such a decision.

Most decisions, however, are much less momentous—how to spend the next dollar or the next hour, whether to hire the next worker, whether to expand the product line to include one more variety or to produce one more run. Most decisions fall into this category. Economists refer to such "next" or "extra" decisions as decisions at the margin. The term *marginal*, in economics, does not mean "borderline" or "of poor quality," but simply "next" or "extra." Marginal decisions determine whether the household or firm is indeed maximizing its output, income, satisfaction, or profit. Will one more hour of income add more to my satisfaction than the value of leisure forgone? Will hiring one more worker add more to costs or to revenue—will it increase or decrease profits? Most of microeconomic analysis is marginal analysis. You will be encountering marginal decisions frequently throughout the rest of this book.

CHAPTER PERSPECTIVE

This chapter sets the stage for an understanding of the decisions that firms make in production and sales, including the contexts in which those decisions are made. Economics is about choices and how choices are made in firms and households. Economists describe those choice-making processes through models that are based on theories. Often these models are described with the aid of graphs and statistics. Models are simplified representations of reality that help to clarify the central decision-making process. The usefulness of models is limited by the inability to measure many subjective factors, by ceteris paribus assumptions, and by self-fulfilling and self-negating prophecies. With these limitations, these models can still be very useful in describing how firms and households minimize costs or losses and maximize satisfaction, output, or profits. In the maximizing and minimizing process most decisions are made at the margin, and it is important to have an adequate measure of opportunity cost.

FOOTNOTES

1 *The reader may be puzzled to see these relationships described as "curves" then see straight-line demand and supply "curves" throughout this book and, indeed, most introductory books in economics. A straight line is a special case of a curve. In reality, some demand curves and supply curves are straight lines, and others are not. It is conventional to refer to the supply function and the demand function as supply curves and demand curves, rather than supply lines and demand lines.*

2 *Some costs and benefits are current, while others are in the future. What is the value of tax breaks to be received five years down the road? A technique known as discounting, which is covered in a later chapter, is used to convert future dollars into current ones for purposes of comparison.*

3 *Capital, in economics, refers to any man-made means of production, ranging from simple tools to roads, factories, and sophisticated communications systems.*

Participants in a Market Economy: Households, Firms, and Government

CHAPTER 2

INTRODUCTION AND MAIN POINTS

The previous chapter identified households and firms as the principal actors in a market economy. This chapter provides a closer examination of how households and firms interact in a market economy, and introduces an important third participant—government.

After studying the material in this chapter:

■ You will be able to explain how self-interest, property rights, and competition make a market economy function.

■ You will be able to describe the workings of a market economy with a circular flow diagram.

■ You will understand the roles of the household and the business firm in a market economy.

■ You will be able to distinguish between the three basic forms of firm organization—partnership, proprietorship, corporation—and identify the advantages and drawbacks of each.

■ You will know what basic role a government performs in a predominantly private, market economy.

MARKET VERSUS NONMARKET ECONOMIC SYSTEMS

The market system is not the only way to determine what is produced and who gets it. In fact, other ways of allocating goods and services have played a larger role in history and continue to play a larger role in many other countries. There are three dominant ways to decide how to allocate scarce resources and distribute output, income, or goods and services among households. One is tradition; a second is command; and the third is the market. All three methods coexist even in modern capitalistic economies. Tradition continues to dominate peasant societies, and command plays the lead role in most centrally planned economies (e.g., the Soviet Union, Poland, Cuba).

Tradition means doing what you did last year and what your parents did before you. In a traditional economy custom governs the kind of work individuals perform, the crops they raise, and their shares of the output. Feudal Europe was governed by traditions about the nobleman's share of the crop, obligations for military service from peasant to lord to king, and the peasant's rights to protection and to use of the mill and other equipment. Some elements of tradition persist in modern societies; children often feel pressure to enter their parents' trades or businesses, and certain occupations are traditionally designated female (such as nursing and teaching). Tradition is a workable method of making economic decisions only in small societies in which change and growth are very slow. For urbanized and industrial societies, which tend to experience rapid growth and technological change, other methods of making decisions are required that are more adaptable to changing circumstances.

Command means that decisions are made by the government. Some central plan or authority determines the desired size and composition of output and how it is to be distributed. Some elements of command decision-making are found even in capitalistic economies such as the United States. There are aspects of command in taxation and public production, although the public sector accounts for only about one-third of total output. At the microeconomic level, command is reflected in government constraints on the kinds and amounts of output individuals can produce and the conditions under which it can be sold. For example, it is illegal to grow marijuana, to operate a taxicab in New York without a license, to build a fast-food restaurant in a residentially zoned neighborhood, or to sell alcohol or tobacco to minors.

Although there have always been markets, the market rose to prominence as the primary method of determining the level and composition of output, prices, and the distribution of income only in the last few centuries and only in more developed economies. A market economy means that no one is in charge. Instead, citizens have the freedom to make transactions as they wish. The composition of output, the distribution of jobs and income, the amount devoted to consumption today rather than investment for tomorrow, are all determined by the sum total of individual decisions of countless market participants—workers, consumers, lenders, borrowers, households, and firms. All these participants let prices guide them in making choices about the use of their resources.

Market transactions existed before recorded history and persist even in largely command societies such as the People's Republic of China and the Soviet Union. Most of this book will be devoted to understanding an economic system in which most decisions are made in the market.

WHAT MAKES A MARKET ECONOMY WORK

What makes a market economy tick? Economists would say that there are three basic elements; self-interested behavior, competition, and clearly defined property rights. If these three elements are present, then the market will do a good job of making sure that resources are put to work, that output is produced, that prices are determined, and that goods and services flow to buyers in an orderly way with no central direction.

Self-interested Behavior

Economists assume that all individuals are interested in pursuing their own self-interest, even though they may define self-interest in different ways. To some, self-interest may mean maximizing income; to others, increasing leisure time; to others, meaningful work, friendship, or other values. Economists take those values as given. Self-interest means that individuals respond predictably to the incentives offered by the marketplace. If teachers' wages rise relative to wages for nurses, enough individuals will switch vocations or change majors to bring about the desired reallocation of workers from one occupation to another. But not all nurses will drop out. A few who were on the borderline—the marginal nurses, who are easily persuaded to switch to another occupation—will make the switch. As these marginal workers change occupations, the wages of the remaining nurses will rise because they have become relatively scarcer. If the summer wheat crop is blasted by drought, flour and bread become more expensive. In response, some consumers will substitute other foods for sandwiches, while profit-minded bakers will search the rest of the world for cheaper wheat to hold down the cost of baking bread. The number-one signal coming from the marketplace is price, and the self-interested response is to shift away from using goods, services, or resources whose prices have risen toward cheaper substitutes. The number-two signal from the market is profit. Profit is a signal to existing producers to expand output and to other entrepreneurs to enter the industry. As output expands in response to profit, a product's price will fall until profits are eliminated. We will look at this process more closely in later chapters.

Competition

Economists also assume the existence of competition in the marketplace. To an economist, competition means a large number of buyers and sellers so that no individual or firm can exercise a great deal of market power. Competition means that individuals are free to respond to market signals without hindrance from others. The antithesis of competition is monopoly, which means possession of market power. If there is no market power, and no restrictions on entry into a particular occupation or industry, you can pursue your self-interest.

Suppose that your self-interest tells you to become an electrician, say, or to enter the semiconductor industry. If there is lack of competition—if a union controls entry into the electrician business, or if a few firms control semiconductors and can drive out their potential competitors—then there is not enough competition for the market to work effectively, and you cannot pursue your self-interest. The signals are still there, but individuals are kept from responding. Monopoly power anywhere in the market keeps the system from functioning as effectively as it should.

Property Rights

In order for the market to send out signals and for individuals to respond appropriately, it is necessary to have clearly defined rights to goods, services, and resources. This is the reason why buyers of houses and cars require a title and a bill of sale as proof of the right to sell the property. Property rights include not only proof of ownership but also some specifications about how the property can and cannot be used. Ownership of a residential lot conveys the right to leave it idle or to build on it, to keep trespassers off, to plant trees, or even to put pink flamingos in the front yard. If you put a hamburger stand on your lot in a residential neighborhood, however, it violates your neighbors' rights to an attractive neighborhood free of intense noise, smell, and litter. The property rights to your lot in a neighborhood with residential zoning do not extend to erecting a burger outlet. Nor do they, in most cases, permit you to build apartments, burn trash, or let your sewage run out through an open pipe in the back yard. The property rights to your car mean you can drive it on public highways provided that you carry liability insurance, have a driver's license, and do not speed or drive under the influence.

Property rights safeguard your rights to the rewards of your efforts, although these rights usually carry restrictions to keep you from infringing on the property rights of others. Without property rights, there would be little incentive to build houses, acquire productive assets, or even work beyond the level needed for subsistence, because people's possessions could be taken from them by force or by government command.

Most property rights are defined outside the market, by government. As we shall see later, defining and enforcing property rights is one of the most important functions of government in a market economy.

A CIRCULAR FLOW OVERVIEW OF A MARKET ECONOMY

One way to envision the market economy is with the aid of a visual tool called a circular flow diagram. Figure 2-1 is a simple circular flow diagram for an economy that consists only of households and business firms. Households own all the productive resources—land, labor, capital, and enterprise. (Remember, a business firm may "own" land and capital, but households own

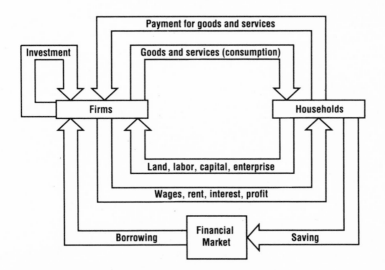

FIG. 2-1 *A Simple Circular Flow Model*

the business firm!) They sell the services of these resources to the firm in the lower half of the diagram in exchange for income—wages for labor, rent for land, interest for capital, and profit for enterprise. The sum total of these incomes is called *national income*, which is a central concern of macroeconomics. This book is addressed to the workings of the individual markets in which these resource transactions occur, which taken together are called the *resource* or *factor market*.

Like most markets, there is no place or building that is "the resource market." Rather, it represents the sum total of thousands of individual markets and transactions. For example, the market for labor consists of personnel offices, employment agencies, help-wanted ads, college recruiting days, and so on. It also includes the lonely individual mailing resumes and filling out job applications.

Firms purchase resources in order to produce goods and services. Most goods and services are destined for consumers and are sold to them in the product market (the upper half of the flow), where households use the income they earned in the resource market to buy goods and services. Some goods and services are capital goods destined for other business firms, or they are added to inventory.[1]

The product market, like the resource market, is not a particular place but a whole network of retailers and wholesalers, street vendors and mail order firms, and other sellers that link the producing firm with the consumer. The flow through the product market of household purchases and business investment are the two largest components of *gross national product* (GNP), also a macroeconomic concept.[2]

You may have noticed that the household did not spend all its income on consumption. A part of its income was saved. When households save, they generally entrust their savings (= income not consumed) to banks, pension funds, stockbrokers, insurance companies, and other entities that make up a third market, the financial market. Business firms offer stock and bonds for sale in this market, or just borrow directly, in order to purchase investment goods for future production. The purpose of the financial market is to match the savings of households with the borrowing needs of business firms. (In the real world, of course, government borrows and some households borrow. While some business firms borrow, others may actually save their surplus in some years and lend it in financial markets. To keep this model simple, however, in this two-sector economy only households save and only business firms borrow.)

THE ROLE OF HOUSEHOLDS

In a market economy, as described in the circular flow diagram, the household plays several important roles. First, it determines what productive resources it will make available to firms at various alternative prices. Changes in household decisions in this regard have important implications for wages and output. When women were less likely to be part of the labor force for most of their adult lives, there were fewer workers and wages were *relatively* higher. As women have entered the labor force, wages became temporarily depressed; but at the same time women chose to have fewer children, reducing the size of the future labor force. If this smaller labor force becomes a reality in the 1990s and after the year 2000, it would mean that labor would become scarcer (and more expensive) relative to capital. Firms would have an incentive to shift their methods of production. Indeed, with the end of the baby boom some such shifts in relatively low-paying entry-level jobs have already been observed, with the development of such things as automatic teller machines at banks and self-service car washes.

If households choose to consume now rather than later, there is more demand for goods but less in the way of saving for business firms to borrow and invest. The price of borrowing (interest) will be higher, firms will invest less, and future output will be lower. Individuals can also choose to invest in themselves, in training and education to enhance their future productivity. These choices affect the quality of labor and the mix of skills available to firms.

On the goods and services side, households have the ultimate power to determine what combination of goods and services are produced. While advertising can sometimes convince consumers to change their tastes, firms learn to their sorrow that the consumer is sovereign. New Coke and premature introduction of miniskirts are just two bad guesses of the late 1980s that cost firms dearly because they did not read consumer preferences correctly. Luckier firms produced more popular items such as VCRs, transformers and gobots for little boys, and four-wheel-drive vehicles for bigger boys.

THE ROLE OF BUSINESS FIRMS

The purpose of the firm is to organize and direct production. The goal of the firm is to make a profit—the more, the better. To make the largest possible profit, firms must correctly anticipate consumer wants and use resources in the most efficient way possible.

Often the firm has choices about how to combine productive resources in order to produce a given output. It is possible to farm, for example, in ways that economize on land (by using fertilizer more intensely), on labor (by using machinery more intensively), or on capital (by using more labor). Which way to choose? In southeast Asia, where capital is expensive, they use lots of their cheap and abundant labor. American farmers choose capital-intensive methods of agricultural production because labor is expensive and capital is relatively cheap. In Japan, farmers use scarce land very intensively in combination with large amounts of both labor and capital.

The people, owners, or firms that organize production performs another important service—taking risks. Traditional societies take no risks; they always do things as they have been done before. A market society, in contrast, emphasizes the new, the better, the different. The pioneer who comes up with a new product or a new technique can increase sales, or cut costs, and make a profit. Eventually rivals will catch up and produce similar products or develop similar methods of production, but in the interim the person or firm that gets there first enjoys a profit. Of course, new techniques and new products are risky. The product may not sell, or it may have hidden defects. The new technique may not work out; it may be more costly or reduce product quality. Along with the hope of profit is the risk of loss. Only those who are willing to take that risk get a share of the profits when they gamble on the winning side.

PARTNERSHIPS, PROPRIETORSHIPS, AND CORPORATIONS

A business firm can be organized in several different ways. Business organization is a complex and highly technical legal subject. In this book we are only interested in the economic implications of the choice of form. Each one has certain advantages and drawbacks in terms of sharing risks, access to capital, and permanence.

The simplest form of business organization is the proprietorship, owned by a single individual. It is easy to set up, usually with just a local business license. Owners take all the risks and earn all the profits or absorb all the losses. When such firms fail, the individual owners are liable for its debts out of their personal assets. Many small farms, retail stores, and service firms are proprietorships. Capital is limited to the owner's personal assets and what he or she can borrow. Banks are reluctant to bet heavily on one individual, so proprietorships cannot usually borrow much. (Small Business Administration loans are intended to help with this problem.)

The owner has total control over business decisions—location, product line, hiring and firing, hours of operation, pricing. Thus, owners have powerful incentives to make good decisions, because they keep all the profits if there are any. On the other hand, management skills are limited to those of the owner, unless business is brisk enough to hire management help. An owner may be good at product development but not at marketing, or strong in accounting skills but weak in personnel management. While good employees can help, employees are not usually in a position to participate in important management decisions. And when the owner/manager dies, the business may die unless a new owner/manager can be identified quickly.

As a proprietorship begins to expand, one way to spread the risks and obtain more capital is to become a partnership. Many firms, in fact, begin as partnerships in order to put together the necessary capital and expertise. Partnerships are particularly common in professional services, such as medicine, dentistry, accounting, and law. The partners can pool their capital and offer the bank or other lenders a more solid foundation for larger loans. They may bring a good mix of management skills together to make the operation more successful. The risks are now spread among the partners, so that each receives an appropriate share of the profits or bears an appropriate share of the losses. One drawback to a partnership is loss of control; decisions are made by committee. Some partners may try to get a free ride, not pulling their weight but collecting their share of the profits. The more partners there are, the more opportunities there are to shirk without incurring a penalty. Partnerships also share some of the drawbacks of proprietorships; the risks of losses still extend to the partners' personal assets, and partnerships must be renegotiated every time a partner dies or wants to sell his or her shares.

The third option is to organize a corporation. A corporation issues stock, or ownership shares, and is owned by the stockholders, who share in the firm's profits or losses in proportion to their holdings. Unlike the proprietorship or partnership, however, the corporation exists as a separate legal "person" from the owners/stockholders. The stockholders' losses are limited to the value of their stock purchases, and do not extend to their other assets. (In the United States, a corporation often puts "Inc."—Incorporated—after its name. In England and elsewhere the equivalent term is "Ltd."—limited liability—which identifies a corporation by the key feature of limited stockholder liability.) Limited liability makes not only the choice of a corporate form of organization but also the decision to purchase stock more attractive to entrepreneurs and financial investors.

It is much easier for corporations to raise capital than it is for sole proprietorships and partnerships; corporations can issue stock or bonds as well as negotiating bank loans. Bonds are a form of loan that are easily transferable from one investor to another. Individuals, banks, and financial institutions are usually more willing to provide either equity (stock) or debt (bonds or loans) financing to corporations than to partnerships or proprietorships because corporations have a longer lifetime and are less risky. (A corporation continues to exist until it is dissolved, goes bankrupt, or, increasingly, is bought out by another corporation.) However, new corporations, with no credit history, are not considered uniformly good credit risks, so that the owners may be asked to put their personal guarantee on any loans.

The corporate form of organization has two drawbacks—tax treatment of corporate income and separation of ownership from control. Corporations pay federal (and state) corporate income taxes on net income, or profit. Part of this profit is reinvested in the firm; the rest is paid to stockholders as dividends, in proportion to shares owned. Stockholders are taxed again on dividend income. Income of a partnership or proprietorship is taxed only once as personal income. This drawback must be weighed against the advantage of limited liability and the possibility of greater profits. For small businesses there is the S corporation alternative, a form that combines the advantages of the corporate form (limited liability) with some of the advantages of the other two forms of business.

The incentives to hold down costs, to be responsive to consumers, and to remain attuned to possibilities for innovation is strongest when the individual manager bears the losses or earns the profits. In a corporation stockholders make profits, while managers make the business decisions. Managers may be more interested in large offices, expense accounts, or power and prestige than in profits, and it is difficult for thousands of fragmented stockholders to organize and protest management inefficiency. Stock options and profit-sharing plans for managers to give them a vested interest in profit are responses to this problem.

While partnerships and proprietorships make up 85 percent of the firms in the United States, corporations are responsible for producing 85 percent of the output. Thus, the corporation is the most significant form of business organization in the U.S. economy today.

THE ROLE OF GOVERNMENT

There is a third partner in the market economy, one whose primary role is to make up for some of the failings of the market, or to make markets work better. This partner is the government. We have already seen that a central role of government is to define and enforce the property rights that are so essential to a market economy. Governments also are called on to promote competition and to discourage or regulate concentration of market power (monopoly). There are also certain goods that will not be produced in market system, or will not be produced in the desired amounts, such as national defense, courts, education, and roads. Where the benefits for some goods are widely shared both by those who pay and those who do not, the market will not produce the goods, or not produce enough. Where the benefits or the costs of producing certain goods spill over to third parties who are not involved in the production or consumption decision, then the market may result in producing too little or too much of that particular good. Education has positive spillovers, so it is subsidized through government. Pollution causes negative spillovers, and is regulated or taxed by government.

Two other roles of government deserve a brief mention. The pattern of income distribution determined by market forces may be very unsatisfactory. Most market economies expect government to make adjustments to the market-determined distribution of income in order to reduce the amount of inequality, especially to relieve poverty at the lower ranges of the income distribution. Finally, a market economy can be very unstable, with ups and downs in output and employment. Governments are expected to try to smooth out such fluctuations through appropriate macroeconomic policy. In this book we only consider the microeconomic actions of government; redistributing income, promoting competition, regulating monopoly, producing public goods, and regulating production of goods with spillover costs and benefits.

CHAPTER PERSPECTIVE

Economic decisions can be made by tradition, command, or the market. In a market economy the mixture of output, prices, and allocation of resources is determined primarily by the interactions of households and business firms in resource and product markets. Households provide resource services and buy goods and services from business firms, which may be organized as proprietorships, partnerships, or corporations. Markets assume self-interested behavior and work when competition is strong and property rights are clearly defined. In a market economy the role of government is to define property rights, produce public goods, promote competition, reduce spillover effects from privately produced goods, redistribute income, and reduce fluctuations in total economic activity.

FOOTNOTES

1 *Inventory is considered a capital good because, like other capital goods, it can produce an income for the firm in future years.*

2 *In a more complete view of the economy, taking into account government activity and a foreign sector, GNP would also include government purchases and exports.*

Elements of Supply and Demand

INTRODUCTION AND MAIN POINTS
Ask an economist a question, and chances are that the answer will involve a supply-and-demand diagram. Supply and demand are the most basic tools of the economist in trying to explain what is produced, how much, and at what price it is sold, as well as why and how much prices and quantities increase or decrease when other influences change. It will take several chapters to develop the basic theory and applications of supply and demand. This chapter begins with a broad overview of the supply and demand model.

After studying the material in this chapter:
- You will be able to explain why demand curves slope down from left to right and why supply curves slope up from left to right.
- You will be able to distinguish between a shift in supply (or demand) and a movement along the supply curve (or demand curve).
- You will be able to identify the factors that can shift a supply curve or a demand curve.
- You will be able to identify equilibrium price and quantity and to predict the direction of change when supply or demand shifts.
- You will be able to use the supply-and-demand model to describe and analyze simple economic problems.

WHY DEMAND CURVES SLOPE DOWN
A demand curve shows the quantities of a particular good that consumers will purchase at various alternative prices. A demand curve can be drawn for an individual or for a market. Your demand curve for movie rentals shows the number of movies you would choose to rent per day, week, month, or year at various prices. Janet's Video, however, is interested in the market

demand curve—the number of movies that consumers in her service area are willing to rent per day, week, month, or year at various prices.

A demand curve, then, refers to a particular time and space—demand for beef in New York in July, for baseballs in Los Angeles this year, for steel in Detroit in the first fiscal quarter, for lemonade on a hot summer day on Pleasant View Drive. Demand curves for different individuals or areas or time periods can be aggregated into demand curves that cover a wider range of potential customers or a broader geographic area.

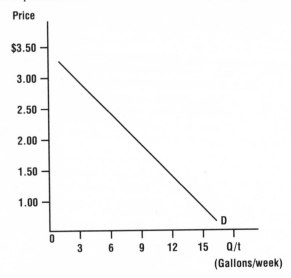

FIG. 3-1 *A Demand Curve for Milk in Waterbury, Connecticut*

Figure 3-1 shows a typical demand curve. The numbers show the various price-quantity combinations that consumers are willing to buy, and the graph plots those numbers with quantity on the horizontal axis and price on the vertical axis. The quantity is expressed as units per time period; in this case, gallons of milk per week. The price is expressed in dollars. This is the demand curve facing sellers in Waterbury, Connecticut. Demand curves normally slope down from left to right, indicating that (ceteris paribus) consumers will purchase a smaller quantity at higher prices and a larger quantity at lower prices. That may seem obvious, but people express a surprising amount of doubt about whether consumers really will respond to price changes. For this reason economists have developed some theoretical arguments to justify the downward sloping demand curve, and have also gathered data to create empirical demand curves. These data almost invariably confirm that demand curves do, indeed, slope downward from left to right.

Diminishing Marginal Utility

In the late 19th century, when the demand curve was born, the explanation for its slope was based on the law of diminishing marginal utility. This law is just one application of the more general law of diminishing returns, which describes what happens when you add more of something (X)—a consumer good or a productive input, for example—to a fixed amount of something else. The output, satisfaction, or whatever you are trying to create will continue to increase (up to a point), but the increases will get smaller and smaller as more X is added. Firms see this law expressed in smaller and smaller increases in output as more and more labor is added to a fixed stock of capital or as more and more fertilizer is applied to a fixed area of land. For consumers the object is not output but satisfaction—or utility, as it was labeled by 19th century economists.

Consider pizza. As you add one slice to an empty stomach, your satisfaction (utility) is considerable. The second slice is tasty, but it doesn't do as much for you as the first. Unless you have a huge appetite, the fourth slice does very little for you, and the fifth may actually have negative value—it could make you sick! The same principle applies to adding cars to the family fleet, rooms to the house, shoes to the closet, or even children to the family! The value of the additions may remain positive, but at least beyond some minimum level, each additional unit adds less happiness, satisfaction, or utility than the one before.

What does this have to do with demand? The amount you are willing to pay for something reflects the satisfaction you expect to receive from it. If the extra unit gives less satisfaction, you are willing to pay less for it. You might be willing to pay $1.50 for one loaf of bread per week, but the supermarket can only induce you to buy the fourth loaf at a price of 50 cents, because it adds much less to your satisfaction than the first loaf. (If the first loaf is providing toast and sandwiches, by the fourth you may be feeding the birds!) Thus, diminishing marginal utility implies that your demand curve will slope down from left to right, and you will purchase additional units only at lower prices.

Income and Substitution Effects

A second explanation for the demand curve is based on how people respond to those price signals coming from the market that were discussed in Chapter 2. A fall in the price of any product sends a signal to substitute it for other goods in consumption. If the price of milk falls, you may substitute it in consumption for other beverages (or sources of calcium and protein) in your diet. You may purchase less orange juice, or less cheese, or less lemonade. Most goods have some close substitutes that consumers can shift to when the price of the good rises. Coffee and tea, beef and chicken, movies and bowling are all examples of close substitutes. A shift among products when the price of one falls and the prices of the others are unchanged (ceteris paribus again) is called the substitution effect. (Some goods are complements; they are consumed together, like bread and butter, movies and popcorn, baseball tickets and hot dogs, bicycles and backpacks. If the price of one rises, less of both goods will be consumed.)

In addition to the substitution effect there is a related effect of the fall in the price of milk that is a little more complicated. Suppose that Jeff goes to the store with $20 and a list that includes "2 gallons of milk at $2.50." When Jeff gets there, he discovers that the store is running a special on milk for $1.50 a gallon. After buying two gallons, instead of having only $15 left for everything else, he has $17 left. The fall in the price of milk is equivalent to a $2 increase in his income! With more money left to spend, Jeff may choose to spend some of this windfall on extra milk. This aspect of a decline in price is called the income effect. Since both income and substitution effects occur together and work in the same direction, it is difficult to tell how much of Jeff's extra milk purchase is due to the income effect and how much to the substitution effect.

The income and substitution effects work together in reverse when the price of milk rises. When milk gets more expensive, consumers switch to other drinks and other sources of calcium and protein whose prices have not risen. When milk gets more expensive, the price rise is equivalent to a reduction in income, so consumers buy less of everything, including milk.

Both the law of diminishing marginal utility and the income and substitution effects lead us to the same conclusion. Ceteris paribus, the demand curve slopes down from left to right, with smaller quantities at higher prices and larger quantities at lower prices.

Individual Demand and Market Demand

For most goods the market-demand curve is obtained by adding up the quantities each individual buyer would like to purchase at various alternative prices. For example, if there were three buyers in the milk market, the market demand would be obtained as follows:

Price	Jeff's Demand	+ Jan's Demand	+ Lew's Demand	= Market Demand
$3.00	1	2	0	3
$2.50	2	3	1	6
$2.00	3	4	2	9
$1.50	4	5	3	12
$1.00	5	6	4	15

The market-demand curve can be obtained by plotting the price figures in the first column and the quantity figures in the last column. Like Jeff's demand curve, the market demand curve slopes down from left to right.

Shifts in Demand

What if ceteris are not paribus? That is, what if something else changes? There are many factors that went into Jeff's decision to buy two gallons of milk at $2.50. These factors included his income, the prices of substitutes (ice cream, cheese, lemonade, orange juice), the prices of complements (cereal, cookies), the number of people in the household, his tastes and preferences, and other factors. If one of these factors changes, then his whole demand curve can shift, and he will demand a larger (or smaller) quantity than before at every possible price. Suppose that Jeff and his wife Sheila adopt two-year-old twins. Children drink a lot of milk; Jeff's weekly milk requirement at $2.50 a gallon rises from two gallons to four gallons. At $1.50, he would have purchased four gallons, to feed the cat, to substitute for orange juice at breakfast, and to make pudding for dessert; with the twins, he will now buy six gallons at that price. In Figure 3-2, D_1 was his original demand curve; D_2 is his new demand curve for milk now that he has the twins to consider. When the twins grow up and go

29

off to college, his demand curve for milk will shift back to the left—back to D_1 or even declining all the way to D_3. He will demand fewer gallons of milk at every alternative price.

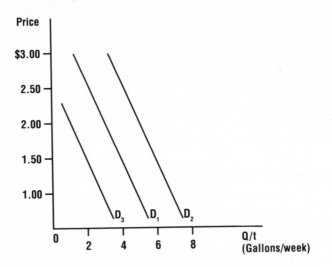

FIG. 3-2 *Jeff's Demand for Milk*

It is not difficult to see how other factors would shift the demand curve. Here is a quick checklist for you to work through.

Factor	Change	Demand curve shifts to:
Price of substitutes	rises	right
Price of substitutes	falls	left
Price of complements	rises	left
Price of complements	falls	right
Number of consumers	increases	right
Number of consumers	decreases	left
Shift in tastes	in favor	right
Shift in tastes	against	left
Income	rises	right
Income	falls	left

WHY SUPPLY CURVES SLOPE UP

A demand curve is of limited use without its faithful companion, the supply curve. The 19th-century economist Alfred Marshall compared the supply-and-demand curves to the two blades of a pair of scissors. It takes both blades to cut. Likewise, it takes both a supply and a demand curve to determine price and quantity in the market.

A supply curve shows the amounts that sellers will offer for sale in the market at various alternative prices, ceteris paribus. A supply curve can be drawn for an individual firm or for the entire market. That is, it could show the supply of milk offered by Jane's Dairy or by all the milk processors in a particular area.

Like a demand curve, a supply curve refers to a particular time and space. Supply curves for different firms or areas or time periods can be aggregated into supply curves that include a wider range of suppliers or a broader geographic area.

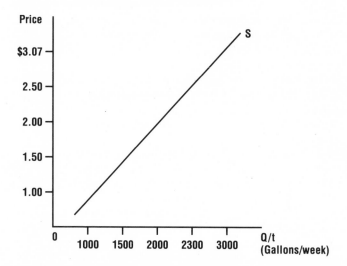

FIG. 3-3 *A Supply Curve for Milk in Waterbury, Connecticut*

Figure 3-3 shows a typical supply curve. The numbers show the various price-quantity combinations that sellers are willing to offer, and the graph plots those numbers. Quantity, again, is on the horizontal axis, price is on the vertical axis. This is the supply curve facing milk buyers in Waterbury, Connecticut. Supply curves normally slope up from left to right, indicating that (ceteris paribus) sellers will offer a smaller quantity at lower prices and a larger quantity at higher prices. This statement seems to cause less difficulty than the matching statement about the demand curve. Usually if people do not believe that supply curves slope upward, it is because they think that the supply is some fixed and given quantity independent of price. We will look at the myth of the vertical supply curve in a later chapter. For a few goods a vertical supply curve may be a possibility, and later we will even encounter a few circumstances when the supply curve slopes downward from left to right, but most supply curves look like the one drawn in Figure 3-3.

Increasing Marginal Cost

The supply curve slopes upward because of increasing marginal cost; that is, beyond some point the extra, additional, or marginal unit of output costs more to produce than the preceding ones. If that is true, the producers will choose to produce that extra unit and offer it for sale only if they can get a higher price for it to recoup their higher costs of production.

The concept of increasing marginal cost can be explained in several different ways. One explanation relies on the general principle of diminishing returns. Extra workers may be added to a fixed supply of equipment, machinery, or floor space. With no extra capital to work with, however, extra workers will add less to output than the preceding workers but they will be paid the same amount. Thus, the per-unit cost of their extra output will be higher. For example, suppose a worker in a shoe repair shop was able to repair ten pairs of shoes an hour. Since the shop has several pieces of equipment, a second worker may have to wait occasionally for a tool or a piece of equipment, but even so can still turn out eight pairs of repaired shoes. A third worker may produce only six units. If all these workers receive $5 an hour, then the labor cost per pair of shoes repaired is 50 cents when output is ten pairs. The next eight pairs generate a labor cost of 62.5 cents per pair ($5/8 units), raising the average labor cost of all units to 55.5 cents ($10/18 units). The third worker's average labor cost per unit is 83.3 cents ($5/6 units), and raises the average labor cost of all units to 62.5 cents.

A second explanation for increasing costs is that the firm may have to pay a higher price for resources—labor or other inputs—in order to bid them away from other jobs. Alternatively, the price of the resource—for example, labor—may not increase as output expands, but perhaps the quality of the resource will fall. If the best or most suitable workers or resources are employed first—the experienced shoe repairers, say—as output expands the firm may have to take on less productive workers or workers with less aptitude for shoe repair. Thus, the labor cost of extra units of output will be higher.

Shifts in Supply

A supply curve shows the relationship between price and quantity supplied, with everything else held constant (ceteris paribus). If there is a change in one of the other factors held constant, or ceteris paribus conditions, then the whole supply curve can shift to the right or the left, as in Figure 3-4. For example, suppose that a drought or a severe winter meant that there was not enough hay to feed cows, so that milk cows had to be slaughtered for beef. The amount of raw milk available to Jane's Dairy and her competitors would be less, and as dairies competed for the limited quantity of raw milk, the price would rise. The same amount of milk would now be offered at a higher price, or smaller amounts of milk would be offered at the same price. Some firms might go out of business in response to higher costs for raw milk, reducing the number of suppliers. In Figure 3-4, the supply of milk would shift from S_1 to S_2.

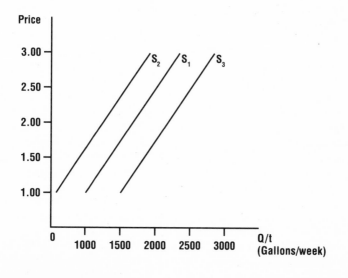

FIG. 3-4 *Shift in Supply*

An improvement in dairy technology could reduce costs of production, and firms might now be willing to supply the same amount of milk at a lower price, or more milk at the same price. Supply would shift to the right, from S_1 to S_3.

Another source of shifts in supply is changes in the prices of other goods the firm could produce. For example, if the dairy can produce either milk or cheese, and the price of cheese rises, some resources will be shifted from milk to cheese, and the supply curve of milk will shift to the left.

Here is a quick checklist of some of the major sources of shifts in supply:

Factor	Change	Supply curve shifts to:
Prices of inputs	rise	left
Prices of inputs	fall	right
Number of suppliers	increases	right
Number of suppliers	decreases	left
Improved technology	increase	right
Prices of other goods	rise	left
Prices of other goods	fall	right
Taxes on business	rise	left
Taxes on business	fall	right

The market-supply curve is obtained in the same way as the market-demand curve. The quantities that will be offered for sale at various alternative prices for each individual supplier are added to obtain the market quantities at each price and, thus, the market supply curve.

DEMAND, SUPPLY, AND THE MARKET

Now we are ready to put the two halves of the pair of scissors together. Figure 3-5 shows the supply and demand for milk in Waterbury, Connecticut in July. The two curves intersect at a point called the equilibrium position, which determines that a quantity of 2000 gallons will be sold per week at a price of $2.00 per gallon. At a price of $2.00 the quantity that buyers want to purchase is exactly equal to the quantity that sellers want to offer for sale. This price and quantity will persist until something happens that shifts the demand curve, the supply curve, or both.

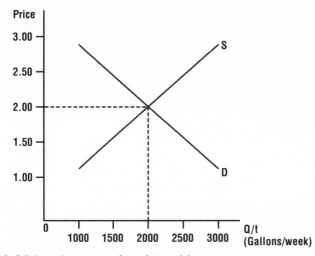

FIG. 3-5 *Supply, Demand, and Equilibrium*

What makes this price and quantity combination equilibrium? Consider what would happen if the average supplier guessed wrong about the demand curve and posted a price of $2.50. At that price suppliers are willing to offer 2200 gallons, but buyers want only 1800 gallons. There is a surplus of 400 gallons of milk, and milk spoils quickly. Some suppliers cut their prices to get rid of their unsold milk. At the same time they cut back their orders for next week. Quantity supplied falls toward the equilibrium level of 2000. As the price begins to fall, some customers that were not buying milk at $2.50 will start buying it at a lower price, and other customers will increase their purchases. Quantity demand rises toward the equilibrium level of 2000. As long as the price is above the equilibrium level of $2.00, there will be unsold milk and pressure to cut price until equilibrium is reached.

If sellers happened to set the price below $2.00—say, at $1.50—the opposite would happen. Retailers would run out of milk in the middle of the day, angering their customers. They would increase their orders to the dairy, but they would also raise their prices. As the price rose, some customers would cut back on their purchases. As long as price is below equilibrium, however, there will be a shortage of milk and angry customers.

Notice the words *shortage* and *surplus*. To an economist these words have a particular meaning. A shortage or surplus occurs at a particular price and can usually be eliminated by lowering or increasing the price. A wheat surplus occurs because the government price-support program does not allow the price to fall toward equilibrium. The shortages of nurses and teachers could be solved if their employers were willing to pay higher salaries for those occupations. It may take time for these adjustments to occur, but price plays a central role in resolving shortages and surpluses.

If the supply or demand curve shifts, the equilibrium price and quantity will change. Figure 3-6 shows several possibilities. In Figure 3-6(a), if demand increases from D_1 to D_2, the price rises from $2.00 to $2.40 and the quantity increases from 2000 to 2250. Notice that we *shifted* the demand curve and *moved along* the supply curve. In the jargon of economists there was a shift in demand and a change in quantity supplied. The supply curve did not move, but there was a change in quantity supplied because of a change in price. A change in quantity supplied or quantity demanded means that sellers or buyers are moving along a fixed supply or demand curve in response to a change in price. A change in demand (shift in demand) or a change in supply (shift in supply) means that the whole curve has moved in response to a change in something other than the price of the product—a change in one of the ceteris paribus conditions. The shift in demand from D_1 to D_2 means that something other than the price of milk has changed—income, number of consumers, price of substitutes, or some other factor.

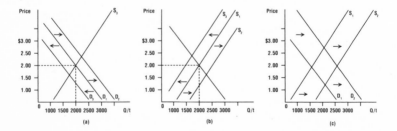

FIG. 3-6 *Shifts in Supply and Demand and Equilibrium*

When demand shifts to the left (D_1 to D_3) in Figure 3-6(a), both equilibrium price and quantity fall as sellers move back along the given supply curve S_1. In Figure 3-6(b) demand is held constant while supply shifts. An increase in supply from S_1 to S_2, perhaps because of an improvement in milking technology or a reduction in feed costs for milk cows, means the best of both worlds for consumers—larger quantity, lower price. A shift in supply from S_1 to S_3 results in a smaller quantity at a higher price.

Finally, it is possible for both supply and demand to shift at the same time. If they both increase (shift to the right), as in Figure 3-6(c), quantity will definitely rise but price may rise or fall, depending on which curve shifts more. Likewise, if both decrease (shift to the left), the quantity will definitely fall, but the price may go either way, depending on which shifts more. You may want to experiment to see what happens when demand increases and supply decreases, or vice versa.

CHAPTER PERSPECTIVE

The supply-and-demand model developed in this chapter is the most basic tool that economists use to describe how the market works in determining prices and quantities of various goods. Later chapters will apply this model to a variety of situations and will go behind the supply-and-demand curves to look at how steep or flat the curves are, how costs affect supply, and how taxes, market power, and the amount of competition affect supply and demand.

Consumer demand is based on a very simple view of how consumers, acting in their own self-interest, respond to changes in prices or to changes in tastes, income, or other factors. This model generally explains very accurately how consumers actually behave. At higher prices consumers buy less, and at lower prices they buy more. These choices reflect both diminishing marginal utility and the income and substitution effects. If something other than the price changes, the entire demand curve can shift. This means that consumers are now willing to buy more (or less) at every alternative price.

Supply, likewise, is based on a view of how firms, acting in their own self-interest, respond to changes in prices or to changes in costs or other factors. At higher prices suppliers will offer more for sale, and at lower prices they will offer less. These choices reflect increasing marginal costs. As we will see in later chapters, there are more likely to be exceptions to this law of supply than to the law of demand. In general, however, supply curves slope up from left to right because of increasing marginal costs. If something other than the price changes, the entire supply curve will shift. A shift in supply means that suppliers are now willing to offer more (or less) for sale at every alternative price.

Applications of Supply and Demand

INTRODUCTION AND MAIN POINTS

This chapter offers an opportunity to become more comfortable in using supply-and-demand analysis in concrete situations by applying it to some real-world questions. We will look at government intervention in setting prices (price floors and ceilings), the effects of taxes on output and prices, and how prices are—or can be—used effectively to help allocate resources in the public sector. All these questions can be analyzed with a supply-and-demand model, and all these policy decisions influence the choices of households and business firms in specific and identifiable ways.

After studying the material in this chapter:

■ You will be able to explain how price floors and ceilings affect buyers and sellers and create surpluses and shortages.

■ You will be able to analyze the effects of various kinds of taxes on the market and determine who really pays the tax.

■ You will be able to explain how prices can be used in the public sector to allocate public services more efficiently.

■ You will have a clearer understanding of the central role of price in directing market activity.

■ You will feel more comfortable with applying the supply-and-demand model to a broader range of economic questions.

APPLICATION 1: PRICE FLOORS AND CEILINGS

One way that governments intervene in the market is to place limits on price changes. A government may establish a minimum price, or price floor, which is the lowest legal price. (The price can be higher, however.) Farm price supports and the minimum wage are examples of price floors.

Farm Price Supports

Figure 4-1 shows a price floor of $5.00 a bushel in the market for wheat. If the price floor had been set lower, perhaps at $3.00 a bushel, which is below market equilibrium, it would have no immediate impact. But since the floor price has been set above the equilibrium level, it has a significant impact. Left to itself, the market would have arrived at an equilibrium price of $4.00 and an equilibrium quantity of 30 million bushels. Consumers purchase less—25 million bushels instead of 30 million—as they move up along the demand curve in response to a higher price. Sellers, however, find the higher price of $5.00 attractive, so they expand output; the amount of wheat offered for sale rises from 30 million to 35 million bushels, moving along the supply curve. As quantity demanded falls by 5 million bushels and quantity supplied rises by 5 million bushels, a *surplus* of 10 million bushels of wheat appears.

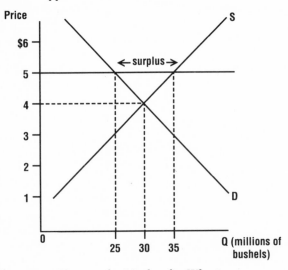

FIG. 4-1 *A Price Floor in the Market for Wheat*

Notice that this surplus exists at a particular price. At a higher price the surplus would be larger, and a lower price it would be smaller. If the price became low enough, the surplus would disappear entirely. Economists do not speak of surpluses (or shortages) without reference to the particular price at which the surplus or shortage occurs.

Governments usually impose price floors or ceilings to address a particular problem of income distribution, usually in response to complaints from powerful constituencies. Farm price supports are usually justified as helping to maintain the income of farmers and guaranteeing a future food supply. However, price floors solve one problem while creating a new one. What do we do about the resulting surplus? And, if indeed we need to help the farmer and assure a food supply, is there a better way?

The history of U.S. farm policy is littered with unsatisfactory ways of dealing with the surplus. The Department of Agriculture has stored it, burned it, given it away abroad, given it to soup kitchens and school lunch programs at home, tried to keep farmers from growing it—the possibilities are limited only by the imaginations of the Secretary of Agriculture and interested members of Congress. In the meantime taxpayers pay twice: They pay taxes to fund government programs to buy and store the surplus, and they pay again at the grocery store in higher prices.

U.S. farm policy is not the worst in terms of high food prices and surplus problems; that honor goes to the European Economic Community, which is drowning in a sea of olive oil and piling up mountains of various farm commodities. However, even in the United States, economists suggest that there are better ways of accomplishing the same goal. "Better" is a loaded term, but to an economist it simply means accomplishing the same goal with a smaller expenditure of resources. One way would be to use farm income supports instead of price supports. If farmers' net income falls below a certain target level as a result of low market prices for their products, the government makes up the difference between market income and target income with an income transfer. Consumers still pay taxes for the income transfer, but they no longer have to pay higher prices at the grocery store in addition to higher taxes to pay for storage and distribution of the surplus. The target-price program introduced in the 1970s, which pays subsidies to farmers on the basis of the difference between the target price and the market price, was a step in this direction.

Minimum Wages

A second illustration of a price floor in the U.S. economy is the minimum wage. Supported by labor unions and opposed by business groups, the minimum wage has been a source of controversy since it was first enacted in the 1930s. This law decrees that workers shall not be paid less than a specified minimum hourly wage, with exceptions for very small firms, certain agricultural occupations, casual employment (e.g. teenage babysitters and yard workers), and a few others. Virtually all workers are covered by the minimum-wage law. At this writing, the minimum wage remains at the level of $3.35 set in 1981, but it is scheduled to be increased in steps in the early 1990s.

The minimum wage is a very appealing idea. A person who worked full-time, year round, at the 1989 minimum wage of $3.35 earned less than $7000 a year. That income was barely above the poverty level for one person and below the poverty threshold for a family of three. However, like farm price supports, a minimum wage creates a surplus of unskilled workers, or unemployment, if it is set above the market equilibrium wage because employers will hire fewer of these workers.

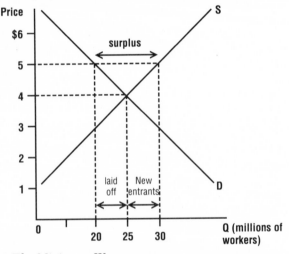

FIG. 4-2 *The Minimum Wage*

Figure 4-2 shows the effects of a $5.00-an-hour minimum wage in a market for unskilled labor where the equilibrium wage is $4.00 an hour. As the minimum wage is increased, some firms eliminate unskilled entry-level jobs—stockboys, extra clerks, cleaning staff. These people are worth hiring at a lower wage, but they do not add enough to the company's earnings and profit to be kept on at the higher price. In this diagram 5 million workers (30 – 25) will be laid off. At the same time 5 million new workers (35 – 30) are attracted into the labor market by the higher minimum wage. At that price it is worth their time and effort to search for a job and perhaps even pay for child care. Moving up the supply curve for labor, we find that an extra 5 million workers have decided to join the labor force. The result is a surplus of 10 million workers at $5.00 an hour, or 10 million unemployed.

Whatever the actual numbers, this diagram points to a basic truth. Some workers—the 25 million who kept their jobs and got a raise from $4.00 to $5.00 an hour—are better off as a result of the minimum wage. On the other hand, some lose their jobs, or some jobs that would have been available never appear. Some people decide to enter the labor market and have no luck finding jobs. The beneficiaries, the 25 million who got a raise, know that their raise came from the minimum wage. Some of those laid off also know what hurt them—the increase in the minimum wage. But for the jobs that didn't appear, or for the workers who searched and found no jobs, the source of the problem is not quite so clear. Thus, a minimum wage is politically appealing because its benefits are clearly visible while its harmful effects are hard to pinpoint.

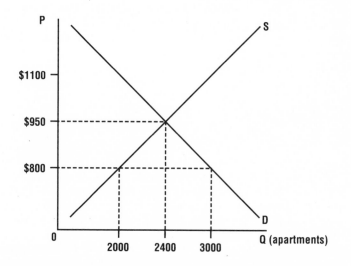

FIG. 4-3 *Rent Control*

Rent Controls

Governments also set ceiling prices, or prices that sellers are not allowed to exceed. Examples of price ceilings are less common than price floors. During the "energy crisis" of the 1970s there were price ceilings on natural gas. Most states used to have usury laws that set maximum interest rates banks could charge for mortgages and other types of loans. One type of price ceiling still in effect in a number of large cities, including New York, is rent control. Figure 4-3 illustrates the effects of rent control on the price and quantity of rental housing.

Rent control typically takes the form of a price ceiling. This price ceiling says that certain types of apartments in particular parts of the city—2 bedroom apartments in the south end of town, for example—cannot be rented for more than $800 a month. (If that price sounds high to you, you must not live near or in a large city!) At that price, the quantity supplied is only 2,000 units, while would-be renters would like to occupy 3,000 apartments at that "bargain" rate. Note that the price ceiling has reduced the quantity supplied (from 2,400 to 2,000) and increased the quantity demanded (from 2,400 to 3,000) compared to the quantities that would be supplied and demanded at the equilibrium price of $950 a month. The quantity supplied declines as apartments are converted to owner-occupied units, allowed to deteriorate, or put into nonresidential uses, all of which will be more profitable for the current owner. (Notice that this is *not* a shift in supply, just a movement along the supply curve in response to a change in price.) The quantity demanded rises because of the lower price; young couples feel they can cut loose of the in-laws, lower income families think that they can now afford to move up from one bedroom to two, or folks living out of town decide that they can now afford to move into town. The result of a price ceiling is a shortage.

One consequence of a shortage is that price ceases to perform a very important function—rationing. Prices decide who gets apartments in an unregulated market. Apartments go to those who want them most as measured by the amount they are willing to pay. When sellers, or landlords, can no longer use price to allocate apartments, then they must turn to other ways of choosing. Chances are the landlord will go for the tenants who are likely to cause the least trouble—no noise, no damage, no complaints. Gone are the families with children or dogs, and in are the quiet, peaceful tenants who promise to paint the walls and fix their own plumbing leaks. Nonmarket methods of rationing replace the market, or the price mechanism, in choosing between competing buyers.

Sellers generally like price floors, to protect them from a fall in price. Buyers like price ceilings, which protect them from a higher price. In reality, neither gains much, especially in the long run. Some sellers may gain, while others lose, as you learned in the minimum wage illustration. The price floor creates surpluses, raises consumer prices, and ultimately turns political support against the seller and the protected product. Price ceilings, likewise, protect a few buyers. However, they keep other buyers from purchasing what they are willing and able to buy at what would otherwise be the equilibrium price, and also create frustration in people who are attracted into the market by the artificially low price but cannot find any apartments.

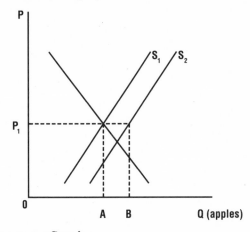

FIG. 4-4 *Temporary Surplus*

How Markets Correct Temporary Shortages and Surpluses

Price controls are not the only source of shortages and surpluses. Shortages and surpluses can also be observed *temporarily* when there is a movement from one equilibrium to another. Consider the market for apples in Figure 4-4. There is a sudden, unexpected increase in supply owing to a bumper crop. Supply shifts from S_1 to S_2, while the demand curve is unchanged. The immediate effect of the supply shift is a temporary surplus at the old price, P_1. Quantity demanded is OA, while quantity supplied is

OB. This temporary surplus looks much like the surplus resulting from a price floor, and indeed it is. The difference is that market forces immediately go to work. Competition among apple sellers to get rid of their surplus leads them to cut prices. As they do so, some sellers take part of their crop off the market until prices improve, while many buyers purchase more for snacks, pies, and apple jelly. As prices fall, the surplus shrinks and eventually disappears.

APPLICATION 2: TAXES AND TARIFFS

A second application of supply and demand curves is to examine the effects of taxes (including tariffs, which are simply import taxes) on prices and quantities and to determine who is affected most. There is a whole range of tax models, but we will examine just two examples, an excise tax on automobile tires and a tariff on imported shoes. Both types of taxes are particularly important to business firms in the affected industries.

Who Pays the Excise Tax?

Figure 4-5 shows the effects of an excise tax on the sales of automobile tires (this tax that actually is used in the United States). The market demand and supply of automobile tires are represented by D_1 and S_1, respectively. The government then imposes a tax of \$1.00 per tire, which is payable by the seller. (It could be made payable by the buyer; the effect will be the same.)

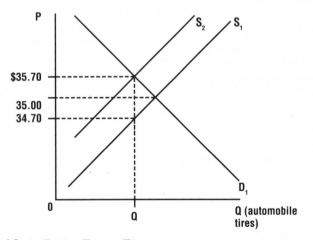

FIG. 4-5 *An Excise Tax on Tires*

If the equilibrium price of tires was $35.00 a tire, does the price rise to $36.00? Not exactly. The seller's supply curve is the same, but the buyer perceives that supply curve as lying just above the old supply curve at a vertical distance of $1.00—same old supply, plus $1.00 of tax. This supply curve perceived by the buyer is labeled S_2. This new supply curve intersects the demand curve at a higher price, $35.70, and a smaller quantity—OA tires instead of OB. The price has risen, but by less than the amount of the tax. What accounts for the other 30 cents?

As the volume of sales begins to fall from OB to OA, sellers move back along the supply curve. In commonsense terms, competition among sellers for a shrinking market means that they cut prices. Perhaps they advertise a sale, offer discounts to preferred customers, or promise free wheel balancing—all forms of price reduction. According to the market-supply curve, sellers who find they aren't selling as many tires at the old price will be willing to cut their price to $34.70 in order to keep sales from falling below an amount OA. In effect, sellers absorb 30 cents of the new tax. Thus, 70 cents of the tax falls on buyers (or, in the jargon of economics, is "shifted forward" to consumers), and 30 cents falls on the seller in the form of a lower price received. Chapter 5 will explore exactly what determines the division of a tax between buyer and seller.

This example illustrates a more general point about taxes. The law usually specifies who pays the tax. General sales taxes, for example, are supposed to be paid by the buyer; property taxes, by the property owner; social security taxes, equally divided between employer and employee. But tax writers cannot legislate the market. The actual division of the burden of any tax depends on market conditions—the steepness of the supply and demand curves, the degree of competition in the market, and other factors that are discussed in more detail in Chapter 5.

Winners and Losers from Tariffs

A second example of using a supply-and-demand model to analyze the effects of a tax is shown in Figure 4-6. U.S. consumers buy shoes from both domestic and foreign producers. Their demand is D_u, and the supply from domestic producers is S_u. American buyers can also buy shoes that are made abroad. For simplicity, we have drawn the foreign supply curve as horizontal at a price level of $30.00 a pair. This curve says that American buyers can buy all the foreign shoes they want at the going world price of $30.00. If buyers are indifferent about choosing between foreign and domestic shoes, American producers cannot charge more than $30.00 a pair or they will not sell any shoes. Thus, American firms produce OA pairs of shoes, American consumers purchase OD pairs of shoes, and the difference (AD) is imported.

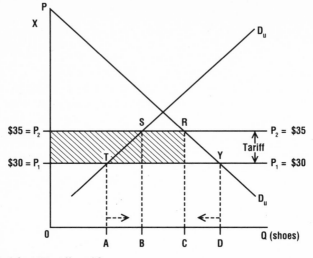

FIG. 4-6 *A Tariff on Shoes*

Suppose U.S. shoe producers persuade the government to protect them with a tariff of $5.00 a pair. This tariff works somewhat like a cross between a price floor and an excise tax. The foreign supply curve perceived by the U.S. customer rises to be horizontal at a price of $35.00 a pair—the foreign supply price plus the tariff. It is easy to see that U.S. consumers are worse off. They are now buying a smaller quantity of shoes (a drop of DC pairs, from OD to OC in Figure 4-6) at the higher price of $35.00. Foreign sellers are exporting less—BC instead of AD. The gainer is the domestic producer, who is now selling more shoes (OB instead of OA) at a higher price. The government also has a gain to show—tariff revenue of $5.00 a pair times the imports of BC pairs of shoes.

It is important to note from this diagram that the losers lost more than the gainers gained. In order to demonstrate that point, it is helpful to develop the concept of consumer surplus. Remember from Chapter 3 that consumers were better off if the price of a good fell—the price fall was equivalent to an increase in income, because they could now buy a larger total quantity of goods. The technical name for this gain to consumers from a decline in price along the demand curve is *consumer surplus*, and it measures changes in satisfaction or utility.

When buyers purchased OD pairs of shoes at $30.00 a pair, they gave up OD times $30.00 worth of satisfaction or utility. For example, if OD = 500 pairs of shoes, they paid $15,000, giving up $15,000 of other goods they could have purchased with that money. However, they gained utility equal to the area under the demand curve up to OD, an area equal to OXYD. The difference between utility gained from purchases of shoes and utility lost by giving up the $15,000 worth of other goods that could have been purchased is consumers' surplus, measured by triangle P_1XY.

The concept of consumers' surplus is easy to envision in terms of a personal demand curve. Suppose that Peter's demand curve is such that he will buy one pair of shoes at $35.00, two pairs at $30.00 each, or three pairs at $25.00. Peter goes to the shoe store and finds that shoes are selling for $25.00 a pair, so he buys three pairs. Peter gives up $75.00 worth of utility (three pairs times $25.00). How much utility does he gain? To Peter the three pairs of shoes are worth, respectively, $35.00, $30.00, and $25.00, for a total of $90.00. His consumers' surplus is the difference between the total value that he places on what he bought (the area under the demand curve, or $90.00) and the value of what he gave up to purchase it ($75.00). Consumer surplus in this case is $15.00.

When consumers move back up the demand curve because of an increase in price, they lose consumer surplus. When the price of shoes rose to P_2 = $35.00, the loss of consumer surplus amounted to the shaded area, or P_1P_2RY. Part of that went to the government and part of it (area P_1P_2ST) went to domestic producers. The rest was just lost. Thus, the losses to consumers from a tariff outweigh the value of the gains to the government (tariff revenue) and to domestic producers. It is for this reason that economists are so strongly opposed to tariffs under most circumstances.

APPLICATION 3: USING PRICE TO ALLOCATE "FREE" GOODS

Our final application of supply and demand is to the pricing of goods and services offered by the government. Consider some of the services that your local government may provide—trash collection, city parks, street maintenance, police protection, downtown parking, and streetlights, for example. Chances are that your city doesn't charge for most of these services. If something is free, how much will citizens choose to consume?

In Figure 4-7 citizens "demand" 800 downtown parking spaces—if they are free. But parking is not free. There is a cost to the city to maintain the parking area, even if it is only painting the lines and picking up the trash and litter. In addition, if parking is free, there may be a shortage at that very low price, so some people who want to park downtown and would be willing to pay can't find a parking space.

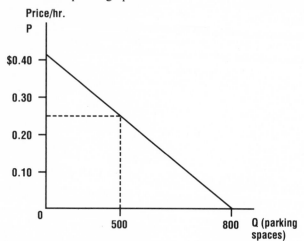

FIG. 4-7 *Demand for Parking Spaces*

The city can look at this pricing problem in two ways. One way is to say that the parking spaces are given, the costs of maintaining them are low enough to be ignored, and the reason for charging a price is (1) to ration the parking spaces available among competing users and (2) to raise some revenue for general purposes for the city. They raise the price a little each day until, through trial and error, they find the price at which the spaces are full but there are not several cars always circling looking for an empty space.

With 500 downtown parking spaces, the city finds that at a zero price there is demand for 800 spaces. Gradually raising the price, the police chief finds that at 25 cents an hour the spaces are pretty well filled during the day, and there are not many cars cruising in search of a space. This price serves to allocate parking spaces efficiently as well as to raise some revenue.

One alternative is to say, "We need more parking!" What this statement really means is that at the zero price, [quantity supplied exceeds quantity demanded.] The two can be made equal by increasing the supply or by raising the price. But adding parking spaces is not costless. Land must be purchased and then graded, paved, and made suitable for this use. Who should pay— taxpayers in general, some of whom never drive downtown, or those who use the parking spaces? If it is the latter, then some of the cost of creating and maintaining the parking spaces should fall on those who "demand" them. In this case charging a price is a way to make sure that those who benefit from the service pay for the costs they create.

Many of the services provided in the public sector are more difficult to charge for than parking. Who should pay for street lights, for example—the neighbors who benefit regularly or the stray passerby who is saved from an accident by a well-placed light? Should society charge the children of the poor (as well as the rest) for their education, knowing they are likely to drop out earlier if they have to pay? Why charge for entrance to a city park when extra users impose no extra costs and there is ample empty space for all to enjoy? At a national level, how should the bill for national defense be allocated? Clearly some of the goods and services produced in the public sector do not lend themselves to a "fee-for-service" approach. But there are opportunities to use prices creatively in the public sector for certain types of goods, and economists encourage governments—especially local governments—to be more alert to such opportunities.

THE ROLE OF PRICE

The last example raised an interesting point. A market system puts a tremendous burden on price as a signal, a rationing device, an incentive, and a means of communication. Here is a quick list of what a market system asks price to do:

* signal consumers to substitute in consumption
* signal producers to expand or contract output
* provide public officials with a measure of demand for certain public sector goods and services
* signal resource owners how best to employ their resources

* signal producers to change the mix of resources they use, shifting to those whose prices are lower
* ration a limited quantity of a good among competing buyers so that it goes to those who are willing to pay the most

Price plays the starring role in a market system. Sometimes it does not work fast enough or effectively enough to suit us; we want instant equilibrium, and adjustments are not always that fast. For example, some Southern states had been using 16- and 17-year-old school bus drivers, paying the minimum wage ($3.35). When the U.S. Department of Labor forced them to switch to adult drivers in 1988, the governments involved relied on the price system to attract drivers, raising the hourly rate substantially. Did it work? Yes and no. The higher price certainly led to a substantial increase in the number of adult drivers available, but when school started in the fall after the switch, many districts were still experiencing a driver shortage. The economist would say that the market was indeed doing a good job, but there were two problems: (1) school districts didn't raise the price high enough and (2) it takes time for the market to adjust. Other examples of price rationing and price signals are easy to find; just look around.

CHAPTER PERSPECTIVE

Supply-and-demand analysis lends itself to explaining a great variety of market events. This chapter explored a few applications—price floors and price ceilings, taxes and tariffs, and public-sector pricing. Price floors, or minimum prices established by government, create surpluses that must be disposed of in some way. Price ceilings, or maximum prices, create shortages, and some other way must be found (other than price) to allocate the limited quantity among competing buyers.

Taxes raise the prices paid by buyers and lower the price received by sellers. They generate revenue to the government but reduce the amount of the taxed product that is produced and sold. Even if the government places the tax on one party, either the buyer or the seller, the burden is shared between the two in most cases. Tariffs on imported goods also raise prices and cause a loss of consumer surplus, although they benefit domestic producers and generate revenue for the government. Price can also be used by the public sector to ration some goods produced by government and to measure how much such goods citizens really want.

This chapter highlighted the important role of price in a market system by showing some of its uses and by examining what happens in the market when the government intervenes in the price mechanism in various ways. One question that was not addressed was how much consumers will respond to a price change: This measure of responsiveness is the main focus of Chapter 5.

Demand, Consumers, and Elasticity

INTRODUCTION AND MAIN POINTS

No firm can make intelligent decisions about setting prices, how much output to produce, or how much inventory to maintain without some sense of the other side of the market—that is, how consumers might be expected to respond to changes in price or other factors. This chapter looks more closely at the demand curve and takes a brief second look at the supply curve. Specifically, this chapter examines consumers' (and producers') responses to price changes, measured by *elasticity of demand* (and supply); what influences elasticity; and how elasticity affects price setting.

After studying the material in this chapter:

■ You will know how to measure elasticity of demand and supply based on price and quantity information.

■ You will be able to use the total revenue test to determine whether demand is elastic or inelastic.

■ You will be familiar with the factors that make demand more or less elastic, and be able to use that information in pricing decisions.

■ You will be able to explain how elasticity is related to the amount of market power a firm possesses.

DEMAND RESPONSE WHEN SUPPLY SHIFTS

Suppose that the local market for paperback books at one bookstore is in equilibrium at P_0, Q_0, as in Figure 5-1. At P=\$3.00, customers are buying 1000 books a week, so the firm's weekly revenue is \$3000. Suppose also that the firm's supply curve looks like the one drawn (S_1), but the manager doesn't know much about the demand curve except that it passes through the equilibrium point. Many demand curves could pass through that point. Figure 5-1 shows two possibilities: D_1, which is very flat, and D_2, which is very steep.

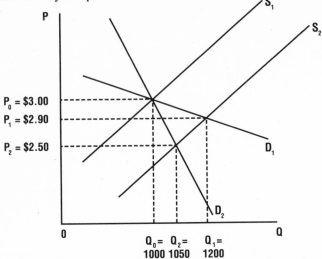

FIG. 5-1 *Elastic and Inelastic Demand and Shifts in Supply*

What happens if this firm's supply curve shifts to the right? (Why the supply shift? Perhaps the firm got a bigger discount from publishers, or perhaps other costs fell.) If the correct demand curve is D_1, then the bookstore will see a large increase in sales volume (to Q_1 = 1200) and a small decline in price (to P_1 = $2.90). It only takes a small cut in price to induce buyers to purchase *lots* more books. The firm's total revenue (price times quantity), increases from $P_0Q_0 = \$3*1000 = \$3000$ to $P_1Q_1 = \$2.90*1200 = \$3480$.

On the other hand, if the correct demand curve is D_2, the results of an increase in supply are not nearly as appealing. The firm still sees a fall in price and a rise in quantity, but now price falls more (to P_2 = $2.50) and quantity increases less (to Q_2 = 1050). Total revenue falls from $P_0Q_0 = \$3000$ to $P_2Q_2 = \$2.50*1050 = \$2625$.

The lesson from this exercise is that it is important for firms to know something about how buyers of their products will respond to changes in price. This measure of responsiveness is called *price elasticity of demand*.

MEASURING RESPONSIVENESS: PRICE ELASTICITY OF DEMAND

The percentage change in quantity demanded in response to a given percentage change in price is measured by price elasticity of demand. Elasticity is computed on the assumption that the demand curve is stable; that is, all other factors remain constant (ceteris paribus) in order to focus on the response of quantity to price. In symbols:

$$E = \%\ \Delta Q/\%\Delta P$$

where E is the elasticity coefficient and Δ means "change in...". While the slope of a straight-line demand curve is constant, its elasticity is not. Because elasticity measures a percentage change, its value changes as buyers move along the demand curve. A little computation will illustrate exactly how elasticity changes.

Recall the demand schedule in Chapter 3, which described the market demand for milk:

Price	Quantity
$3.00	3
2.50	6
2.00	9
1.50	12
1.00	15

This set of numbers and the formula given above are all the information needed to compute the elasticity of demand between any two prices. Consider the change from P = $3.00 to P = $2.50. The percentage change in quantity is $\Delta Q/Q$. The change in quantity is 3. What should be used for the denominator—the original quantity, 3, or the new quantity, 6? Neither! If you use the original quantity, you will get a different answer for elasticity when price falls from $3.00 to $2.50 and when it rises from $2.50 to $3.00. To get the same measure in both directions, use the average of the two quantities, or 4.5. Thus the percentage change in quantity is 3/4.5, or 66.6%.

Likewise, to compute the percentage change in price, divide the price change ($0.50) by the average of the old price ($3.00) and new price ($2.50). This average is $2.75; the percentage change in price is .50/2.75, or 18.2%. Finally, the elasticity coefficient, E, is computed as percentage change in quantity divided by percentage change in price, or 66.6%/18.2%, giving an elasticity coefficient of 3.66. (Note that along a downward-sloping demand curve price and quantity always move in opposite directions, so that the coefficient of price elasticity of demand will always be negative. Economists usually ignore the minus sign in computing elasticity.)

Try one more calculation. What is the value of the elasticity coefficient when price falls from $1.50 to $1.00? The percentage change in quantity is now only 22.2% (3/13.5), but the percentage change in price is much larger, 40% (.50/1.25). Elasticity is much smaller; the elasticity coefficient is 22.2%/40%, or .555. Moving down the demand curve, the price base in the calculation gets smaller while the quantity base in the calculation gets larger, so elasticity always gets smaller at the lower range of the demand curve. You may want to experiment with calculations at other points on the demand curve.

If the elasticity coefficient is greater than one, demand is *elastic*. Elastic demand means that when a price changes, the buyers' response in terms of quantity purchased is more than proportional to the change in price. If the elasticity coefficient has a value less than one, demand is *inelastic*. The quantity response by buyers is less than proportional to the change in price. If the elasticity coefficient is equal to one—which occurs at one point on every straight-line demand curve—demand is of *unitary elasticity*. The percentage change in price will meet with an equal change in quantity demanded. You should be able to identify a point of unitary elasticity on the demand schedule for milk given earlier.

While all straight-line demand curves have an elastic and an inelastic range and pass through a point of unitary elasticity, it is possible to compare demand curves in terms of their relative elasticity. If two demand curves pass through the same point, as in Figure 5-1, but one is steeper than the other, the steeper demand curve is usually described as "relatively inelastic" and the flatter one as "relatively elastic." Thus, in Figure 5-1 demand curve D_1 is relatively elastic and demand curve D_2 is relatively inelastic. This rather casual use of these terms is useful in discussing alternative market structures in future chapters.

Elasticity is not a purely theoretical concept. Economists have used actual market data to compute elasticity of demand for a variety of products. Airline travel, for example, has a higher elasticity of demand than television sets, but lower than tomatoes or medical care. Elasticity is used to forecast auto sales, to set bus fares, to decide whether to offer "cents off" coupons and to whom they should be sent, and for a variety of other marketing purposes.

The Total Revenue Test

A quick way to determine whether demand is elastic, inelastic, or of unitary elasticity is to observe what happens to total revenue when price changes. Here is a guide:

If...	and...	then...
Price rises	Total revenue rises	demand is inelastic
Price rises	Total revenue falls	demand is elastic
Price falls	Total revenue rises	demand is elastic
Price falls	Total revenue falls	demand is inelastic

If price rises and quantity demanded does not respond very strongly (demand is inelastic), then the rise in price will more than offset the decline in quantity, and total revenue will rise. You can work through the reasoning for the other three cases. Now apply this test to the demand curve for milk:

Price	Quantity	Total Revenue	Demand is
$3.00	3	9	—
2.50	6	15>	elastic
2.00	9	18>	elastic
1.50	12	18> .	unitary
1.00	15	15	inelastic

Determinants of Elasticity

Is there a quick way of guessing how elastic or inelastic demand for your product is, without experimenting with price changes and making costly mistakes? There is no substitute for the marketplace test, but there are some commonsense guidelines that tell you for which products and in which markets demand is likely to be elastic.

Demand is more elastic for products with many good *substitutes*, less elastic for products with few good substitutes. These substitutes may be highly similar products (aluminum foil for plastic wrap, apple juice for orange juice) or products from other sellers—Joe's gas station instead of Alice's, Kroger instead of Safeway. If there are many good substitutes for your product, or lots of competing sellers, your customers are likely to be very sensitive to even small price changes. If you own the only copy shop for miles around, you can charge 20 cents a copy and still make sales; but if there are competitors nearby, you can't charge much more—if any more—than your competitors do and still make any sales. The local power company doesn't have that problem; it is much harder to find good substitutes for electricity, and there is no competing electric producer for customers who would like to switch. Thus, demand for electricity is relatively—but not totally—inelastic. Substitute products and substitute suppliers are the most important determinants of price elasticity of demand.

Sellers expend a great deal of time and money trying to convince customers that competing products and competing sellers aren't really good substitutes—the quality is inferior, the location is inconvenient, the service is poor. One major function of advertising is to make demand less elastic for a particular product, like Nike shoes, or a particular seller, like K-Mart stores.

Demand is also likely to be more elastic if the product carries a *high price* relative to the consumer's budget. Thus, consumers are more likely to shop carefully for price differences when buying cars, appliances, and furniture than when buying bread or renting video cassettes. Furthermore, a large percentage change in the price of a car or a washing machine translates into a large dollar chunk of the consumer's budget. A $300 saving on a used-car purchase is worth a large investment of a buyer's time, even if it is only 5 percent of the price of the car.

A third important determinant of elasticity of demand is *time.* Demand is much less elastic in the short run because it takes time to identify substitutes, gather price information, change habits, or make other adjustments to changes in price. If Jeff needs a quart of milk right now for the twins' breakfast, he is probably willing to pay a high price at a convenience store. After several such experiences, however, he will plan better and buy enough lower-priced milk at the supermarket to last through the week.

When gasoline prices rose sharply in the mid-1970s, consumers' initial response was moderate. Over time, however, they cut down on pleasure driving and formed car pools, shifted to smaller cars, used public transportation more frequently, and even moved closer to their work-places. As gasoline prices fell in the 1980s, likewise, consumers were slow to adjust their habits by buying larger cars and doing more recreational driving, and in the short run lower prices did not result in much of an increase in gasoline sales. By the mid-1980s, however, the larger and less fuel-efficient cars were beginning to make a comeback, "cruising" had become a way of life among small-town teenagers, and the volume of gasoline sales began to rise again.

Long-run elasticity is greater than short-run elasticity. There is an important lesson for business pricing in long-run elasticity. A firm may see an opportunity to increase revenues by raising prices because short-run elasticity of demand is low. Over time, however, the decision to raise prices may prove costly, as customers identify substitutes or as other suppliers see an opportunity to get a foothold in the local market with lower prices. Likewise, the short-run effects of cutting prices may be discouraging, but if the firm can hold on until customers get word of price change, adjust their habits, and start responding, the long-run gains from price cuts may be substantial.

Elasticity, the Firm, and the Market

A demand curve facing an individual firm is much more elastic than the market demand curve. The individual firm may be a retailer, a wholesaler, or a producer of a particular brand or product line. Thus, while the demand curve for running shoes may be relatively inelastic, the demand for Reeboks or Nikes is much more elastic, and likewise the demand for running shoes at Smith's Sport Shop or at the competing Discount Athletic Wear will be very sensitive to price. Any runner can tell you that there are no substitutes for good running shoes, but there are many good substitutes for a particular brands or a particular store.

Sometimes the firm *is* the market. In a small town there may be only one gas station, one beauty shop, one fast-food place. These firms can charge somewhat higher prices because their customers are not likely to travel any great distance for those goods and services. Even so, such firms are limited in their price discretion. As the town grows, competitors are likely to come in. If local prices get too high, some families may choose to make a weekly expedition to a larger town to fill the tank, get haircuts, and go out for a burger all in one trip. Every firm has some kind of competition, or substitutes, if the price gets high enough.

Perfectly Elastic Demand Curves

At the other end of the scale your firm may be one among so many producing virtually identical products that you may have no price discretion at all. Suppose you run one of hundreds of copy shops in a large city, and the going rate for copies is 10 cents a page. You can do all the business you want at 10 cents a page. If you raise the price even a little, to 11 cents a page, most of your customers will switch to competitors. You could cut your price to 9 cents a page, but that seems silly when you can get all the copying business you can handle at the going rate of 10 cents a page. Your firm's demand curve is horizontal at 10 cents a page.

What determined the price of 10 cents a page? The market for copying services represents the sum of the supply curves of all producers, like yourself, and the sum of the demand curves of all the individual potential customers. The market for copying services is represented in Figure 5-2(a), with an equilibrium volume (quantity) of copying services of 500,000 copies a day at a price of 10 cents a copy. Your firm, in Figure 5-2(b), takes that price as given. Your firm's supply curve intersects that horizontal demand curve at an equilibrium quantity of 1000 copies a day.

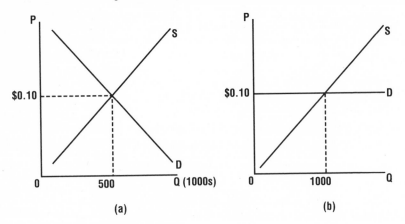

(a)   (b)

FIG. 5-2(a) *Market Demand*   FIG 5-2(b) *Firm Demand*

Perfectly elastic demand curves are not uncommon. They apply particularly to agricultural products, where there are many producers of virtually identical products. In other product lines different brand names, location, reputation, or service may give an individual firm a slight edge, so that its demand curve is flat but not perfectly horizontal.

Perfectly Inelastic Demand Curves
One popular misconception is the idea of a vertical demand curve—the belief that people "need" a certain amount of water,

gasoline, etc. and will consume the same amount regardless of price. If you were going to consume 200 gallons of water a day, whether it cost a penny a gallon or a dollar a gallon, your demand curve for water would be vertical. You would buy the same quantity at every possible price. In reality, while there are some very inelastic (almost vertical) demand curves, the perfectly inelastic demand curve is a mythical beast.

Consider salt. Your household uses some salt in cooking, and you may not even know the price of a box of salt—10 cents? 25 cents? 75 cents? If you buy a box of salt every six months, you will pay any one of those prices without thinking twice about it. But what about $2.00 a box? or $10? Until you cut back your salt purchases because of higher prices, the seller just hasn't arrived at the price range where you will respond. Furthermore, even if it takes an enormous price hike for you to respond, there are other people for whom price matters. Low-income families on a tight budget will buy a smaller box rather than a larger one when pennies count. Highway departments that use large quantities of salt to melt ice on the roads in winter will switch to sand or chemical substitutes if salt becomes more expensive. Restaurants that deal in high volume may switch to shakers with fewer holes to subtly reduce salt usage and save some expenses where it won't be noticed. Even if not every buyer is sensitive to price, it only takes a few buyers who are responsive to give a market demand curve a negative slope.

Even addictive drugs—heroin, nicotine, cocaine—show some sensitivity to price. As the price of cigarettes has risen (mainly because of higher tobacco taxes), some smokers have cut back. However, it is difficult to separate the effects of prices from the effects of a strong antismoking campaign. When the price of street heroin goes out of sight, more addicts enroll in methadone maintenance programs. There are no vertical demand curves. How much individuals "need" of anything depends on its price and on how much of other goods and services they must give up in order to obtain it.

Market Power and Consumer Response

Most buyers want demand to be elastic so that sellers will cut prices to entice them to buy more. Most sellers want to face a highly inelastic demand curve so that they can raise prices, produce less, and still take in more revenue. This tension between buyers and sellers is part of what makes markets work.

A major goal of business firms is to make their demand curves less elastic. They try to do this through advertising, superior service, creating brand/store loyalty, discounts for repeat customers, and other tactics. Fortunately for consumers, but unfortunately for the seller, the firm's rivals compete in the same way. The result? Better service, better products, lower prices—but not necessarily a less elastic demand curve. The competition, however, benefits consumers.

Another way that business firms try to make demand curves less elastic is to drive out or forestall development of competing firms. If XYZ Office Products can have the local market all to itself—a local monopoly—then its demand will be inelastic and it can raise prices, operate fewer hours, and still get plenty of business. Unfortunately, the landscape is littered with failed firms that thought they could safely rest on their laurels inside the protective fortress of a local monopoly. Such behavior is an open invitation to competitors to come in and offer better hours, better service, and lower prices. Even a local monopoly has to behave like a firm that has competitors, because it does have potential if not actual competitors. Thus, business firms are constantly trying to convince customers that there are no satisfactory substitutes, while consumers try to impress on these same sellers that they do, indeed, have plenty of alternatives. This tug of war over the elasticity of the demand curve ensures that consumers have some degree of market power, even where there are few firms in the market.

ELASTICITY OF SUPPLY

It is also possible to measure elasticity of the supply curve. Supply curves are important not only to consumers and public policymakers but also to business firms, because firms are both buyers and sellers. They sell to other firms and to consumers, but they buy in the resource market. They may buy semifinished products as well. Wholesalers and retailers buy from producers in order to distribute to other customers or final users.

Consider Figure 5-3, which shows a demand curve D_1 and two supply curves, S_1 and S_2, for soup. Both supply curves pass through the original equilibrium, P_0, Q_0. Suppose that as a result of very cold weather and more interest in hot lunches, the demand curve shifts to the right (to D_2). Regardless of which is the correct supply curve, the price of soup and the quantity supplied will both increase, but in what combination? That depends on how steep or flat the supply curve is. If the supply curve is relatively flat, like S_1, there will be a large increase in quantity (to Q_1) and a small increase in price (to P_1). If the supply curve is steeper, like S_2, there will be a smaller increase in quantity (to Q_2) and a larger increase in price (to P_2).

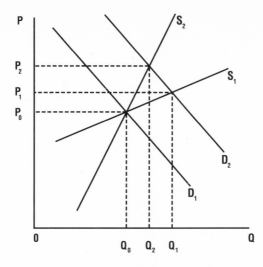

FIG. 5-3 *Elasticity of Supply and Shifts in Demand*

Elasticity of supply is defined in the same way as elasticity of demand:

$$E_s = \% \Delta Q / \% \Delta P$$

Since price and quantity move in the same direction, elasticity of supply is always positive. An elasticity coefficient of less than 1 means that supply is inelastic; greater than 1, elastic; and equal to one, of unitary elasticity. The computations are the same as for elasticity of demand.

Supply elasticity is affected chiefly by the cost and availability of inputs, a topic considered more closely in the next few chapters. Like demand curves, supply curves are more elastic in the long run, when there are opportunities to adjust to changing signals. Supply curves can be horizontal or perfectly elastic in some cases. An apple buyer in season can pick from many roadside stands with identical prices. A small firm hiring unskilled labor in a large market can hire all the workers it wants at the going wage; it faces a perfectly elastic supply curve of labor.

Unlike demand, supply can be vertical for a few products and/or for very short time periods. The supply of Super Bowl tickets is given once the stadium has been selected. The number of Michelangelo sculptures was fixed once the artist died (although the number offered for sale by current owners may vary with market price). The supply of milk in Pasadena today is fixed, or close to it, although it can be increased tomorrow.

With a few rare exceptions, however, most supply curves slope upward. When the price of gold rose sharply in the 1970s, this higher price called forth more gold. The quantity in existence was fixed, but the supply was not. Higher prices led to melting old jewelry and opening old mines. Super Bowl tickets are fixed in supply once the stadium is chosen, but an excess demand for Super Bowl tickets one year means that the next year sponsors may search for a site with more seats. In the long run vertical supply curves are almost as rare as vertical demand curves.

CHAPTER PERSPECTIVE

The elasticity of the demand curve determines how much consumers will respond to a price change—whether the change in quantity or volume of sales will be large or small. This measure of responsiveness is useful to producers in making decisions about pricing. Elasticity of demand is lower in the short run than in the long run, higher for items with many substitute products or substitute suppliers, and lower for items that are small relative to the total budget. Some firms face horizontal, or perfectly elastic, demand curves; vertical demand curves are mythical or nonexistent. Firms try to make their demand less elastic through advertising or other means.

Supply elasticity measures the response of quantity supplied to changes in price. Supply is more elastic in the long run. Supply elasticity depends on the cost and availability of inputs. It is possible for a supply curve to be vertical, at least for a few special (unique and irreproducible) products and/or in the very short run.

The Theory of Production

INTRODUCTION AND MAIN POINTS

Most of the last chapter was devoted to a closer examination of the demand curve. This chapter and the two that follow look at the determinants of supply, namely production theory and costs. We begin with some basic production concepts in this chapter. These concepts will provide a foundation for understanding how costs behave as output expands and contracts, which is the subject of the following two chapters.

After studying the material in this chapter:

■ You will understand how the principle of diminishing returns can be applied to simple production decisions.

■ You will know how changes in marginal product relate to changes in total product and average product, and be able to apply this knowledge to other kinds of total, average, and marginal relationships.

■ You will be able to draw and interpret a production-possibilities curve, using it to describe choices between two alternatives, to measure opportunity cost, and to identify output combinations that represent technical and allocative efficiency.

■ You will be able to describe the relationships between inputs and outputs using such techniques as a production function and an isoquant map.

ECONOMIC EFFICIENCY

A basic goal of production is efficiency; that is, to get the most output from a given quantity of resources, or to produce a given output with a minimum expenditure of resources in terms of inputs. In a narrow, technical sense, we can talk about physical efficiency—minimizing the number of worker hours, kilowatts of electricity, or acres of land as an input to the productive process.

However, none of these measures gives a complete view of efficiency, because they do not allow the producer to add units of different inputs or to compare them.

Economic efficiency means minimizing the *value* of inputs to produce a given *value* of output, or maximizing the value of output that is generated from a given value of inputs. This measure of efficiency calls for economizing on resources that are scarce and expensive, and looking for ways to substitute other resources that are more abundant and therefore cheaper. It also requires that producers be attentive to what consumers would like to have produced, as measured by the prices they are willing to pay. The value of output is the sum of the quantities times the prices, or the amount that consumers are willing to pay. Inputs are valued by their opportunity costs or their value in the next best alternative use.

There are several tools that economists use to visualize the choices of inputs and outputs and the input-output relationship. These tools include production functions, production-possibilities curves, and isoquant maps. Underlying all three of these tools or models is a basic economic principle, the *law of diminishing returns*.

THE LAW OF DIMINISHING RETURNS

This law, introduced briefly in Chapter 3, states that as a producer adds more and more of a variable quantity to a fixed quantity, the increase in output, satisfaction, or other products continues to increase, but at a decreasing rate. Additional units of input result in less and less additional output. This general principle has widespread applications to economic processes of all kinds as well as to some noneconomic processes. Students can tell you that the additional increase in their grade per hour of studying gets smaller and smaller with each extra hour. Try pushing on a bicycle pump and see if the tenth push generates as much increase in tire pressure as the first few.

For consumers, the law of diminishing marginal utility states that as one adds more and more consumption of one good to a fixed stock of other goods, then beyond some point the additional satisfaction from the extra units gets smaller and smaller. Note that it does not mean that consumers suffer diminishing marginal utility from goods-in-general, just from more and more pizza or more and more shoes with no increase in consumption of soft drinks, chicken, socks, or T-shirts.

For producers, the law takes the form of the law of diminishing marginal product or increasing marginal cost. Assume that one input—usually land, physical plant, or capital equipment—is fixed and that we continue to add more units of another input—usually labor or raw materials. Beyond some point the extra units of labor or raw materials add less and less to total output, simply because they do not have enough of the fixed inputs to work with. There is no point in hiring more than two typesetters in a print shop if there is only one typesetting machine. One typesetter can keep the machine in use; two typesetters allow for breaks and doing other tasks; three typesetters will be waiting in line for a turn at the machine. If each worker is paid the same as the others, then diminishing output per extra worker translates into increasing cost per unit of output, as we will see in the next chapter.

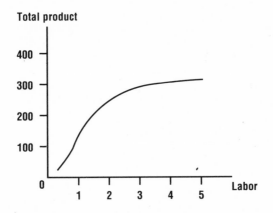

FIG. 6-1 *Total Product*

What Is a Production Function?

The relationship between inputs and outputs is called a *production function*. A particularly useful type of production function is the kind that shows the relationship between one varying input, such as labor, and the amount of output, while holding other inputs fixed. Figure 6-1 shows the relationship between total output of a print shop (pages per day) on the vertical axis and the number of worker hours on the horizontal axis. As you can see, initially output rises rapidly as more worker-hours are added, but beyond some point output increases at a slower and slower rate, and finally begins to drop off. Perhaps the sole worker is putting in overtime and getting careless, or there are too many workers relative to the equipment available, but eventually extra worker-hours generate little if any extra output.

Total, Average, and Marginal Product

Figure 6-1 does not indicate to the manager of this print shop how many worker-hours to use. That depends on other factors not yet discussed, such as the price of labor and the price of output. However, this diagram is the first of several that you will encounter that express some important relationships between total, average, and marginal values of something; in this case, total, average, and marginal product. Total product is just what it implies; in this case, pages per day. Average product is the number of pages per day divided by the number of workers. When total product is 220 pages, the production function shows that the firm is using two workers for an average product per worker of 110 pages. When total product is 320 pages, the firm is using five workers and average product has fallen, as the law of diminishing returns predicts that it will, to 64 pages per worker. The numbers below correspond to the points on the graph in Figure 6-1:

Worker-hours	Total Product	Average Product	Marginal Product
0	0	—	
1	100	100	100
2	220	110	120
3	270	90	50
4	300	75	30
5	320	64	20
6	330	55	10
7	330	47	0
8	320	40	−10

Here, *marginal* means "extra." In this case marginal output is the extra output generated by one additional (marginal) worker. When the number of workers rose from two to three, output increased (according to the production function) from 220 to 270. Marginal output was 50. When a fourth worker was added, output increased again, but by less (law of diminishing returns!). The fourth worker added 30 pages to output. The sixth worker hour added only 10 pages to daily output. Figure 6-2 graphs the average and marginal product curves.

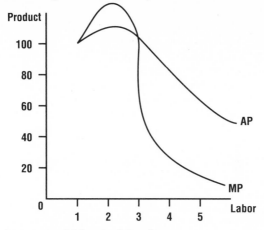

FIG. 6-2 *Average and Marginal Product*

If you compare the numbers and the graphs, you will notice some important relationships between total, average, and marginal. Total can be increasing even as average and marginal are falling, as long as marginal is positive. Total product will fall only if marginal product is negative. Second, if marginal product is greater than average product, it will pull up the average. If marginal product is less than average product (i.e., if the next worker adds less than the average amount to output), the average will fall. This pattern holds true for all kinds of average and marginal relationships. If your sales today are greater than your week's average, the average will rise; if they are lower, your week's average will fall. If they are exactly equal to the average, the average will be unchanged. This relationship between total, average, and marginal will be very useful in the next two chapters, which describe the behavior of costs.

OTHER TOOLS FOR LOOKING AT PRODUCTION DECISIONS

The production function in Figure 6-1 shows the simplest of all possible relationships between input and output; one input, one output. Production decisions are more complicated when there is the possibility of more than one output, or product, and more than one input. This chapter describes two simple models of the relationship between inputs and outputs in a firm. The first graphic model, the production-possibilities curve, shows the various combinations of outputs that can be produced with a fixed stock of inputs. The second, an isoquant map, shows the various input combinations that can be used to produce a given output.

Production-Possibilities Curves

A production-possibilities curve such as the one in Figure 6-3 represents the various quantities of two goods that can be produced with a given amount of resources or inputs. This particular curve takes the form of a straight line and shows the various quantities of apples and pears that can be produced with a given quantity of resources. On production-possibilities curve AB, if all resources are devoted to apples, it is possible to produce 1000 bushels; if all resources are devoted to pears, it is possible to produce 800 bushels.

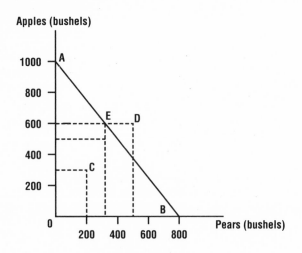

FIG. 6-3 *A Production-Possibilities Curve*

It is also possible to produce various intermediate combinations, such as 400 bushels of pears and 500 bushels of apples, or 100 bushels of pears and 875 bushels of apples, both of which lie along line AB. It is also possible to produce combinations to the left of line AB, such as 200 bushels of pears and 300 bushels of apples at point C, but such a combination would be *inefficient*. This combination would not fully utilize the available resources.

Efficiency requires getting the most out of available resources, and "most" is represented by combinations of apples and pears along line AB. Combinations to the right of AB, such as 600 bushels of apples and 500 bushels of pears (Point D), are not attainable; there are not enough resources to produce that large a combination.

The slope of line AB represents the opportunity cost of each good in terms of the other forgone. Since AB is a straight line, the opportunity cost—the amount of apples that must be given up to get another bushel of pears, or vice versa—is constant. Each time production is reduced by one bushel of apples, enough resources are released to produce another 0.8 bushels of pears.

Along the line AB, which of the possible combinations will be produced? AB tells us what we can produce, but it does not tell us what can be sold. That depends on the preferences of consumers as represented by the prices they are willing to pay. Bidding in the marketplace will determine which of the various combinations they want. In Figure 6-3 we assume that consumers place the highest value on combination E, with 600 bushels of apples and 320 bushels of pears. This combination is efficient in two ways. It is *technically efficient*, in that all resources are being fully utilized, and it is *allocatively efficient*, in that resources are being allocated to the production of an output mix with the highest value to consumers.

Like supply and demand curves, a production-possibilities curve is drawn with ceteris paribus conditions. The two most important ceteris paribus conditions underlying this curve are technology and available resources. An improvement in technology means that more apples *and* more pears can be produced with the same resources. If the technological improvement only applies to production of apples, the production-possibilities curve will shift to A′B in Figure 6-4. Along this line the maximum amount of apples that can be produced increases to A′=1200 bushels. If all resources are devoted to pears, the maximum output of pears remains at B = 800 bushels. The opportunity cost of apples has fallen from 0.8 bushel of pears to only 2/3 bushel of pears—the slope of line A′B. (Looking at the other side, the opportunity cost of pears has risen from 1.25 bushels of apples to 1.5 bushels.)

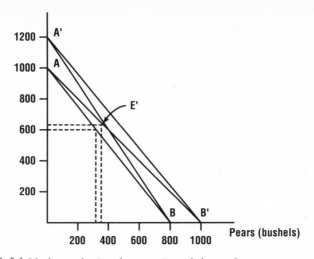

FIG. 6-4 *Shifts in the Production-Possibilities Curve*

Note, however, that it is now possible to produce more of both goods, not just apples. At E′ buyers can now consume more of both goods; instead of 600 bushels of apples and 320 bushels of pears, they now have 650 bushels of apples and 340 bushels of pears. This is an important feature of improvements in technology. By reducing the resource cost of one good, the benefits spill over to other products as well.

If the improvement in technology only affects production of pears, the curve will shift to AB′; if the change in technology benefits both products equally, the curve will shift out in parallel fashion to A′ B′. An increase in resources will shift the curve outward as well, increasing total possible output.

Figure 6-5 draws a slightly different view of the same production-possibilities curve. This curve is convex. The opportunity cost of apples in terms of pears, or of pears in terms of apples, is no longer constant but now changes along the curve. This shape reflects the law of diminishing returns discussed earlier. As this firm, region, or country becomes more specialized in one product, such as apples, resources initially transferred from pears to apples will be those most suited to apples and least productive in the pear business. These resources will be highly productive in apples relative to what they were able to produce in pears. As more and more resources are diverted from pear production to apple production, however, eventually resources are transferred that are less and less suited to apples. The increase in output from additional units of such resources gets smaller as the resources transferred are less and less suited to the task at hand. The opportunity cost of apples (= pears forgone) gets larger and larger. The first 100 bushels of apples only cost 20 bushels of pears (reducing output from 820 to 800). The increase in apple production from 500 to 600 bushels cost 90 bushels of pears (reducing from 700 to 610). The last 100 bushels of apples (increasing, on the diagram, from 900 to 1000 bushels) meant a sacrifice of 300 bushels of pears. It is unlikely that this firm, region, or country will choose to totally specialize with increasing marginal costs, because the last few units produced have such a high opportunity cost.

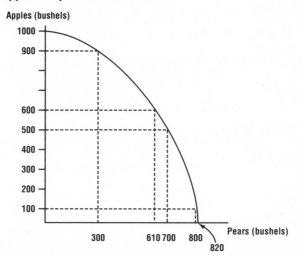

FIG. 6-5 *A Production-Possibilities Curve with Increasing Costs*

Isoquants and Budget Lines

Paralleling the production-possibilities curve as a description of output choices is a curve, or set of curves, that describes the choices facing the producer who is trying to choose a resource mix for producing a particular product. This curve is the iso-quant, which is a Greek compound that simply means "given quantity." An isoquant curve (curve I in Figure 6-6) shows the various quantities of two inputs, such as labor and capital, that can be used to produce a given level of output of one good, such as bicycles. Bicycles can be produced with highly capital-intensive methods, as at point A on Isoquant I_1, which represents production of 100 bicycles. Machines, including robots, do most of the stamping and assembly work with a minimum of labor input at point A. Alternatively, bicycles can be carefully assembled by hand with a minimum of capital equipment, as at point B.

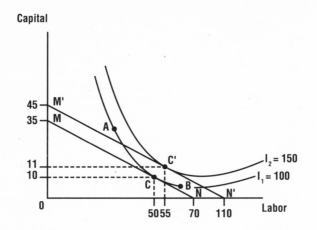

FIG. 6-6 *An Isoquant Map*

Like the convex production-possibilities curve, the concave isoquant reflects the law of diminishing returns. As more and more labor is combined with less and less capital, the extra output from the extra worker or extra worker-hour gets smaller and smaller. Conversely, there are diminishing returns to mechanizing the production process. At least a few workers must supervise the machines, and as the process becomes more capital-intensive, machines are doing most of the work without enough attention from humans. Breakdowns, errors, and other problems develop. Extra output per extra machine continues to fall.

If the firm wants to expand the output of bicycles, it will probably choose to use more of both inputs. Isoquant I_1 represents production of 150 bicycles. If this firm had been producing 100 bicycles with input combination C (50 labor, 10 capital), then expansion to 150 bicycles can be achieved with an increase in labor input from 50 to 55 and of capital from 10 to 11 units on isoquant I_2. Each isoquant in Figure 6-6 represents a different level of output, and shows the various combinations of inputs that can be used.

While many different combinations of inputs can be used to produce a particular level of output, the choice of a specific input mix is based on the prices of the two inputs. In Figure 6-6 the price ratio is given by line MN, which is known as an isocost line (or sometimes simply a budget line). The firm has a budget of $2100 for the two inputs, labor and capital. If all of the budget is spent on capital, and the cost of a unit of capital is $60, this firm can purchase 35 units of capital. (The units can be measured in various ways; for example, the price of $60 per unit might represent one hour's or one day's worth of time of a leased machine, or the hourly cost of paying off the loan to buy the machine.) If labor is measured in worker hours, and the hourly wage is $30 an hour, then the firm could purchase 70 units of labor if all of its budget is spent on labor.

Faced with these prices, the firm will try to maximize the output it gets out of its given ($2100) expenditure on these two inputs. That is, the firm will try to reach the highest possible isoquant. In this case the firm is able to reach isoquant I_1, producing 100 bicycles with 10 units of capital and 50 units of labor. Note that is could expend the $2100 on different combinations of capital and labor, but the result would be a lower isoquant and less output. Only where the isocost, or budget line, touches the highest possible isoquant is the firm spending its money in the most efficient way possible.

A larger production budget—say, $3300—would shift the isocost line to the right in parallel fashion, to M'N', enabling the firm to increase output by purchasing more capital and labor. It will wind up on an even higher isoquant, such as I_2.

A more interesting possibility, one to which every business firm should be attuned, is a change in the slope of the budget line, which simply means a change in the relative prices of inputs. Perhaps labor costs rise from $30 to $40 per hour because of a new union contract or a hike in the social security tax rate. In Figure 6-7 this increase in labor costs per hour is represented as a shift in the budget line from MN to MN". The amount of capital that the firm can buy if all of the budget is spent on capital does not change, because the price of capital has not changed. However, if the firm spent all its funds on labor, the maximum amount of labor that the firm can purchase with a $2100 budget has fallen from 70 ($2100/$30) to 52.5 ($2100/$40). How will the firm respond?

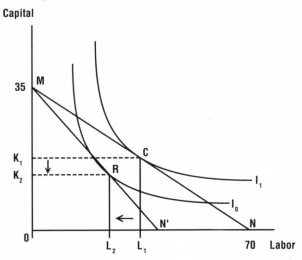

FIG. 6-7 *A Change in Labor Costs and Factor Substitution*

First, the firm cuts output. Its budget of $2100 will not buy as much in the way of total inputs, so it cannot attain as high an isoquant. The firm chooses input combination R, which represents a lower output of bicycles (moving from Isoquant I_1 to I_0).

Second, the firm substitutes relatively cheaper capital for relatively more expensive labor. Notice that while purchases of both labor and capital have fallen, the use of labor has fallen much more sharply (L_1 to L_2) than the use of capital (K_1 to K_2). Automation is not merely a buzzword but is a real and reasonable response to higher wages if the cost of capital or other inputs is not rising at the same rate. Successful firms are always attuned to changes in the relative prices of inputs—not just labor and capital, but different kinds of labor and capital as well as land, raw materials, semifinished goods, and other inputs—and look for ways to change the input mix to get the most output out of their expenditures on inputs.

Isoquants suffer from a myth similar to the vertical-demand curve myth. The myth is that there is one way, and only one way, to produce a particular output—just one technically suitable combination of resources. A look around the world shows that this is untrue. In Asia rice cultivation uses a large amount of (cheap) labor and almost no (expensive) capital; peasants work the paddies with sticks and water buffalo, harvesting the rice by hand in baskets. The water buffalo, sticks, and baskets are the only capital. In the United States, where farm labor is scarce and expensive, rice is planted from airplanes and harvested in motorboats.

This example is extreme, but a creative business manager will always be attuned to opportunities to change the input mix. Examples are easy to find. Automatic car washes substitute capital for labor, while high-rise and other multifamily styles of housing substitute capital, raw materials, and labor for land in areas where land is scarce and expensive. Sometimes consumers are offered a lower price for substituting their own labor for the firm's labor; cleaning up after yourself in a fast-food restaurant and pumping your own gas are two such opportunities that represent a creative form of input substitution.

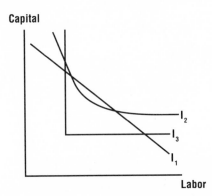

FIG. 6-8 *Isoquants and Factor Substitutability*

Some products have many opportunities for input substitution, some do not. If inputs are largely interchangeable, the isoquant map will be relatively flat; a typical isoquant curve might look like I_1 in Figure 6-8. Other products have a limited range of substitutability between inputs. The isoquants for such products will be more curved, like I_2 in Figure 6-8. Finally, there may indeed be some products for which there is only one technically feasible combination of inputs, such as requiring two laborers per unit of capital. Extra workers without extra capital, or extra capital without extra workers, will yield no increase in output. In this extreme case the typical isoquant would be L-shaped, like I_3 in Figure 6-8. Most products lie between the extremes of nearly perfect substitutability of inputs (I_1) and fixed coefficients, or a rigid capital-labor ratio (I_3).

CHAPTER PERSPECTIVE

This chapter is a first look at the production process from an economic perspective. A primary goal for the economy as a whole as well as for the individual firm or household is economic efficiency—allocating scarce resources among competing uses in such a way as to get the maximum value of output. In attempting to maximize output out of a given stock of inputs, both firms and households are faced with the law of diminishing returns. For firms, this law means that adding more and more of one input (labor or raw materials) to a fixed stock of other inputs (land, capital equipment, buildings) will eventually reduce the marginal product of the extra input. Beyond some point, adding more units of labor (or other input) will result in smaller and smaller increases in output.

The law of diminishing returns is reflected in the production function. A simple production function shows the total output resulting from various quantities of a particular input, usually labor. The production function makes it possible to determine not only the relationship between inputs and total product but also average product and marginal product.

Often production choices involve several outputs or several inputs. A production-possibilities curve shows the various combinations of two outputs that can be produced with a given quantity of inputs. An isoquant map shows the various input combinations that can be used to produce various levels of output of a particular product. Both of these models reflect the law of diminishing returns. Each one is also a good way to visualize the choices facing a particular producer in terms of output mix and input substitution.

Costs in the Short Run

INTRODUCTION AND MAIN POINTS

The most important determinant of supply, one of the two primary determinants of profit and loss, and one of the most powerful signals in the marketplace is *cost*. Firms try to produce output at minimum cost. Rising costs can make the difference between survival and bankruptcy. Because costs are so important, and somewhat complicated, we devote two chapters to them. This chapter looks at costs in the short run, when some inputs can be changed but others are fixed. The next chapter looks at costs in the long run, when no commitments are fixed and anything can be changed, including staying in or going out of business.

After studying the material in this chapter:
- You will be able to identify and distinguish between accounting costs and opportunity costs, fixed and variable costs, and total, average, and marginal costs, and to explain how they are related to each other.
- You will be able to explain how the firm decides how much to produce in the short run.
- You will know when a firm should shut down operations even in the short run.
- You will be able to explain how a change in costs affects the level of output and the profitability of the firm.
- You will understand the cost relationships that lie behind the upward-sloping supply curve.

MEASURING COST AND PROFIT

The typical firm will list its costs and revenues on an income statement and subtract costs from revenues to determine its "profit," or at least its net operating income. The costs that are listed on the income statement, however, are usually not the same as the costs that an economist would list. They may be more inclusive in some ways and less inclusive in others, but most often economists criticize accounting costs as not inclusive enough. Income statements usually omit some important costs.

Accounting Costs

If you were going to draw up an accounting statement for Fred's Barbecue, you would begin by looking at the flow of cash. Sales represent most of the income, or inflow of cash. We'll assume that Fred's gross annual sales come to $95,000. Gross income (before subtracting any costs) is usually pretty close to the same number for both the accountant and the economist.

You would also look at the outflow of cash. Fred has to pay his employees, and he has to buy pork or beef, barbecue sauce, napkins, electricity, and other supplies, or inputs. Those generate an outflow of cash—$8000 for his part-time help, $22,000 for food and other inputs.

Perhaps Fred also has a loan at the bank to cover his equipment. That generates another regular outflow of cash—monthly payments of $1000, or $12,000 per year. So far, of his intake of $95,000, we've seen $42,000 flow out to pay for inputs of various kinds. Does this mean that Fred is making a profit of $53,000? No.

Opportunity Costs

Labor, materials, and debt payments are not his total costs. Suppose Fred has $30,000 of his own cash tied up in the business. That $30,000 could be earning interest in a bank, or it could be invested in another company's stock and earning dividends. Suppose it could earn a return of 10%, or $3000. This income forgone on Fred's investment is an opportunity cost of staying in the barbecue business. It is just as real a cost as the other $42,000, even if it doesn't show up on his income statement. Subtracting this $3000 brings Fred's net earnings down to $50,000.

Fred also could be earning a salary if he wasn't devoting full time to the barbecue business. He could be managing a burger franchise for someone else and earning, say, $18,000 a year. This salary is another opportunity cost of being in this business. Fred should be paying himself a salary of at least $18,000 a year, bringing his net income down further to $32,000.

Fred also owns the building in which his barbecue place is located. He inherited it from his grandmother, so it "doesn't cost him anything" to use it. Right? Wrong! If he didn't house his barbecue place there, he could rent it to another commercial operation for $1000 a month, or $12,000 a year. That income forgone is another opportunity cost of doing business. Subtract that, and Fred's net income or "profit" falls further, to $20,000.

Are we through shrinking Fred's profits down to size? Almost. Economists argue that one cost of production is a "normal" profit that represents a return to the entrepreneur (Fred)—the risk-taker, innovator, owner, manager that started this business and keeps it going by taking risks and trying new ideas. This return is over and above the salary that Fred should be paying himself. Estimates of the approximate amount of return to an enterprise vary, but a typical figure for a "normal" profit is 6% of gross income, or about $5000. Anything over and above this "normal" profit—the resource payment to the enterprise input—is called economic profit. After this last subtraction the final figure for Fred's actual, economic profit is $15,000—a far cry from the $53,000 in net income on his income statement. Recognizing all of the opportunity costs provides a much more realistic estimate of profit.

Here is a recap of Fred's calculations:

Gross revenue			$95,000
less	Accounting costs:		
	Labor	$ 8,000	
	Food, materials	22,000	
	Bank loan	12,000	
equals	Net accounting income		$53,000
less	Other opportunity costs:		
	Interest forgone	3,000	
	Salary forgone	18,000	
	Rent forgone	12,000	
	Normal profit	5,000	
equals	Economic profit		$15,000

The economic profit of $15,000 is Fred's income as an entrepreneur. It is a reward for risk-taking, innovating, and organizing production. This reward is over and above his salary as a manager ($18,000) and his return on invested capital ($3000).

In addition to paying for enterprise, profit also serves as a signal. Other potential barbecue sellers will become aware of how well Fred is doing. If the barbecue business in this area is profitable, perhaps there is a place in the market for a second barbecue producer. Or perhaps another fast-food place will broaden its offerings to include barbecue. As competitors enter the market, Fred's profits will decline. Thus, profit has sent a signal to expand output, and in the process profits have been reduced back to "normal" levels.

Fred could be running at a loss. It is possible that his total costs, both accounting costs and implicit costs such as his own salary, normal profit, and return on his invested capital, are greater than his revenue. This loss sends a signal not only to potential competitors but also to Fred! Competitors are less likely to enter a market where an established firm is unable to show a profit. If Fred's losses are substantial enough, he may leave the barbecue business. After analyzing costs more carefully, we will return to the decision to enter or leave the industry.

FIXED COSTS AND VARIABLE COSTS

In the short run a firm has two categories of costs that merge in the long run: fixed costs and variable costs. Variable costs depend on the level of production. If a store is open more hours or if a factory turns out more units of its product, there will be extra costs for labor, electricity, and heat as well as extra stock for the store or extra materials for the factory. More sales may call for more marketing or advertising expenditures or for more miles on the delivery truck.

There are also some costs that are independent of the level of output, the hours of operation, or other measures of the amount of activity that is occurring. The rent or mortgage (even if it is an opportunity cost rather than an explicit or accounting cost) is fixed and given. The amount is independent of the level of production. This obligation has to be paid even if nothing at all is going on at the firm, at least until the lease expires or the building is sold. The same is true of insurance, capital equipment (or store fixtures), basic telephone service, and a business license. All of these expenses are independent of the level of output and will continue to be incurred whether output is expanded or contracted or even if the firm temporarily shuts down.

Variable costs represent a choice to producers; fixed costs do not. A producer can compare variable costs to selling price and decide whether the extra unit of output is worth producing or not. Fixed costs are irrelevant to this decision, because they will have to be paid whether or not the extra output is produced.

Total, Average, and Marginal Cost

Total costs consist of variable costs plus fixed costs. Total fixed costs are a given amount, but total variable costs depend on the level of output. You can probably guess how total, average, and marginal costs behave as output expands from the discussion of the production function and the law of diminishing returns in Chapter 6. If each extra unit of input produces less and less extra output beyond some point, then each extra unit of output is going to cost more (in terms of expenditures for inputs) than the one before.

Total costs always increase as total output rises, but at first they rise more slowly because more labor and materials are being added to a fixed quantity of land and capital, and thus the firm is making better use of its fixed inputs. As the firm continues to add more variable inputs, however, the extra output from the extra units of variable input get smaller and smaller, so both average and marginal cost start to rise. Total cost at first increases slowly and then more rapidly as output expands in the short run.

The cost figures in Table 7-1 for production of picture frames are graphed in Figure 7-1. Figure 7-1(a) shows total cost; Figure 7-1(b) shows average variable cost, average fixed cost, average total cost, and marginal cost. Note that total fixed cost is equal to total cost when output equals zero.

TABLE 7-1

Units of Output	Total Fixed Cost (TFC)	Total Variable Cost (TVC)	Total Cost (TC)	Average Fixed Cost (AFC)	Average Variable Cost (AVC)	Average Total Cost (ATC)	Marginal Cost (MC)
0	10	0	10	—	—	—	—
1	10	10	20	10	10	20	10
2	10	18	28	5	9	14	8
3	10	24	34	3.3	8	11.3	6
4	10	32	42	2.5	8	10.5	7
5	10	40	50	2.0	8	10	8
6	10	49	59	1.7	8.2	9.9	9
7	10	59	69	1.4	8.4	9.8	10
8	10	72	82	1.3	9	10.3	13
9	10	87	97	1.1	9.6	10.7	15

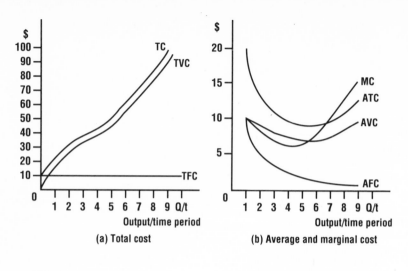

FIG. 7-1(a) *Total cost*

FIG 7-1(b) *Average and marginal cost*

USING COSTS TO MAKE PRODUCTION DECISIONS

Given this cost information, how does the producer decide how much to produce and what price to charge? This decision can be simplified to just one choice, the level of output, by assuming that this producer is a small firm and takes the market price as given. That is, this firm is a price taker, facing a horizontal demand curve at a price of $13.00. This firm will incur the fixed costs of $10.00 whether or not it produces any output, so fixed costs do not enter into the firm's decision in the short run. The only question is whether each extra unit of output will cover its extra variable cost, or marginal cost. Since the first unit adds more to revenue ($13.00) than it does to cost ($10.00), it is worth producing because it increases the firm's net revenue by $3.00. The second through the seventh units, likewise, each add more to revenue than to cost, so they are worth producing. The firm will be indifferent about producing the eighth unit, because it adds just as much to revenue as it does to costs. Economists generally assume that the firm will go ahead and produce this last unit. However, the ninth unit will not be produced, because it adds more to cost ($15.00) than to revenue ($13.00). This step-by-step decision process gives the profit-maximizing rule for a firm that is a price-taker: produce that output or quantity (Q) for which

$$P = MC$$

—the marginal (extra) cost of producing the last unit—is just equal to the price it will bring. (The profit-maximizing rule for other firms, which do not take price as given but have some influence over their market price, is discussed in Chapters 9 and 10.)

Figure 7-2 adds a horizontal demand curve at $P = \$13.00$ to the average and marginal cost curves of Figure 7-1(b). $Q_1 = 8$ is the quantity this firm will choose to produce. Is this firm making a profit? Yes! To determine profit, look at the difference between total revenue and total cost, using the numbers in Table 7-1. Total revenue is price times quantity, or $\$13.00 \times 8$ units, which is $\$104.00$. (On the diagram total revenue is the rectangle OP_1RQ_1.) Total cost is average cost times quantity, or $\$10.30 \times 8$, which is $\$82.40$. (On the diagram, total cost is the rectangle OC_1SQ_1.) Total profit is the difference between the two—$\$21.60$, or the shaded area on the diagram. Because price is greater than average cost, this firm is making a profit.

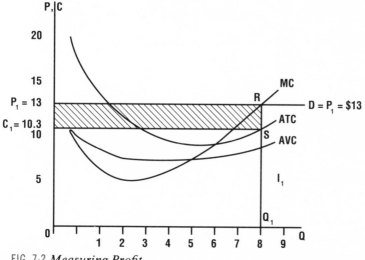

FIG. 7-2 *Measuring Profit*

Given the price of $13.00, the profit at this level of output is greater than it could be at any other level of output. You can verify this fact by calculating profit at each of the levels of output shown above. For example, at a level of output of four units, total revenue would be $52.00 (4 x $13.00) and total costs are $42.00, so profit would only be $10.00. As long as an extra unit adds more to revenue than to costs, the firm is not producing at the profit-maximizing level.

Suppose this firm was faced with a lower price, such as $9.00. The profit-maximizing rule of MC = P for a firm that is a price-taker calls for an output of six units, resulting in revenue of $54.00. Total cost, however, is $59.00. This firm is losing $5.00. The only consolation in this situation is that six units of output yield the smallest possible loss. You can check this by using the figures given above to measure profit or loss at each level of output. You should also try redrawing Figure 7-2 with a horizontal demand curve at a price of $9.00 and determine output and profit or loss at that price level on the diagram.

You may have noticed in Table 7-1 that for some prices there are two output levels from which to choose. For example, if price is equal to $10.00, then P = MC when output is one unit and again when output is seven units. Which of these two output levels is correct? You can calculate profit at both levels and find that the firm is losing $10.00 at an output of one unit and making a profit of $1.00 at an output of seven units, so the correct answer is seven units, not one.

Why? When marginal cost is falling, the next unit will add more to revenue than to cost, so it should also be produced. It is only when marginal cost is rising that the MC = P rule gives the correct answer, because then the next unit will add more to cost than to revenue and should not be produced. So the profit-maximizing rule should be modified to say that the most profitable (or least unprofitable) level of output occurs where P = MC *and* marginal cost is rising.

This profit-maximizing rule is one of the most important contributions of economic theory to management. Sometimes firms do not have precise marginal cost information and must guess at the profit-maximizing level of output, but as they experiment with different levels of output, they are groping their way toward an equilibrium where P = MC.

Many business managers would argue that while this rule is theoretically correct, it is very difficult to apply in practice because marginal cost is hard to measure. Total cost is easy, and average cost is not difficult to determine, but it is not always easy for a firm to determine how much it costs to produce the last unit of output or to estimate the extra cost of a small increase. Costs are particularly hard to measure in a multiproduct firm. Over time, however, the firm gathers experience with increasing and decreasing output, hiring an extra worker, running an extra shift, or staying open an extra hour. Based on these experiences the firm's managers can make a reasonably accurate guess at marginal cost in the neighborhood of the current level of output, even if it is not possible to trace out the entire marginal-cost curve.

CUTTING YOUR LOSSES: THE SHUTDOWN DECISION

Until now we have considered marginal cost to be the most important information for the firm's output decision. Total and average cost only entered into determining whether the firm was making a profit or loss, not how much it should produce. The firm was committed to producing; the question was, how much? Since the next unit of output is a marginal decision, marginal cost provides the relevant information. Sometimes, however, the firm needs to make larger decisions. For such decisions total cost and average cost—especially total cost and average variable cost—also play an important role.

If the firm is making a profit or breaking even, there is no problem about what to do in the short run. This firm is doing something right and should go on doing it. But what if a firm is incurring losses? Should it shut down? The answer is not a simple yes or no; it depends on the relationship between total (or average) revenue and total (or average) variable costs.

In the example we have been using, as long as the price is more than $8.00, the firm should always continue producing in the short run even if it is creating losses. Why? Because at any selling price over $8.00, the firm's revenue is enough to cover all of its variable costs (labor, electricity, raw materials, etc.) and to pay at least part of its fixed costs of $10.00. If the firm shuts down, it still has to pay those fixed costs. So as long as losses are less than the fixed costs, the firm should continue operating in the short run.

Suppose, however, that the price of the product falls to $7.00. The profit-maximizing (or loss-minimizing) level of output from Table 7-1 is four units. Total revenue is $28, and losses are $14. The revenue of $28 is not even enough to cover the total variable cost of $32, let alone contribute to fixed costs.

This firm could cut its losses to $10.00 without bothering to produce anything! Obviously, in this case, the firm is better off shutting down, eliminating its variable costs, and just losing its fixed costs of $10.00. As long as the price is greater than average variable cost, however, the firm is better off if it continues producing in the short run, because the losses would be smaller than if it shut down.

The shutdown rule, then, is

If $P > AVC$ continue to produce
If $P < AVC$ shut down

where AVC = average variable cost, and P = price.

CHANGES IN COSTS

These cost functions were calculated on the assumption that both technology and the prices for all of the inputs were given. If one of these ceteris paribus conditions changes, then the cost figures and the cost curves will shift, changing the profit-maximizing (or loss-minimizing) level of output. The price of labor could rise, a new, cheaper method of production could become available, or capital could become cheaper. How will such changes affect the level of output?

Figure 7-3 shows the effects of an increase in costs on the output decision. (It is possible to solve this output problem with numbers, but it is simpler just to visualize it on the graph.) Assume that the market price (P_1) for this price-taker firm is $15.00 before and after the change in costs. The profit-maximizing output in Table 7-1 was nine units, because at that level of output P=MC>AC. The firm was making a profit of $38 (total revenue = 9 x $15.00 = $135.00; total cost = $97.00). Now the firm has to pay a higher price for labor, increasing its variable cost by $2.00 per unit for each unit of output. Both average variable cost and marginal cost increase, or shift upward, by $2.00, from AVC_1 and MC_1 to AVC_2 and MC_2. (If you want to go back to Table 7-1, just add $2.00 to the AVC and MC columns.) If the price remains at $15.00, the new profit-maximizing level of output where $P = MC = 15 is eight units instead of nine. Profit has fallen to $18.70 (total revenue of $120.00 minus total cost of $101.70).

The profit-maximizing level of output will not change unless the marginal cost changes. An increase in fixed costs will reduce profits or increase losses, but it will not affect either the profit-maximizing level of output or the shutdown decision.

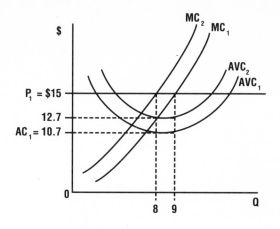

FIG. 7-3 *Effect of A Change in Costs on Price and Output*

If costs fall, you can trace through the effects in Figure 7-3 by shifting the AVC and MC curves downward and to the right. As you might expect, the result of lower variable and marginal costs is to increase the level of output and the firm's profit.

COST CURVES AND SUPPLY CURVES

Recall from Chapter 3 that costs are an important determinant of the firm's supply curve. Now that you are familiar with cost curves, it is possible to describe exactly how costs are reflected in supply curves. The firm's marginal cost curve *is* the supply curve, as long as marginal cost is above average variable cost. (If MC = P is below average variable cost, the firm will not supply anything; it will shut down.) Why? Recall from Chapter 3 that the supply curve shows the various quantities that the firm will offer for sale at various alternative prices. Since the profit-maximizing rule for determining what quantity to produce and sell is P = MC, the marginal cost curve also shows the quantities that the firm will offer for sale at various alternative prices. As long as P = MC is the firm's decision rule, the marginal-cost curve and the supply curve will be the same. Likewise, in an industry composed of many small firms, the industry's supply curve is just the sum of all the firms' marginal cost curves. If marginal costs change, the supply curve will change in the same amount and the same direction.

The cost curves and the supply curves in this chapter apply only to the short run, when some factors are fixed and cannot be changed. The next chapter will look at the firm's costs and production decisions in the long run, when nothing is fixed and anything can be changed.

CHAPTER PERSPECTIVE

Before a firm can make a good economic decision about production, it needs to have a firm grasp of exactly how much each unit costs to produce. A simple accounting statement will tend to understate costs (and overstate profit) because it is likely to omit some implicit or opportunity costs, especially in a small proprietorship or partnership. These opportunity costs might include interest on the owner's invested capital, salary, normal profit, or even the rental value of a building owned by the firm. Economic profit is the difference between total revenue and total costs, including all opportunity costs.

In the short run some costs are fixed. The firm may have a lease on a building, payments on capital equipment, or contracts with suppliers that cannot be changed for a while. These fixed costs will be incurred whether or not the firm produces, and are thus not relevant to deciding how much to produce. Variable costs, which depend on the level of production, are much more important in deciding how much to produce.

Average cost is total cost divided by the level of output. Marginal cost is the additional cost of an additional unit of output. A firm that is a price-taker will maximize profits by producing that level of output for which price is equal to marginal cost, as long as marginal cost is above average variable cost. If marginal cost and price are less than average variable cost, the firm will minimize its losses by shutting down. The marginal-cost curve is also the firm's supply curve. If marginal costs increase (MC shifts upward to left), the price-taker (small) firm will reduce its level of output in order to maximize profits or minimize losses. If marginal costs fall (MC shifts downward and to the right), the profit-maximizing level of output will increase.

FOOTNOTE

1 *For simplicity, we are assuming that all costs are variable costs; fixed costs are zero.*

Costs in the Long Run

INTRODUCTION AND MAIN POINTS

In Chapter 7 we looked at the decisions that a firm makes in the short run, when options are rather limited. Certain inputs may be fixed in supply in the short run. Potential new firms do not have enough time to respond to profit signals by entering the industry. Existing firms may shut down or scale down production temporarily, but they do not permanently leave the industry or shift to an entirely new product line. But all of these circumstances and options are open to change in the long run, when no costs are fixed and no decisions are cast in concrete.

The short-run model of Chapter 7 is realistic for many day-to-day business choices about output and pricing, but it ignores some critical decisions about the future of the firm. These long-run decisions give rise to the fixed costs in the short run of the future. Should we build a new plant? buy new machinery? merge with another firm? buy out a competitor? invest in new technology? change product lines? give up the business? These are all long-run decisions. They do not sound like the marginal decisions of Chapter 7—to raise or lower the price a little, to expand or contract output by a few units—but they are governed by the same profit-maximizing rules. This chapter explores the process of making some critical long-run decisions on the basis of a few simple assumptions about the nature of costs in the long run.

After studying the material found in this chapter:

■ You will be able to distinguish between short-run and long-run decisions.

■ You will be able to describe the behavior of costs in the long run and how they affect the firm's choice of a size of plant.

■ You will understand what economies and diseconomies of scale are and how they affect a firm's pricing and output decisions.

HOW LONG IS THE SHORT RUN?

Although the terms "short run" and "long run" are common parlance, they have no clear dividing line. How long is the short run; when does it turn into the long run? In other words, where does the short run end and the long-run planning horizon begin? a month? six months? two years? a decade? Economists do not have a single answer to that question; it varies from firm to firm. However, there are some general criteria for distinguishing between short-run decisions and long-run decisions.

In the short run certain options or choices are excluded. It is not possible to expand the size of the physical plant, to increase certain other "fixed" inputs, to enter or to leave the industry (although a temporary shutdown is possible if revenues are less than variable costs). Contracts may mean that the rent will be due, the attorney's monthly fee must be paid, and that orders for certain products and product lines must be honored regardless of the firm's sales and revenues. Inevitable time lags in delivery or problems of availability may mean that new equipment cannot come on line, that specialized labor or raw materials cannot be obtained easily, or that the product line cannot be quickly expanded.

The long run is defined as the period when anything and everything can be changed, in contrast to the short run when certain obligations or costs are fixed. Consequently, if some factor that significantly affects production cannot be changed within a particular time frame, then that time frame—whether it is a week, a year, or a decade—belongs to the short run.

There are two problems with this definition. First, the long run will not be the same for different products or industries. Some industries lend themselves to quick and easy expansion. It doesn't take long to get into the photoprocessing business or to open a video store. It takes longer to start up a textile factory or a major restaurant, still longer to enter the medical profession or set up an automobile factory, and a very long time to get into or out of the aircraft industry. For some industries the long run may be only six months; for another, ten years.

The second and more difficult problem is that any firm faces multiple time horizons for different kinds of decisions. Perhaps a retail store has a six-month contract with a supplier, an annually renewable business license, a two-year lease on a building, and a loan for the purchase of equipment to be repaid in monthly installments over five years. In other words, decisions that create fixed short-run costs do not all come up at the same time.

Which of these fixed-cost decisions determines what is the firm's long run? Is it the shortest? the longest? the average? Six months is probably too short a time to be "the long run" for this retail store, because two major costs (the lease and the monthly loan payment) remain fixed at the end of that time. Five years, however, is too long. In two years, when both the lease and the business license are up for renewal, the current six-month supplier contract can also be reconsidered; in addition, the balance of the loan will be much smaller. With a smaller loan balance, alternative financing is possible. The firm's net worth should have increased enough to make sale of the firm feasible. Perhaps the firm has even accumulated enough funds or built a large enough clientele to consider expansion. There are enough major options open at this point so that two years is a good candidate for the long run for this retail firm.

COSTS IN THE LONG RUN

With no fixed costs and no fixed inputs—the conditions that define the long run—then the total, average, and marginal cost curves on which the firm bases its long-run decisions will look different for two reasons. First, with no fixed costs, there is no distinction between variable costs and total costs. TC is equal to TVC, and AC is equal to AVC. Second, and more important, the explanations for the shape of the average total-cost curve are no longer valid. Recall from Chapter 7 that the ATC curve has a sort of U-shape. Average total costs decline for a while as output expands because of declining fixed costs. As output continues to expand, increasing marginal costs (diminishing returns) will eventually cause it to turn upward at larger and larger output levels. If no costs are fixed, then there is no longer a reason for the downward-sloping first part of the average cost curve. The upward-sloping part is also no longer necessarily valid, because it was based on the law of diminishing returns, or increasing marginal costs. This law explains what happens when you add more of a variable factor to a fixed factor. With no factors fixed, the law of diminishing returns does not apply to the long run. The average-total-cost curve could take any of a variety of shapes. It could even be horizontal, or constant, as output expands in the long run.

Selecting the Plant Size

One way to think of the long-run average-cost curve is to consider it as the summation of a series of short-run alternatives.

The biggest long-run decision, and the hardest one to change, is the size of the plant—the number of square feet in the factory or the showroom floor—and the amount of capital equipment it will contain. Once a firm has chosen a plant size that will be fixed for a year, two years, or even five years, that firm is operating in the short run with a fixed plant size. At that point its decisions are short-run decisions—hiring or firing labor, buying more or fewer raw materials or inventory, and expanding or contracting output within the limits set by the existing physical plant. Each size of plant will have its own U-shaped short-run average-total-cost curve.

In practice "size of plant" is a rather loose term that includes not only the square footage of production or sales space but also the equipment needed to make that space operational —machinery, computers, office equipment, display shelves, etc. For the purpose of developing cost curves size of plant is defined not in terms of dollars of expenditure to construct it or in terms of square feet, but rather by the range of output levels a given plant is capable of producing.

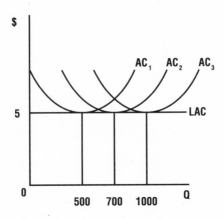

FIG. 8-1 *Plant Size and Long Run Average Cost*

Figure 8-1 shows the average-total-cost curves for three different plant sizes. AC_1 allows the firm to hit a minimum average total cost of $5.00 per unit with an output level of 500 units per week. If the firm expects the output level to be in the range of 500 units per week, a plant of the size corresponding to AC_1 would be preferable to a larger plant (corresponding to AC_2), because high fixed costs mean that this larger plant has higher average costs at every level of output up to about 600 units. If the firm expects to produce 600 to 800 units per week, it would be better off the plant size corresponding to AC_2. This is the best choice for output levels of 600 to 800 units. For output of 800 or more units a week the firm should choose the plant size corresponding to AC_3.

The practical explanation of the choice of plant size is fairly straightforward. A plant that is expected to produce 500 shirts a week doesn't need the capacity of one designed to produce 5000 shirts a week. If the 500 shirts have to bear the fixed costs of a plant with the capacity to produce 5000, the average cost of a shirt will be much higher. The same principle applies to the appropriate size of retail stores, day-care centers, dance studios, or any other establishment where size of plant determines the feasible level of output (measured in sales, child-hours, and lessons taught, respectively).

Economies and Diseconomies of Scale

Figure 8-1 connects the minimum points of the three short-run average-cost curves. The line connecting these points is labeled LAC, or long-run average cost. In order to fill in the rest of the points, it would be necessary to draw the short-run average-cost curves corresponding to other sizes of plant that are larger, smaller, or in between the sizes represented by AC_1, AC_2, and AC_3. LAC is horizontal, suggesting that as the size of plant increases there is a proportional increase in output, so that the minimum point (lowest average cost) on each successive average cost curve is the same. In other words, doubling or tripling the size of the plant would double or triple the firm's output, and at the most efficient level of output (at minimum average cost), the average cost would be the same for each size of plant. This kind of relationship between average cost, output, and plant size is know as *constant returns to scale*. Many industries exhibit constant returns to scale, particularly if the industry tends to consist of small firms, if it utilizes relatively simple technology, and if the industry itself is small relative to the economy as a whole. With constant returns to scale, the long-run marginal-cost curve is also horizontal and is equal to the long-run average-cost curve.

In other industries, however, the long-run average cost curve may slope downward because of economies of scale, or it may slope upward because of diseconomies of scale. That is, the mini-mum average cost on successive short-run average-cost curves may decline as output expands, or it may rise as output expands. If average cost in the long run falls as plant size is increased and output expands, the firm is enjoying economies of scale, techni-cally known as *increasing returns to scale*. With increasing returns to scale, the marginal-cost curve also slopes downward and lies below the average-cost curve. Figure 8-2 shows the cost curves for a firm with increasing returns to scale.

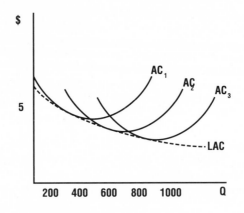

FIG. 8-2 *Increasing Returns to Scale*

Increasing returns to scale can arise from several sources. Even in the long run there may be some factors that are "indivisi-ble"—that cannot be purchased in fractional units, such as one-third of an accountant or one-quarter of a machine. Doubling the plant size may not require a second plant manager or a second accountant; such a move may simply make use of the existing ones more efficiently. The firm may be able to purchase in quan-tity and get a discount. Perhaps it can use technology that was not economical at lower output levels. A print shop can justify a computer-driven typesetter if volume is large enough. Supermar-kets can install sophisticated cash registers that would be hard to justify as cost-effective in a corner neighborhood store or a con-venience store. Assembly-line methods or robot-driven opera-tions are generally feasible only at high output levels. The nature of economies of scale will vary from industry to industry, but they clearly exist in many industries where average costs fall as the firm grows.

It is important to distinguish between economies of scale along the long-run average-cost curve (LAC in Figure 8-2) and declining fixed costs on the short-run average-cost curve. Electrical utilities (which are examined more closely in Chapter 10) have very high fixed costs and very low variable costs of producing electricity, so their short-run average cost curves slope downward over a long range of output. They also enjoy scale economies because they can adopt more efficient technology at higher levels of output, so their long-run average cost curves also tend to slope downward. Some industries may enjoy falling fixed costs over a long range of output in the short run even though they do not achieve any long-run economies of scale.

If average cost in the long run rises as plant size is increased and output expands, the firm experiences diseconomies of scale, technically known as *decreasing returns to scale*. In this case the industry will probably consist of many small firms rather than a few large ones, because smaller firms will have lower costs. With decreasing returns to scale the long-run marginal-cost curve, like the short-run average-cost curve, will rise even more steeply than the average-cost curve.

Diseconomies of scale, which cause the long-run average cost (and marginal cost) eventually to turn upward as output gets very large, also can be found in some industries. Diseconomies of scale mean that the long-run average cost per unit increases as output continues to expand. Diseconomies of scale may be the result of difficulties in managing a large and unwieldy effort. In some industries a firm may be the principal buyer of some particular inputs—a particular type of computer chip, or a machine that is only used to make a particular style of shoes, a certain specialized type of chemist. As the sole buyer, or the dominant buyer, of such specialized inputs, the firm may be able to attract or acquire more of those specialized inputs only by offering higher prices.[1]

If there are diseconomies of scale beyond some level of output, the long-run average-cost and marginal-cost curves will turn upward. Note that the explanations for diseconomies of scale (a long-run problem) are quite different from the explanations of increasing average and marginal cost in the short run, which are based on adding more of a variable factor to one or more fixed factors. Nothing is fixed in the long run.

Diseconomies of scale are relatively uncommon. In general, the existence of many small firms in an industry reflects other factors, such as high shipping costs or a need to be close to a local market in order to serve customers, rather than diseconomies of scale.

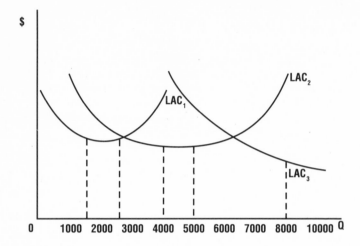

FIG. 8-3 *Scale of Economies and the Number of Firms*

Figure 8-3 shows three different long-run average-cost curves, each representing the situation of the typical firm in three different types of industries. (For simplicity, no marginal-cost curves are shown.) Industry 1, represented by a firm with long-run average-cost curve LAC_1, experiences some rapid declines in average costs up to the plant size associated with 1500 units of output a week, and then has constant average long-run costs until output hits 2500 units a week, beyond which there are diseconomies of scale. In this industry, firms of a size to produce 1500 to 2500 units a week are the optimum size.

Firms in Industry 2 do not reach all their scale economies until output is 4000 units a week (LAC_2), but then quickly encounter diseconomies of scale at output levels beyond 5000. The best choices for the size of a plant or firm in this industry fall within a fairly narrow size range, measured in terms of output.

Finally, Industry 3's typical firm has a long-run average-cost curve (LAC_3) that declines over a long range, perhaps until it is large enough to adopt the most efficient technology. The typical firm in this industry must produce more than 8000 units a week in order to achieve the fullest economies of scale. Within the output range shown on the diagram there are no diseconomies of scale; no firm in Industry 3 has been observed to reach an output level that high.

We would expect Industry 1 to consist of many small firms, because it is not difficult to attain economies of scale at a relatively small output level, and diseconomies of scale are likewise encountered fairly quickly. Industry 2 would consist of larger firms, but they too would be discouraged from becoming too large by the diseconomies of scale they quickly encounter. Industry 3 is likely to be dominated by one large firm or at most two or three firms. Thus, economies and diseconomies of scale can play an important role in determining how much competition there is in an industry at the local as well as at the national and even international level.

Maximizing Profit in the Long Run

The profit-maximizing rule for the short run is also the profit-maximizing rule for the long run. Each additional unit should be produced as long as it adds more to the firm's revenues than it does to the firm's costs. All costs are variable or marginal in the long run, so costs that do not influence short-run decisions play an important role in long-run decisions. However, the rule is more difficult to apply in the long run because, in general, the longer the time frame, the greater the uncertainty. Since the firm must make long-run decisions, however, the managers must guess at the future price of the product as well as at the future course of variable short-run costs before choosing a plant size. The rule is the same, but there are more uncertainties in applying it.

The collection of decisions labeled long run are usually focused on one particular decision, the choice of plant size. The firm needs to know the range of output it is likely to produce in order to build, buy, or lease the optimum-size plant in which to produce that output. In turn, the firm must know something about the behavior of average long-run costs in order to determine the range of plant sizes that it can build and operate while taking advantage of any available scale economies and avoiding becoming so large that it encounters diseconomies of scale. Thus, long-run profit maximizing is primarily a decision (a) to be in the industry at all (to enter or not to leave) and (b) to choose a physical facility and to enter into contracts that form the fixed costs of short-run decision-making.

The Long-Run Supply Curve

In the long run all costs are marginal costs. If the firm experiences scale economies, its long-run supply curve may slope downward, because additional units cost less to produce. If it experiences scale diseconomies, the long-run supply curve will slope upward like the supply curves of earlier chapters. In either case the long-run marginal-cost curve is equal to the long-run supply curve; for the industry as a whole the long-run supply curve is the sum of the marginal-cost curves of the individual firms in the industry.

MAKING INVESTMENT DECISIONS: A PREVIEW

One of the most important long-run decisions that firms have to make is to invest in plant and equipment. Usually the decision is more complex than simply selecting a plant size. There may be alternative production techniques for expanding output, using different combinations of inputs. Equipment may be coming close to the end of its useful lifetime, and the decision must be made to repair or to replace it. Households face the same kind of decisions about the family car.

The firm may have the option of expanding on the present site or moving to a new location, which may be closer to markets and workers but involve higher costs than expanding on site. The firm may have several kinds of new equipment that would be useful, but it cannot purchase them all at once, so choices have to be made among new computers, new company cars, or new machinery in the plant. Some choices may be much more expensive than others but have the potential to produce large increases in revenues. Others may yield immediate returns and look more attractive than those with payoffs that may be large but lie far in the future.

Is there a way of comparing these different choices? The technique used by economists to compare alternative investments by the firm is called discounting and present value. This technique makes it possible to compare the present and future costs and revenues from various alternative investment decisions so that the firm can choose the one that generates the highest net revenues, i.e., the one that is most profitable. Because this set of long-run decisions is so important to the firm, and because the technique of discounting and present value is so important, most of Chapter 9 is devoted to this topic.

CHAPTER PERSPECTIVE

This chapter considers how the firm makes long-run decisions. The long run is the time period in which no inputs or costs are fixed. Capital can be purchased, firms can enter or leave the industry, contracts can be renewed or canceled, leases expire, equipment wears out. The long run will vary from one industry to another; it is not a fixed time period but a planning horizon for the firm.

There are no fixed costs in the long run. All costs are variable costs. The long-run average-cost curve connects the minimum points (the lowest possible cost for each level of output) on a series of short-run average cost curves, each corresponding to a different size of plant. If the firm knows the range within which output is likely to fall, it can pick the appropriate plant size so as to minimize average long-run cost. Once this decision is made, the firm is back to the short-run pricing and output decision of the previous chapter.

The long-run average-cost curve is not necessarily U-shaped. It can be horizontal if there are no economies or diseconomies of scale. If there are economies of scale, the long-run average cost curve will slope downward until all economies of scale have been exhausted, then become horizontal. Marginal cost will lie below it, getting closer to average cost as average cost approaches horizontal. If there are diseconomies of scale beyond a certain level of output, the long-run average cost curve will turn back upward, and so will marginal cost. Thus, if both economies and diseconomies of scale are present, the long-run average and marginal cost curves will have the same shapes as the short-run average and marginal cost curves, but for different reasons.

If the long-run average cost curve shows some scale economies but attains all those scale economies at a fairly low level of output, there is room in the industry for many small firms, setting the stage for intense competition. This is especially true if there are also diseconomies of scale that show up fairly quickly. If economies of scale persist up to very large output levels, it is more likely that there will be only one or very few firms in the industry.

The firm maximizes profits in the long run by setting marginal revenue equal to marginal cost. Marginal cost may be horizontal (no scale economies), downward sloping (scale economies), upward sloping (scale diseconomies), or it may first fall, then become horizontal, then rise. The firm's long-run supply curve is equal to its long-run marginal-cost curve.

FOOTNOTE

1 *This may not sound intuitively plausible, because we think of large firms as benefiting from quantity discounts. Consider, however, competition among the teams in professional sports for prized athletes, a highly specialized input. For example, every time the NFL attempts to expand "output" by creating another franchise, the bidding competition for players seems to heat up.*

Investment Decisions and Capital Markets

INTRODUCTION AND MAIN POINTS

Households, business firms, and governments all have to make complex choices among alternative ways of using their limited resources. These choices become even more difficult when their impact on costs and revenues extends far into the future. The three types of economic agents need a simple, understandable technique for comparing purchases or outlays with very different time paths of current and future expenses and revenues. While the focus in this chapter is on the business firm's decisions, the techniques described are also useful for household and government decisions.

After studying the material in this chapter:
▬ You will understand the meaning of present value and how it is used to compare alternative investment decisions.
▬ You will be able to use a simple table of discount factors to analyze investment decisions.
▬ You will know how to identify the interest rate that is appropriate for your investment decisions.
▬ You will understand the advantages and disadvantages of debt and equity financing and the circumstances under which each type is more appropriate.
▬ You will understand the basic working of capital markets.
▬ You will be able to explain the reasons for different interest rates on different types of borrowing.

THE DECISION TO INVEST

The firm's decision to invest—to purchase new plant and equipment—is made on the same basis as any other decision. If the investment will add more to revenue than to cost (i.e., if it will increase profit), it should be undertaken. However, there are three important qualifiers to this simple rule.

First, a large part of the revenues and the costs are in the future and must be converted into current dollar values before they can be compared. For example, a particular investment may incur costs of $1500 in the first two years and yield $1600 in revenues five years down the road. Is this profitable? It depends on the interest rates, because those five-years-down-the-road dollars are worth less than the "up-front" dollars.

The second qualifier is uncertainty. Firms always face uncertainty in whatever decisions they make, but the longer the time horizon, the greater the uncertainty about future costs, revenues, competitors, and customers. Faced with uncertainty, the firm may proceed with greater caution on long-run decisions than short-run ones.

Finally, the firm is likely to have a budget constraint. There may be limits on its ability to raise cash for investment purposes, so that such purchases may have to be spread over many future years rather than made all at once. If this is the case, the firm may be facing a number of profitable investment alternatives, and thus must choose from among those that fall within its budget constraint. Perhaps the firm can only fund one project, or two, or three, so it will choose those that offer the promise of the greatest profit.

Discounting-and-present-value analysis was designed to help the firm answer these questions; that is, to determine which investments are potentially profitable and to rank them in order of profitability.

DISCOUNTING AND PRESENT VALUE

The basic principle underlying discounting and present value is that dollars in the future are worth less than dollars in the present. If you were offered the choice of $100 right now or $100 one year from now, even if there was no doubt that the future $100 would be paid, you—or any other rational individual—would take the $100 right now. Why? Because at the end of a year, the $100 right now will be worth more than the $100 you would receive then. If the current interest rate is 7%, you could bank the money and have $107 ($100 × 1.07, or $P \times (1 + i)$, where P is the principal amount and i is the interest rate. Even if you spend the $100 instead of banking it, you are likely to come out ahead. If there is even moderate inflation, say 4%, you could spend the $100 on something that would (on average) cost $104 a year from now, and have its use for an extra year as well.

If $100 is worth $107 a year from now (at 7% interest), then what is $100 payable in a year worth right now? If the value of a current dollar amount P one year from now is $P * (1 + i)$, then the present value (PV) of a future amount (F) payable in one year must be

$$PV = F/(1 + i).$$

Thus, the $100 one year from now is worth

$$\$100/(1.07) = \$93.46.$$

In other words, to have $100 one year from now, you would have to invest $93.46 at 7% interest. At lower interest rates you would have to invest more, and at higher interest rates, less. This formula also indicates that future dollars are worth less at higher interest rates and more at lower interest rates.

What if the time period is longer than one year? The calculations get more complicated, but the principle is the same. The sum of $100 invested for two years at 7% will grow to $100 * (1.07)(1.07) = $114.49. At the end of one year it is $107, which is then reinvested at 7% to grow to $114.49. If the process is reversed, so that the question is now the present value of $100 two years from now, the answer is

$$PV = F/[(1 + i)(1 + i)] = F/(1 + i)^2, \text{ or}$$

$$100/[1.07*1.07] = 100/1.1449 = 87.34.$$

Thus, $87.34 is the present value of $100 to be paid two years from now, or alternatively, the sum you would have to invest in order to have $100 two years from now.

Future costs as well as future revenues can be discounted (converted to present values) by this technique. A firm that is considering several alternative expenditures with different present and future costs and different present and future revenue streams can discount these future values (i.e., compute present values) for all of these alternatives so that they can be compared directly. Present value and discounting is one of the most powerful tools of business decision-making.

Computing and Comparing Present Values

Let's apply this technique to some investment decisions. Table 9-1 gives some discount factors for interest rates from 3% to 10% and time periods from one to ten years. Each of the values in the table is of the form

$$1/[(1 + i)^t],$$

where i is an interest rate and t = a number of years. Now rewrite the present value formula as

$$PV = F/[(1 + i)^t] = F * 1/[(1 + i)^t].$$

PV can be calculated simply by multiplying the future value, F, by the discount factor, DF, from the table. For example, the discount factor for four years and 8% interest is

$$1/[(1.08)^4] = .734$$

so that \$100 delivered four years from now is worth

$$\$100 * .734 = \$73.40.$$

If there are several future payments or revenues, they can simply be added. For example, the value of a \$100 payment each year for the next four years at 6% interest is

$$\$100*1/[(1.06)] + \$100*1/[(1.06)^2] +$$

$$\$100*1/[(1.06)^3] + \$100 * 1/[(1.06)^4]$$

or

$$\$100*.839 + \$100 *.792 + \$100 * .745 +$$

$$\$100 * .704 = \$308.00.$$

TABLE 9-1
Discount Factors for Present-Value Calculations

$$[DF = 1/(1 + i)^t]$$

Number of Years t =	i = 3%	4%	5%	6%	7%	8%	9%	10%
1	.971	.962	.952	.943	.935	.926	.917	.909
2	.943	.925	.907	.890	.874	.857	.841	.826
3	.916	.890	.863	.839	.817	.794	.771	.751
4	.889	.856	.823	.792	.764	.734	.707	.682
5	.864	.823	.783	.747	.714	.680	.648	.620
6	.839	.792	.745	.704	.667	.630	.594	.564
7	.750	.762	.709	.664	.624	.583	.545	.737
8	.790	.733	.677	.627	.584	.539	.500	.465
9	.768	.704	.644	.592	.545	.499	.458	.423
10	.746	.677	.613	.558	.510	.462	.420	.384

Consider a retail firm that is examining three investment options. Given its cash assets and its line of credit at the bank, it cannot undertake all three right now, so it wants to undertake the most profitable one over the next five years, which is the firm's planning horizon. The bank is offering an interest rate of 9%. The choices are to buy a new computer system, expand the building, or buy two new delivery vans. Each option will cost $20,000. The new computer system will increase the firm's operating costs by $1200 a year immediately. It will take a full year to get the system operational, at which point it will increase the firm's revenues (sales minus other operating costs) by $12,000 a year for the second through fifth years.

The vans will incur operating costs of $1500 a year, but by expanding home delivery service it is expected that sales revenue after other expenses will increase by $10,000 a year immediately and for the entire five-year planning period. The expanded building is the slowest of the three to come on line, because it has not yet even been designed. There will be a two-year delay in getting this one operational. Once it is usable, it will increase costs by $6000 a year but will increase revenues by $20,000 a year. Which is the best choice?

The computer system's present value over a five-year planning horizon is measured as the present value of the additional revenues minus the present value of the additional costs. The additional costs of $1200 a year must be discounted for each of the five years:

$1200 * [.768 + .704 + .644 + .592 + .545] = $3904.60

The additional revenues for the second, third, fourth, and fifth years, likewise, must be multiplied by the appropriate discount factors for $i = 9$ percent and $t = 2,3,4,$ and 5 from Table 9-1:

$12,000 * [.704 + .644 + .592 + .545] = $12,000 *

$$2.485 = \$29,820$$

The present value of the computer system is the present value of the additional revenue of $29,820 minus the present value of the additional operating cost of $3904.60, or $25,915.40. This is a profitable investment, since the present value of the income stream exceeds the current outlay of $20,000.

The same computations can be made for the other two alternatives. The net present value of the vans (additional sales less additional operating costs) is $27,650.50. The net present value of the additional sales space is $24,934. (The reader is left to verify these computations.) Thus, the vans are the best of the three alternative ways to invest the $20,000. Note that all of these alternatives are offering a higher rate of return than the going interest rate of 9% because even discounted at that interest rate their present value is still higher than $20,000, the current sum invested. If they had all turned out to have a present value of less than $20,000, the firm's best choice would have been not to borrow or, if it had that amount in cash, to have invested the $20,000 at the market rate of 9 percent.

Planning Horizons and Salvage Value

Note, too, that this firm has only a five-year planning horizon. This assumes that the firm will junk the investment at the end of five years—there is no salvage value. This assumption may be valid for the vans and perhaps even for the computer system, since they tend to become obsolete quickly, but the additional space may still have considerable value at the end of five years. Suppose the additional floor space has a "salvage value" of $15,000 at the end of five years, while the vans and the computer system have become worthless.

How does this change the computation? Simply add the discounted value of the $15,000 for five years at 9 percent to the value of the investment. Thus, $15,000 at the end of 5 years at 9% is worth $8175, bringing the value of this investment up to $33,109. Now this investment ranks first instead of third and should be chosen over the other two.

Choosing an Interest Rate

The choice of an interest rate has a great deal of effect on the outcome of the calculations. High interest rates favor projects with quick payoffs and lower earnings in the future, while lower interest rates can make delayed-payoff projects more attractive. A slight difference in interest rates can convert a profitable project into an unattractive one, or vice versa.

In the loanable funds market the "real" interest rate is the price paid for the privilege of spending now instead of later. Those who borrow pay for the privilege. Those who give up the privilege—savers or lenders—are rewarded with interest payments. The suppliers in the loanable funds market are savers and lenders, and the demanders are borrowers. Generally, savers channel their loanable funds through banks, which act as brokers between lenders and borrowers.

A household, business, or government can be either a saver/lender or a borrower, changing roles from one year to the next. The supply curve slopes upward because it takes a higher interest rate to coax people to forgo more present consumption and postpone spending until a later date. The demand curve slopes downward because borrowing becomes more attractive at lower interest rates. In fact, at lower interest rates projects that were not profitable suddenly look attractive enough to induce additional borrowing.

There are two other important determinants of interest rates. One is risk. The lender takes a chance that the interest will not be paid or even that the principal itself will not be fully repaid. The greater the risk, the higher the interest rate that the lender requires.

The other determinant is inflation. If lenders expect that the dollars repaid will have less purchasing power than the dollars lent, they will demand a higher interest rate to offset this loss. Suppose, for example, that A lends B $100 for one year at an interest rate of 5%, expecting no inflation. Suppose that actual inflation is 8%. At the end of the year A is repaid in full—$105— but the purchasing power of the repayment has fallen to $97.22 ($105/1.08). The effective interest rate paid by B is negative, because less purchasing power was repaid than B originally borrowed. In order to have the purchasing power lent plus 5% A would have to receive $100 × 1.08 × 1.05 = $113.40. The extra 8.4 percent represents an inflation premium applied to both principal and interest.

Expected inflation rates vary among lenders and borrowers and also for different time horizons. Risk also varies greatly from one customer to another. Because of these two factors the market does not offer only one single interest rate but a whole family of rates. The lowest interest rates are those for short periods to very low-risk customers, such as the rates on U.S. Treasury bills (Treasury borrowing for periods of less than one year). Corporate bonds, home mortgages, and car loans all run for longer periods and carry more default risk as well as more inflation risk, so the interest rates are higher.

Table 9-2 lists some representative interest rates for various types of assets in the 1970s and 1980s. Note that longer term and higher risk assets carry higher interest rates in most years, although there were some periods in the late 1970s and early

1980s when other rates adjusted more slowly and Treasury bill rates temporarily rose relative to the others. Note, too, that by and large the various interest rates tend to rise and fall together.

TABLE 9-2
Representative Interest Rates, 1975-1987

Year	Treasury Bills (3 mo.)	Treasury Bonds (10 yr)	Corporate Bonds*		Home Mortgages
			Aaa	Baa	
1975	5.8%	8.8%	8.8%	10.6%	9.0%
1977	5.3	7.4	8.0	9.0	9.0
1979	10.0	9.6	9.6	10.7	10.8
1981	14.0	13.9	14.2	16.0	14.7
1983	8.6	11.1	12.0	13.6	12.6
1984	9.6	12.4	12.7	14.2	12.4
1985	7.5	10.6	11.4	12.7	11.6
1986	6.0	7.7	9.0	10.4	10.2
1987	5.8	8.4	9.4	10.6	9.3

*Aaa are top-rated investment-grade bonds; Baa are medium-grade bonds, carrying more risks; so-called junk bonds are not rated.

How does a firm choose from among all the interest rates in the market to find one to fit into the present-value formula? If the firm is borrowing, it should use the interest rate at which it can borrow. If the firm is financing an investment with its own funds, it still has an interest cost—the interest it could have earned in the market if it had lent those funds instead of investing them in the business. The rate it could have earned on bonds, bank deposits, or other financial investments is the appropriate interest rate to use in such calculations.

TYPES OF INVESTMENT FINANCING—DEBT AND EQUITY
The firm has a variety of financing options when it is considering making an ivestment. One source is internal financing—using funds accumulated out of previous revenues to purchase new plant and equipment. This is an important source—essentially lending to oneself rather than to others—but it is rarely adequate for a growing firm. If financing is sought from sources external to the firm, it must choose between incurring debt or increasing equity.

Debt Financing, Bond Prices, and Bond Yields

Debt financing is simply borrowing with an obligation to repay. A firm can borrow from a bank or other financial institution in the same way that a household does. A corporation also has the option of borrowing in more formal and impersonal fashion by issuing bonds. A bond, like any loan, is a promise to repay a fixed sum of capital and interest at a stated date. Bonds, unlike loans, are easy for lenders to buy and sell. They come in convenient denominations (usually $1000). There is an active market in outstanding bonds where buyers can find bonds to their liking in terms of maturity (date due), risk, and yield (interest rate as a percentage of price).

People who invest in bonds are buying a reasonably certain commitment of repayment of a specific sum with interest by an agreed-on date, in a form where their investment can be sold at any time. They are taking some risks, however, particularly with longer term bonds of ten years or more. Some of the risks may be apparent at the time of purchase. If the bonds are not highly rated (less than Baa), they carry a significant risk that the issuer may default on interest and/or principal. These bonds usually carry a higher yield to compensate for this risk.

A risk that applies to all bonds, even those of the safest borrowers, is that interest rates will change. Suppose, for example, that you bought a $1000 bond with 20 years to maturity at its full issue price with an annual interest rate of 6%. You receive $60 a year in interest and at the end of 20 years will receive your principal of $1000 back. (The interest rate on your bond at the time of issue is the annual dollar yield divided by the price.)

Suppose, however, that bonds issued next year carry an interest rate of 8% while your old bond is still carrying its fixed commitment of 6%. If you try to sell your old bond, you will receive less than $1000 for it because $1000 will buy a bond with an 8% yield. For a bond with 19 years to maturity, the price will fall approximately to the level at which the yields are equal. At the current yield of 8%, a bond yielding $60 per year is only worth $750. ($60 is equal to 8% of $750. In general, if Y = $ yield on the old bond, i = current interest rate on new bonds, and P = price of the old bond, the price of an outstanding bond that is far from maturity can be approximated by solving the relationship $i = Y/P$ for $P = Y/i$.)

Rising interest rates spell disaster for bondholders; falling interest rates increase the value of their holdings. Inflation represents a double threat because it erodes the purchasing power of the dollar at the same time that it drives up nominal interest rates and drives down the prices of old bonds issued at lower interest rates.

The attraction of owning bonds is that bondholders have a prior claim on the earnings of the firm, while the stockholders get the residual. Bonds are safer than stocks but do not participate in the firm's success if it does well.

Stock and Ownership Rights

An alternative for corporations is to issue stock, or ownership rights. If the firm has already issued stock, it can issue additional shares. Preferred stockholders have no voting rights but are guaranteed a fixed dividend before anything is paid to common stockholders. They fall below bondholders and other creditors but above common stockholders in priority of claim on the firm's assets. Common stock represents ownership rights to the firm, including voting at stockholders' meetings and a share of the firm's net earnings. The dividends on common stock and the value of a share rise and fall with the firm's fortunes. Common stockholders are risk-takers; some win big, others lose big. Buying common stock is an entrepreneurial activity, undertaken in the hope of profit.

Issuing additional stock to raise capital for investment dilutes the ownership claims of existing stockholders, but it may be worthwhile if the additional investments undertaken increase the profitability of the firm. Issuing bonds increases the firm's liabilities. Payments on interest and principal represent a prior claim before anything goes to stockholders. In addition, a firm that is heavily in debt will be less attractive both to lenders (or prospective bond-buyers) and to potential stock buyers, so there are limits on the amount of debt financing a firm can undertake relative to its current sales and earnings. The firm must weigh market conditions, look at present and future interest rates, and consider what is in the best interests of its owners (stockholders) in deciding whether to use debt or equity financing.

CHAPTER PERSPECTIVE

This chapter takes a closer look at one of the most important long-run decisions the firm makes, the decision to expand the stock of fixed assets by investing. A firm is usually faced with multiple investment alternatives and needs a way to rank them. Discounting-and-present-value calculations make it possible to compare such alternatives. The present value of a project repre-sents the sum-total of future costs and revenues, adjusted for the difference in values of current and future dollars. Present values can be compared to make an investment choice.

The outcome of a present-value comparison depends on the planning horizon and the interest rate chosen. The interest rate used is either the interest the firm could earn on its own financial assets or the interest rate it must pay if it borrows. Interest rates reflect time preference, risk, and expected rate of inflation. There is a whole array of different interest rates for different borrowers and time periods.

The firm can finance externally either by issuing more debt (borrowing or issuing bonds) or by issuing more ownership rights (stock). Bond prices fall when interest rates increase and rise when interest rates decrease while stock prices are less directly tied to interest rates. Bondholders have a prior claim on the firm's assets; stockholders are risk-takers with a residual claim on the firm's earnings.

The Firm and the Market: Competition

INTRODUCTION AND MAIN POINTS

The last several chapters have focused on the decisions made by firms in isolation without looking at the market conditions in which they operate. Yet it is clear that the firm that is the sole supplier will act very differently from one of many small firms competing in a large market. This chapter and the two that follow look at competitive conditions in the marketplace and how they affect a firm's decisions. We begin with an extremely competitive case called pure competition, then look at its polar opposite, monopoly, in Chapter 11. Finally, Chapter 12 will develop some intermediate, more realistic descriptions of market structures in which firms experience some competition but also enjoy a little monopoly power.

After studying the material in this chapter:

▬ You will be able to describe how a perfectly competitive firm makes output, pricing, and investment decisions in the long run and the short run.

▬ You will have a better understanding of the relationship between the firm and the industry.

▬ You will understand the benefits to the consumer from competition, and the drawbacks to the firm and the economy from having many small and virtually identical competitors in a market and an industry.

▬ You will understand why and how some firms can continue to enjoy above-average profits in an industry that is purely competitive, even when most firms are only making "normal" profits.

▬ You will have the first of two parts of a theory of industrial organizations that explains differences in the behavior of firms in terms of different market structures.

THE PURELY COMPETITIVE MODEL

The first model to be developed is one that describes the behavior of the firm as a price-taker—too small to influence the market, taking price as given and responding to it. This model, which has a long history in economic theory, represents a theoretical extreme, but it comes close to describing the behavior of sellers as well as buyers in certain kinds of markets—the sellers of agricultural products, the sellers of unskilled labor, and the buyers of most consumer goods. The first of these three kinds of markets, competitive markets in the sale of goods and services, is the one examined in this chapter. Competition in resource markets, and competition and monopoly on the buyer's side of the market, are discussed in later chapters.

What Is Competition?

In sports and other contexts competition often suggests an intensely personal rivalry between a small number of individuals. Economists do not use the term in precisely the same way. Competition in the marketplace in its most intense form is highly impersonal. While everyone has favorite teams and individual athletes, buyers are indifferent among competing sellers of wheat, apples, or shares of General Motors stock in the competitive marketplace. To an economist, when competition is perfect or pure, there is no personal rivalry at all. As the number of competitors gets smaller and the rivalry becomes more direct and more personal, the economist would regard this situation as one of less competition, not more. Unlike sports editors, economists define competition primarily in terms of the number of competitors in the field rather than the intensity of the rivalry between opposing sides.

Assumptions

The basic assumption of the purely competitive market is that there are many, many buyers and sellers in this market, so that each individual is too small to have any impact on the market. If Farmer A stops producing and selling wheat, there is no measurable impact on the price of wheat. If the Smith household boycotts lettuce by itself, the lettuce market doesn't notice.

The large number of sellers in this market means that the long-run cost curve hits its minimum point at a fairly low level of output. Recall the discussion of the optimum size of plant in Chapter 8. In a perfectly competitive industry the *optimum size of plant is quite small* relative to the size of the market.

A second and closely related assumption is that the products of the various firms are completely interchangeable (*homogeneous products*). Farmer A's wheat is perceived by the buyer as exactly like the wheat of all the other farmers, so buyers have no reason to have the slightest preference for one supplier over another. If the products or the suppliers were different in ways that mattered to buyers, then the firm would have a small amount of power over price; a slight increase in price would not drive all customers away, and a small cut in price would be very successful in attracting customers away from competing sellers.

A third assumption of the purely competitive model is that buyers and sellers have *complete information* about prices and quantities and where to find alternative sellers and customers. A buyer of potatoes for Campbell's soup can read the price of potatoes in the daily commodity listing, but a small firm buying paper for its copying machine or packaging materials for its final product may have to work harder to find out what sellers are available and what prices they offer. This assumption is quite valid for agricultural products, raw materials, and the stock market, but not necessarily for many other markets, where good and complete information is harder to find.

A fourth assumption is that firms can easily enter and leave an industry. That is, there are no *barriers to entry and exit*—licenses, regulations, patents, or high costs of getting in or out of this market—that limit the number of competing firms.

These four assumptions—many buyers and sellers, homogeneous product, complete information, and no barriers to entry and exit—can be combined with the supply-and-demand model of Chapter 3 and the cost and production models of Chapters 7 and 8 to describe the behavior of the firm and the industry in a purely competitive situation.

Equilibrium in the Short Run

The most important consequence of these assumptions is that the firm in pure competition faces a horizontal or perfectly elastic demand curve. Figure 10-1 shows the relationship between the industry and the firm. Panel (a) shows the industry's market-equilibrium position of price P_1 and quantity Q_1, where quantity is measured in millions of units. Panel (b) shows the demand curve for the firm, which is horizontal at price P_1. Quantity is measured in hundreds of units.

This firm is so small relative to the market that it can sell as much as it likes at the going price of P_1 without affecting industry supply and industry price. Since each additional unit sold adds P_1 to the firm's revenues, the demand curve also represents the firm's marginal revenue.

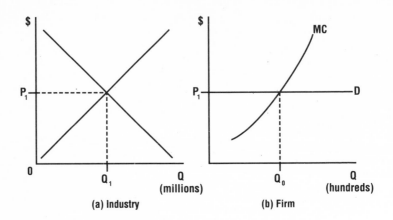

(a) Industry   **(b) Firm**

FIG. 10-1 *The Firm and the Industry in Perfect Competition*

The firm's marginal cost curve is also shown in Figure 10-1(b). The profit-maximizing rule tells us that this firm will maximize profit if it expands output up to the level at which $P = MR = MC$. For the firm the most profitable level of output is Q_0. If output is less than Q_0, additional units will add more to revenue than to cost and should be produced. If output is greater than Q_0, the extra units of output will add more to costs than to revenues. These extra units should not be produced. This firm takes the price as given and chooses a level of output that maximizes profits.

Average Cost, Profit, Entry, and Exit

Figure 10-2 completes the picture of this firm by adding the average cost curve. Note that the firm in Figure 10-2(a) is producing where price is equal to average cost as well as marginal cost. Is this a coincidence? No! In the short run a firm in pure competition may make a profit if price is greater than average cost, as it is in Figure 10-2(b). In the long run, however, profits will attract new firms into the industry. The entry of new firms will shift the supply curve for the whole industry to the right. Looking back at Figure 10-1, if supply shifts to the right in panel (a), the market price faced by all firms in this industry will fall. Each firm will face a new horizontal demand curve at the lower market price.

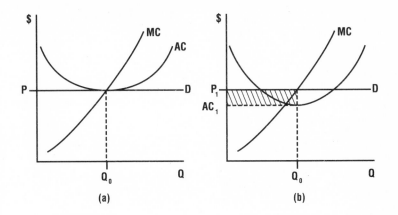

FIG. 10-2 *Long-run Equilibrium in Perfect Competition*

At the same time competition for similar productive resources may raise the prices of inputs and drive up the costs faced by all firms in the industry. This process of falling market price and rising costs will continue until the average firm is again making no profit, or at least only the normal profits that are included in the average cost curve.[1]

Suppose that the average firm was incurring losses, as in Figure 10-3, where average cost is greater than price. The loss to this firm is equal to the difference between average cost and price times the number of units produced, or the shaded area on the diagram. In response to losses some firms will leave the industry. If enough firms leave the industry, the industry supply curve will shift to the left. Market price will rise, reducing losses for the surviving firms. Costs may also fall with fewer firms competing for the same resources, which will also reduce losses for remaining firms. In both cases the process of firms exiting the industry will continue until the average firm is again producing where

$P = MR = MC = AC$ and is making only normal profits. In the long run the average firm in a purely competitive industry produces at the minimum point of its average cost curve.

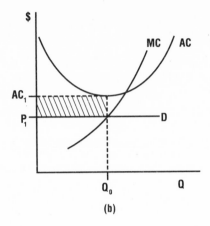

(b)

FIG. 10-3 *Firm Making Losses in Perfect Competition*

Response to Changes—the Long Run

Most of the changes that affect the profit-maximizing decisions of the firm occur in the market or the industry rather than within the firm. Demand for the industry's product may shift, changing the given price that each firm faces. Supply conditions may change. If technology changes, or if there is a change in the cost or availability of inputs, it usually affects all firms, not just one firm, and thus shows up in the market-supply curve as well as the marginal- and average-cost curves of the individual firms. The diagrams just developed can be used to describe how the firm in pure competition responds to some of these changes.

In Figure 10-4 the demand for the product of this industry has increased. The new market price in Panel (a) is P_2, shifting the horizontal demand curve facing the firm in panel (b) upward. The typical firm's profit-maximizing output has increased from Q_1 to Q_2. This firm is making a profit measured by the shaded area, C_1P_2AB, which is the difference between price and average cost times the number of units produced. These profits will attract new firms to the industry, shifting supply to the right until the price is restored to P_1 and a larger industry quantity. As the price falls, old producers cut back output to their original levels, with new firms providing the extra output to meet additional demand.

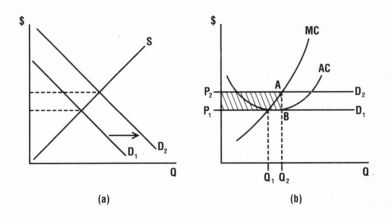

(a)   (b)

FIG. 10-4 *Long-run Adjustment to Change in Demand*

In Figure 10-5 the market supply has increased, perhaps because of a good harvest for agriculture, the entry of foreign competitors, or a reduction in costs. In the first two cases the cost curves of the average firm will not change. The increase in supply is caused by factors external to the average firm. If something changes the costs facing all firms in the industry—for example, a drop in interest rates or raw materials costs—then the cost curves of the individual firm will also change. For simplicity, the first case considered is one in which the supply curve shifts for some reason that does not affect the cost curve of individual firms. Then we will look at the more complex case where the shift in market supply is a result of changes in the cost curves of the individual firms.

As supply increases, the market price falls from P_1 to P_2. The average or representative firm in Figure 10-5(b) responds in the short run by cutting output from Q_1 to Q_2. However, it is now experiencing losses because even at the lower level of output, price is less than average cost. This firm is still covering average variable cost and making some contribution to fixed cost, so it will not shut down in the short run. (If this statement is not entirely clear, you should go back to Chapter 7 and review the shutdown decision in the short run.) Firms whose costs are a little higher, however, may find a shutdown in the short run to be their best option.

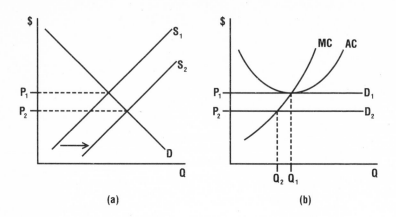

FIG. 10-5 *Change in Industry Supply*

As the firm gets into the long run, it will elect not to renew leases or replace worn-out equipment. Some firms that did not shut down in the short run will do so when they have to make a decision about making a recommitment to pay those fixed costs in the long run. As firms leave the industry, the market-supply curve shifts back to the left, increasing market price and restoring the average firm to the position at which P = MR = AC = MC. At this point there is no profit or loss; exit from the industry ceases; and the average firm is back in equilibrium with only a normal profit and no economic profit or loss.

It is more likely that the shift in supply will be related to the firm's total, average, and marginal costs. If something happens to shift the average firm's marginal-cost curve, then the market supply curve will also shift, because it is simply the sum of the supply curves of the firms in the industry. Suppose, for example, that wheat farmers are faced with a steep increase in the price of fertilizer. Average- and marginal-cost curves for all the firms in this industry shift up and to the left, so that for any given level of output the average cost and the cost of the last unit produced are both higher. Firms, or farmers, will find that their profit-maximizing output is lower than before. If they were in equilibrium before this change, they will now be experiencing losses. This situation is depicted in Figure 10-6. In this diagram the firm is shown in panel (a) and the industry in panel (b) because the direction of causation is now from the firm to the industry or market. Changes in costs of each of the firms in the industry have shifted the individual- and market-supply curves to the left. Price is higher and output is lower in the short run.

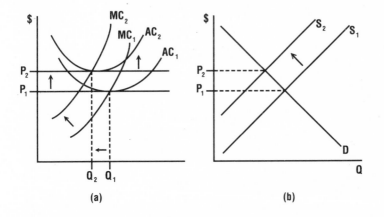

FIG. 10-6 *Change in Costs in Perfect Competition*

What will happen in the long run? By now the story is almost familiar, but this one has a new twist to it. Until now entry into or exit from the industry has always restored market price to its previous level, where price was equal to minimum average cost for the average firm. But now the cost curves have also shifted, so minimum average cost is higher than before. The new equilibrium is at price P_2, which is also higher than before. At this price, after all adjustments have occurred, the average firm still in the industry is producing output Q_2 at an average cost that is equal to price P_2, and is making neither profit nor loss (except for normal profit). Thus there is no incentive to enter or to leave the industry. The higher costs of production have been "passed on" to consumers, but the firms in this industry are still making only normal profits, as they were before the cost change occurred.

When changes in demand or costs signal that some firms should leave the industry, which ones leave? Farming, which is the sector that has shrunk the most, provides us some indicators.

Firms that are most flexible at the time of the changed signals will leave. Perhaps a son or a daughter has just inherited the family farm, or the old equipment has broken down and is in need of costly repair or replacement. As these entrepreneurs leave, the reduced supply will raise the price that the surviving firms can charge.

BENEFITS AND DRAWBACKS OF PURE COMPETITION

From the short-run standpoint of the consuming public the firm in pure competition represents an ideal of sorts. The firm produces the optimal level of output and makes no profits above the normal level required to keep resources in this firm and industry. These two benefits should not be underrated, because they reflect efficient use of resources. In a world of scarcity, efficiency is a very important virtue.

In pure competition price is equal to marginal revenue, and both are equal to marginal cost. The last unit produced costs society exactly the same value of resources as the buyer has to sacrifice to pay for it. Production is at the optimal level. Price is also equal to average cost; there are no economic profits. Profits performed their function of attracting new firms to the industry and then disappeared. Finally, marginal cost equals average cost, a signal that average cost is at its minimum point. These efficiency advantages of the purely competitive model have been the basis for advocating use of the market in preference to other decision-making methods. Those who argue from this model point to efficiency as its most positive attribute.

However, from the standpoint of the firm, of society as a whole, and of the long run interests of consumers, pure competition has some drawbacks to be weighed against its undeniable virtues. First, the typical firm in pure competition lives a day-to-day existence that does not allow it the luxury of a long-term perspective. It is unlikely to undertake any research and development, not only because it may not be around long enough to reap the benefits but also because it is so difficult for the firm to keep to itself the beneficial results of such research. Some entity outside the industry must conduct the research and development needed to keep it viable. In the case of agriculture this research and development has been funded partly by government and partly by suppliers—seed companies, tractor manufacturers, fertilizer firms. Farmers have no incentive to undertake such an expensive and long-term program when they are in an industry that puts a premium on short-run survival.

Second, the process of entry and exit is likely to result in a great deal of waste. Buildings lying idle, unused capital equipment, and labor trained in skills with no current demand are some of the major casualties of the typically high failure rate in a purely competitive industry. Such waste is costly. It takes time to shift these resources into other uses, and in the meantime the production they could generate is lost forever. It is not difficult to spot the empty storefronts, silent factories, and idle fields as living testimony to the cost and waste associated with easy entry and exit in highly competitive industries.

Third, other market structures offer a benefit to consumers in variety that is not found in a purely competitive industry. While some observers find the proliferation of detergents, auto body styles, and other products wasteful, others see this process as accommodating differing consumer tastes and enhancing the range of consumer choice.

Finally, the purely competitive situation is very unappealing to the firm. If the firm can raise some barriers to entry, perhaps make its product a little different, or do something else to get a little slope to its demand curve—managing to keep some customers even if it raises prices—then it has the possibility of longer-term profits and a little more certainty about its future. These elements—product differentiation and barriers to entry—give the firm a little monopoly power (the subject of the next chapter).

PURE COMPETITION ON THE BUYERS' SIDE

While examples of pure competition among sellers is rare, pure competition is the norm on the buyers' side of the market. The retail store is largely indifferent among its customers, selling at the same price to everyone. While buyers as a group face an upward-sloping supply curve, the supply curve facing one buyer is horizontal. Jane Smith can buy all the milk she wants at the going price of $2.00 a gallon, because her purchases are so small relative to the market that she is a price-taker. Retail firms buying business services and unskilled labor are also small enough so that they buy what they need at the going price.

Some buyers are large enough to make a difference, particularly if the buyer is a firm rather than a consumer. For example, a small number of large wine producers buy a significant share of the grape crop in California. They are not price-takers, and they face an upward-sloping supply curve. A single employer in a small town may hire a large enough share of the work force to affect the price. A single buyer of a product or service is called a *monopsonist* (only buyer). The effect of monopsony on output and price is discussed in Chapter 12.

REALISM, RENT, AND THE PERFECTLY COMPETITIVE MODEL

Even in perfect competition, where there are many small firms and the products are identical, firms are not all exactly alike. In farming a particular firm may enjoy better soil, more rainfall, or a more convenient location to market than another. Location is particularly important in retail sales and services, where firms may be virtually identical in every other respect. Such advantages will be reflected in costs that are lower than the average firm's. This modification of the perfectly competitive model brings it a little closer to reality.

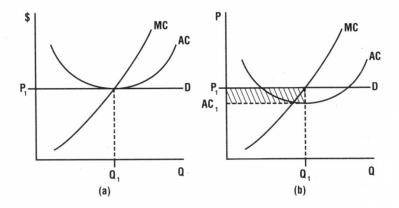

FIG. 10-7 *Economic Rent in a Competitive Industry*

Figure 10-7 shows two such firms in the long run. Panel (a) is the average firm, producing where market price P_1 equals average and marginal cost. In panel (b) the firm with the special advantage also sells at that market price, but it is lower than average cost because the special advantages the firm enjoys are reflected in lower average costs. This firm is making a "profit" represented by the shaded area—the difference between price and average cost multiplied by the number of units produced. This profit is different from the profits discussed earlier, those that provided a signal to enter the industry and then disappeared.

These profits persist but should not attract new firms to the industry, principally because such firms cannot reap profits unless they enjoy the same special advantages as the firm in Panel (b).

Economists call this "profit" by the name *rent*—not the familiar kind of rent paid on an apartment, but the less familiar rent paid to land as well as some other factors. This kind of rent, as defined by economists, is any payment in excess of what is needed in order to call a resource forth. For example, if a gold mine can operate at $100 an ounce (enough to cover costs and make a normal profit), but the price of gold is currently $300 an ounce, there is $200 rent paid to gold as a natural resource over and above what it costs to "call it forth," as 19th-century economists said.

The return to land (unimproved land) is all rent, because land is just there, and the payment for the use of land merely serves to determine who gets it. Ultimately the rent payment goes to the owner of the land. If the firm owns the land, what appears to be profit simply reflects the higher opportunity cost of that resource—what it could earn in other uses. Rent is a return to land, not to risk-taking or enterprise. If the firm does not own the land but leases it from someone else because of its fertility or location, it will have to pay a higher price to obtain the use of such a desirable asset, so that its costs will not be lower than those of competing firms. Such advantages as location, rainfall, and fertility are quickly reflected in the market price of land or similar assets.

CHAPTER PERSPECTIVE

Competition, to economists, is impersonal. More competitors represent more competition, and fewer competitors, less competition. In the purely competitive model there are so many sellers (or buyers) that they have no impact on market price; they are price-takers.

The purely competitive model assumes a large number of buyers and sellers, easy entry and exit for the industry, perfect information, and homogeneous products. If these assumptions hold, then the firm selling in a perfectly competitive market will face a horizontal demand curve at the market price. Price will be equal to marginal revenue and marginal cost in the short run and to average cost in the long run. The firm will produce the optimal level of output. Profits and losses will signal firms to enter and to exit the industry; as they respond, profits and losses will disappear. Firms that appear to make long-run profits in purely competitive industries are actually receiving economic rents because they own land or other assets with some special advantage that reduces their costs relative to the costs of other producers.

The chief benefits of the competitive market structure lie in efficiency. Price is equal to marginal cost, and there are no long-term profits or losses. The drawbacks are lack of incentives for research, wasted resources from frequent entry and exit, and lack of variety for consumers.

FOOTNOTE

1 *Recall from Chapter 7 that one of the elements of cost is a normal profit, or a return just adequate to keep the entrepreneur in this firm and this industry. It is the return to enterprise as a productive resource, and is considered a cost of production. In a corporation, if stockholders do not receive some minimum return that is more than just interest on their capital, that includes some reward for risk-taking, either in dividends or in a higher price per share, they are likely to transfer their capital to other firms and other industries. This minimum required return to risk-taking and organizing production is the normal profit included in the cost curve.*

The Firm and the Market: Monopoly

INTRODUCTION AND MAIN POINTS

At the opposite end of the spectrum of market structures from pure competition is monopoly. Monopoly means that there is a single seller for the entire market. The market in which the seller enjoys a monopoly may be national, regional, or local. (No firms enjoy a world monopoly, although deBeers diamonds comes close; very few firms enjoy a national monopoly, but local monopolies are very common.) All firms seek some degree of monopoly power because it allows them more freedom to raise prices and creates the possibility of persistent profits.

After studying the material in this chapter:
■ You will understand what kinds of conditions give rise to monopoly and why firms seek monopoly power.
■ You will see why consumers object to monopoly and why governments attempt either to regulate monopolies or to break them up.
■ You will be able to compare the monopoly market structure to the market of pure competition.
■ You will be able to distinguish between a natural monopoly and one that is artificially created.

WHY MONOPOLIES EXIST

A monopoly is the sole seller of a particular product in a particular market. The monopoly may be in a limited and shrinking market or a large and growing one. The firm may be a monopoly only if the product is narrowly defined. Walt Disney Studios, for example, has a monopoly on Mickey Mouse cartoons, but not cartoons in general or even mouse cartoons. The monopoly may or may not be profitable. What all monopolists have in common is that their demand curves are the same as the market-demand curves for their products, and they do not have supply curves in the usual sense, although they have cost curves just like any other firm. Because the monopoly is the sole supplier of a product with few good substitutes, it faces a fairly inelastic demand curve.

Monopolies exist and persist because of barriers to entry. These barriers take many forms. There may be a technological barrier—a process, method, or patent that prevents competitors from producing a satisfactory substitute. Polaroid was able to maintain a monopoly on instant picture cameras for decades through renewal, refinements, and extension of patents. The established firm may have control over raw materials or other essential inputs, or it may own a network of retail distributors that competitors cannot crack. All of these are examples of how one firm can create barriers to entry and protect its monopoly position.

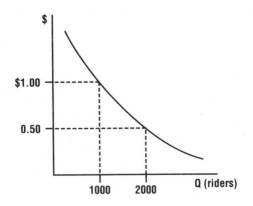

FIG. 11-1 *Average Cost for One Firm vs. Two*

Barriers to entry can also be natural. There may only be room for one firm in the market if the product is one that enjoys substantial economies of scale. In most communities there is only sufficient demand to support one water supplier, one electric utility, one bus system at an average cost that is at or near the minimum level. Figure 11-1 shows what would happen if a community that had average bus ridership of 2000 per week was served by two equal-size bus systems instead of a single system. The monopoly bus system has an average cost of 50 cents per ride, while the two competing bus systems have average costs of

$1.00 per ride. Two bus systems would each have many empty seats and idle buses. One bus system can make better use of its capital equipment. Monopolies that exist because the market is too small to support more than one supplier are called *natural monopolies.*

Finally, there are monopolies that exist because of government policies. Licensing limits entry into certain professions—doctors, lawyers, barbers, realtors. Local governments grant exclusive franchises to cable TV systems, and football and baseball leagues grant franchises as well. Some barriers to entry are created by government in order to help particular firms or particular industries. Tariffs and quotas are ways to protect domestic monopolies from foreign competition. All of these artificial barriers to entry ensure that a monopolist's position is unchallenged.

In reality, of course, no barrier is totally insurmountable. Most monopolists face some competition, even if it is remote and indirect. The sole supplier of electricity in an area must compete with other ways to heat and cool houses (natural gas, oil, solar panels) and with other forms of energy for commercial uses. If the monopolist controls a strategic raw material, substitutes or synthetics can be developed. Governments that were persuaded by the monopolist to erect barriers to entry can be persuaded by other firms to dismantle those barriers.

Even so, there are firms that enjoy monopoly power in varying degrees and for varying lengths of time. Let us examine the consequences of monopoly power before considering what, if anything, can and should be done to restrict it.

Demand and Marginal Revenue for a Monopolist

The purely competitive firm faced a horizontal demand curve. Since the price was constant, so was marginal revenue. Each additional unit sold added the same revenue as the previous one to the firm, and that additional revenue was equal to the product price. The monopolist, however, faces a downward-sloping marginal-demand curve, and a relatively inelastic one as well, since consumers have no good substitute products or suppliers. (Inelastic demand is a major clue for identifying monopoly firms.) Each time the monopolist wants to sell another unit, it has to reduce the price. When it reduces the price on the last unit, it also has to reduce the price on all units it sells. The demand curve in Figure 11-2 indicates that the monopolist's customers will purchase three units at $9, four units at $8, five units at $7, and so forth. In order to sell five units instead of four, the firm must reduce the price it charges on all units from $8 to $7. The fifth unit sells for $7, but it only adds $3 to the firm's revenues, because the other four units that could have been sold at $8 each must now be offered at the going price of $7.

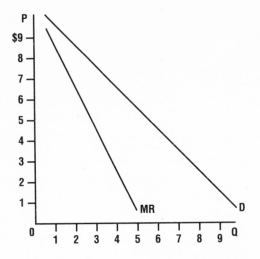

FIG. 11-2 *A Monopolist's Demand and Marginal Revenue Curve*

Another way of computing marginal revenue is as the change in total revenue along the demand curve:

At four units: 4 × $8 = $32.

At five units: 5 × $7 = $35.

Marginal revenue is $35 − $32, or $3.

Note that the marginal revenue curve in Figure 11-2 bisects the distance between the vertical axis and the demand curve. This is always the case for a linear-demand curve. Remembering this principle makes it easier to sketch a marginal-revenue curve that lies in a correct relationship to its demand curve even if you do not know any actual numbers.

Note, also, that at some quantity marginal revenue becomes negative. It makes no sense for the monopolist even to consider producing in this range unless the demand curve shifts to the right, because additional units will not only reduce profits, they will also reduce revenues!

In order to identify the profit-maximizing level of output for the monopolist, the marginal- and average-cost curve must be added to the diagram. This is done in Figure 11-3. The monopolist follows the same profit-maximizing rule as the pure competitor, namely MR = MC, but the results are different. As you can see in Figure 11-2, at the output (Q_1) where MR = MC, price is greater than marginal cost, and marginal cost is not equal to average cost. This firm is producing less than the optimal level of output (where price is equal to marginal cost) and charging a higher price than would be charged if output was at the optimal level.

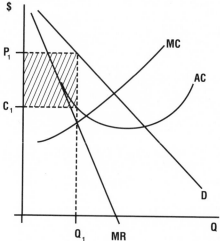

FIG. 11-3 *Price and Output Under Monopoly*

This firm is also making a profit, shown by the shaded area. As always, profit per unit is equal to the difference between price and average cost at the chosen output level, and total profit is profit per unit multiplied by the quantity of output. Like the purely competitive firm in the short run, the monopolist's profits in the diagram are those in excess of normal profits. Recall that normal profits are a cost and are reflected in the average and marginal cost curves.

Not all monopolies make profits. Consider the sole surviving supplier of slide rules, the rather primitive ancestor of the hand-held calculator. In the 1950s and 1960s every engineering student wore one on his belt (the occasional female engineering student carried one on top of her stack of books). Figure 11-4, for example, shows this slide rule monopoly following the profit-maximizing rule; that is, it produces that quantity for which MR = MC. This firm is making a loss, shown by the shaded area. Average cost is higher than price, and the best this monopoly can do is to minimize its losses. The profit-maximizing rule at least ensures that losses are lower at output Q_1 than at any other output level. However, this firm is likely to leave the business soon unless something changes.

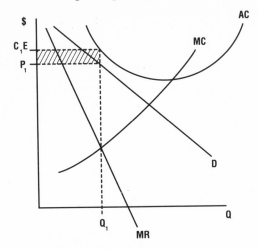

FIG. 11-4 *A Monopoly Making Losses*

Monopoly Profits and Barriers to Entry

The important difference between profits in monopoly and profits in pure competition comes in the long run. In pure competition, when there are short-run profits, new firms are attracted to the industry. As new firms enter, supply increases, price falls, and economic profits are eliminated in the long run. Profits serve their function as a signal to produce more output, then they disappear. One of the distinguishing features of monopoly, however, is high barriers to entry. Profits are sending out a signal, but no one is able to respond because they cannot enter the industry. The long-run solution is the same as the short-run solution; if there are profits in the short run, there are profits in the long run, and if there are losses in the short run, there are losses (or shutdown) in the long run.

Shifts in Demand

In pure competition an increase in demand created short-run profits, called forth more output from both existing firms and new entrants, and eventually resulted in a larger quantity at the original price. What happens in monopoly?

In Figure 11-5 demand for the monopolist's product increases from D_1 to D_2. Since the marginal-revenue curve is not independent of the demand curve, but is derived from it, marginal revenue also shifts from MR_1 to MR_2. The monopolist increases the level of output from Q_1 to Q_2 and raises the price from P_1 to P_2. If you measure profit on the diagram, you will find that profit has also increased. Like pure competition, an increase in demand does call forth an increase in output, but the price rises and stays higher. The increased profits are unable to attract new firms into the industry because of barriers to entry.

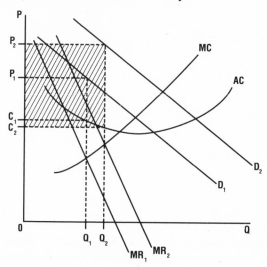

FIG. 11-5 *Monopoly and an Increase in Demand*

You can use the same diagram to trace through the effects of a decrease in demand or a change in the monopolist's costs. Note that if demand decreases enough, even the monopolist must come to terms with the shutdown decision as losses pile up. A monopoly in the production of whale oil lamps, slide rules, or 78-rpm records is of little value in the face of very limited demand.

MONOPOLY VERSUS PURE COMPETITION

Four criticisms of monopoly emerge from this analysis, all in comparison to pure competition. First, the monopoly firm produces less output and charges a higher price than a purely competitive firm would, given the firm's cost curves and the level of product demand. The purely competitive firm sets price equal to marginal cost. The monopolist sets marginal revenue equal to marginal cost, and since marginal revenue is less than price, price is higher than marginal cost and output is therefore smaller.

Second, the monopolist produces at an average cost above the minimum. Only when the firm's demand curve is horizontal will it intersect the marginal-cost curve where marginal cost equals average cost, at the low point of the average-cost curve. As long as the demand curve facing the firm has some downward slope, the marginal-revenue curve will intersect the marginal-cost curve to the left of the minimum point on the average-cost curve.

Third, while profits fulfill their purpose (attracting new firms and calling forth more output) in pure competition, in monopoly profits can persist indefinitely, because high barriers to entry prevent new firms from taking part of the market. Profits thus do not serve any useful social purpose in monopoly as they do in pure competition.

Finally, many valuable resources are wasted in creating and maintaining barriers to entry to prop up a monopoly. Some resources are spent on getting favorable legislation passed and keeping it from being repealed. Other resources are spent cornering sources of supply, building loyal networks of dealerships, maintaining examining board and licensing committees. Some of these expenditures of resources serve a useful public purpose, but most are simply to protect, preserve, and extend monopoly power.

Is it possible to say anything good about monopoly? Compared to the pure competitor, the monopolist has a longer lifetime and therefore more opportunity to engage in research and development from which the firm will reap the benefits. Thus, the firm is more likely to do research and innovate than a purely competitive firm. However, the security of barriers to entry can make the firm lazy. If the protected monopoly is secure, why bother to stay one jump ahead of nonexistent competition? Research and innovation are more likely to occur in market structures between these two extremes.

About the only defenses of monopoly are that (1) no monopoly lasts forever (sooner or later entry barriers are surmounted or destroyed) and (2) some industries lend themselves to monopolies in order to take advantage of economies of scale. These natural monopolies are probably the best alternative in a situation where competition would be wasteful and expensive.

NATURAL MONOPOLY

Figure 11-6 depicts a natural monopoly. Typically this firm's short-run average and marginal costs continue to fall throughout the range of output that the market is likely to demand. As long as marginal cost is falling, it is below average cost because it is "pulling" average cost down. Thus, MC is less than AC throughout the range of output shown in the diagram. This cost pattern is one of the defining characteristics of natural monopoly. A second characteristic of natural monopolies is that they tend to occur in industries for which the short run is a very long time period, because the capital equipment, which is the principal cost, has a very long useful lifetime and cannot be easily converted to other uses. Finally, as is the case with all monopolists, the demand curve is likely to be quite inelastic because there are no good substitutes.

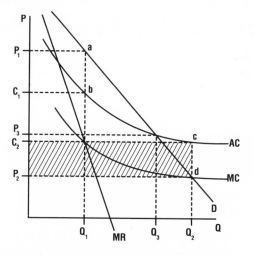

FIG. 11-6 *Natural Monopoly*

Left to itself the monopoly will choose an output level for which MR = MC, which occurs at output Q_1. Price is P_1, determined by following Q_1 up to the demand curve, and the firm is making a profit of C_1P_1ab. However, this solution is unsatisfactory from the standpoint of public welfare. Additional units would be cheaper to produce as the monopolist moves down along the average and marginal cost curves. The social optimum is the solution that would be chosen by the purely competitive firm, which is to produce where price (on the demand curve) equals marginal cost, at Q_2. Unfortunately, at this level of output and at this price the firm is incurring losses of P_2C_2cd, because price is less than average cost. Thus, if regulators require the firm to produce at this level, the deficit must be made up in some other way. This is the dilemma facing public utilities commissions in every state; to find some middle ground between the unsatisfactory (high price, restricted output) private solution and the losses that the firm incurs when regulators impose the purely competitive solution.

There are two intermediate regulatory solutions to this problem: One is average-cost pricing; the other is the two-part tariff.

Average-cost pricing chooses a quantity where the price (on the demand curve) is equal to average cost—resulting in an output of Q_3 and a price of P_3 in Figure 11-6. This output is higher and this price is lower than the monopoly solution, but price is higher and output less than the competitive solution. The firm is breaking even, including a normal profit that is reflected in the average-cost curve. This solution has proved very attractive to public utilities commissions. However, there are two risks. One is the incentive for management to inflate costs in the form of executive salaries, offices, and other "perks." The other is to inflate normal profit. Since regulatory agencies usually compute a normal profit as a percentage rate of return on invested capital, the natural monopoly's owners have an incentive to use more capital-intensive methods of production, creating a higher capital base on which to compute normal profit.

The second solution is the two-part tariff. In Figure 11-6 the cost per unit can be broken into two components, marginal cost and fixed cost (P_2C_2cd). The cost can then be allocated among customers or households according to a formula that divides fixed costs among households and charges each a flat rate. For example, if a firm serving 1000 households had fixed costs per month of $50,000, each household would pay a flat fee of $5 regardless of the number of units consumed. In addition, there would be a charge per unit that reflected marginal cost—$1 per 1000 gallons of water or two cents per kilowatt of electricity. The flat fee covers fixed costs, and the per-unit charge covers marginal cost. The price of the marginal unit can be set equal to marginal cost without inflicting losses on the firm. Two-part tariffs are a useful pricing policy for firms with heavy fixed costs as well as for natural monopolies.

If the government chooses to address the problem of natural monopoly by creating a public entity to produce the product or service, then the fixed costs can be covered out of tax revenues and marginal or operating costs can be covered by per-unit charges. The effect is similar to the two-part tariff, except that the fixed costs are now paid for by taxpayers rather than by a per-household fee.

DO MONOPOLIES EXIST?

Many economists believe that the problem of monopoly is greatly exaggerated. Barriers to entry are not insurmountable and often erode with time. Many of the persistent barriers to entry are actually created and maintained by government in the form of licensing requirements or exclusive franchises. Even where there is only one firm, there are often substitute products or services, at least for some uses.

Whether or not there are many monopolies in the narrow sense—the sole producer of a product with no good substitutes— clearly there is monopoly power in some industries. The insights of the monopoly model suggest some of the problems that arise from monopoly power—restricted output, higher prices, persistent profits. Like pure competition, monopoly may be rare, but the model of monopoly is helpful in understanding the behavior of firms with temporary monopoly or with very little competition.

MONOPOLY AND THE ROLE OF GOVERNMENT

If there is monopoly power, what is the role of government? Governments have three roles to play in dealing with the problem of monopoly power. First, a government may be the sponsor and patron of monopoly by granting exclusive franchises, continuing to extend patents, permitting licensing that limits entry into certain industries or occupations, granting contracts that create monopoly suppliers to government, or restricting foreign trade that is often the main source of competition. A government that wishes to reduce monopoly power can often begin by looking at public policies that create or encourage monopoly.

Second, as noted earlier, governments at all levels are involved in regulating natural monopolies. If it is clearly inefficient to allow many small firms to serve a market where average cost would be much lower with a single firm, then a regulated private monopoly or a public sector firm (such as the post office or a public water supply) may be the most feasible alternative.

Finally, if the monopoly has arisen because a strong firm has driven out competitors or forestalled their development, the government has the power to use the antitrust laws to increase competition in that industry by forbidding mergers, breaking up powerful firms, or using other remedies. This power is discussed in a later chapter.

CHAPTER PERSPECTIVE

A monopoly is a single seller of a product with no good substitutes in a particular market. Usually a monopolist is protected from competition by barriers to entry—patents, control of inputs or distribution networks, exclusive franchises, licensing requirements, international trade restrictions, or simply the fact that there are substantial economies of scale.

Monopolists produce that output level for which marginal revenue is equal to marginal cost. Since monopolists usually face a fairly inelastic market demand curve, they will produce less and charge a higher price than a competitive firm. If profits occur, they will persist because of high barriers to entry.

A natural monopoly is one that exists because economies of scale make it more efficient for a market to be served by a single large firm rather than by several small firms. Often natural monopolies are regulated by the government in order to ensure a larger output and lower prices than would occur in the absence of regulation. If the regulator tries to ensure that price is equal to marginal cost, however, the firm will experience losses. Two solutions to this problem are average-cost pricing and the two-part tariff. In some cases the government creates a public-sector entity (such as a city water department) to provide the service.

Persistent monopolies are rare, but local monopolies are fairly common. Often where monopolies exist and persist it is the result of barriers to entry created and maintained by government. Even if actual monopolies are rare, the monopoly model provides some useful insights into the effects of monopoly power. Governments can respond by regulating natural monopolies, by using the antitrust laws to restrict the growth of monopoly, by limiting government actions that foster monopoly, or by creating public-sector monopolies to provide certain goods and services that lend themselves to natural monopoly.

The Firm and the Market: Monopolistic Competition and Oligopoly

CHAPTER 12

INTRODUCTION AND MAIN POINTS

Intermediate between the polar types of firms, competitive and monopolistic, are some market structures that will be more familiar and more realistic to most readers. Most firms face some competition but also enjoy at least a modest degree of power over price. They do not lose all their customers with a small price hike, and they can capture new customers with sales, discounts, and other forms of price cuts. Unlike monopolists, they have rivals; unlike pure competitors, they may have to take the reactions of those rivals into account in making decisions about pricing, output levels, expansion, location, and other matters. There are barriers to entry, but they range from very low to quite high. The two intermediate market structures are called monopolistic competition, which is near the competitive end of the spectrum, and oligopoly, where a few firms compete directly with each other under conditions closer to monopoly.

After studying the material in this chapter:

▬ You will be able to classify industries according to the four market structures.

▬ You will have a better understanding of how firms make price and output decisions in industries with many sellers, low barriers to entry, and differentiated products (monopolistic competition).

▬ You will be able to describe how firms make price and output decisions in industries with few sellers and high barriers to entry (oligopolies), where firms cannot make decisions without considering how their rivals will respond.

▬ You will know why certain types of products tend to be produced in particular market structures.

▬ You will be able to classify your industry and your firm in terms of market structure, degree of market power, barriers to entry, and other defining characteristics, and use that knowledge to make better decisions for your firm.

HOW REALISTIC ARE MARKET MODELS?

The market models of the last two chapters are difficult to relate to real-world firms. While agriculture is close to perfect competition, and there are some local monopolies and public utilities (regulated natural monopolies), most firms have some competition and some market power. The two principal sources of market power are product differentiation and barriers to entry.

Many industries produce differentiated products, or consist of firms that are differentiated in other ways. *Differentiation* means that consumers observe differences in products or suppliers that cause them to prefer one over another; a particular brand of soft drink or jeans, or one store's location and sales staff. The whole field of marketing is based on the concept of product differentiation. Most industries also have some kinds of barriers to entry, whether natural or created by government or by the existing firms in the industry. Rarely, however, are these barriers so high that new firms cannot get over or around them if the industry is attractive enough. Real firms, for the most part, lie in that vast expanse between competition and monopoly and operate under conditions that include elements of both.

In the 1930s, economists Joan Robinson and Edward Chamberlain filled in some of that space between competition and monopoly with intermediate market models. It was much easier to find real-world counterparts to these newer models. The model of monopolistic competition, with many small firms each possessing a modest amount of market power, fit most retail operations and personal services, a large number of manufacturing industries, and most wholesale trade. The model of oligopoly, with few firms and high barriers to entry, fit most of the industrial giants of the twentieth century—automobile firms, steel, movie producers, appliance manufacturers, oil refiners, and more recently, firms that produce computers.

SOURCES OF IMPERFECT COMPETITION

Imperfect competition exists when firms are affected by the decisions of their rivals. The number of firms may be smaller than required for perfect competition for two reasons. One explanation for a smaller number of firms is the existence of barriers to entry. A second reason is that some firms in the industry may have something unique to offer—style, reputation, location—that gives them a degree of customer loyalty. All kinds of uniqueness are captured by the general term "product differentiation."

Barriers to Entry

Somewhere between the total freedom of entry and exit of the purely competitive industry and the absolute barriers to entry of monopoly lies the situation of most real-world firms. Barriers to entry may include established dealer networks or supplier relationships, proprietary information, patented products, established customer loyalty, substantial economies of scale, licensing, or franchises.

Some industries or market structures have relatively low barriers. It is not difficult to get into most kinds of retail operations—insurance, real estate, restaurants, hairstyling salons, convenience stores. Some of these firms can be started as franchise operations, with a parent company offering considerable assistance in overcoming the barriers to entry of supplier relations, brand loyalty, and initial learning costs by providing suppliers, an established brand name, and training and consulting in exchange for a share of the net earnings. Other small retail firms can be set up with a relatively small amount of capital, a little training, a business license, and a network of friends to spread the word and provide a startup clientele.

High barriers to entry often take the form of substantial fixed costs (in the short run) or significant economies of scale in the long run that limit the number of firms that the market can support. Both of these barriers exist in such heavy industries as automobiles, trucks, and aircraft. In the early days of the U.S. auto industry there were dozens of firms, but over the years the industry gradually evolved toward a market structure with a few giant corporations, each with a number of large plants, a dealer network, and close supplier relationships that a newcomer would find hard to challenge or to penetrate. Japanese and European automakers were well established in their own domestic markets before they challenged their U.S. competitors.

Barriers to entry can also be created artificially. Supposedly "the mob" creates barriers to entry in the "crime industry" (which would otherwise have many small "firms") by threats of violence. Less dramatic steps are taken elsewhere to discourage potential rivals. An established firm may offer discounts or price cuts temporarily to keep a new rival from getting a toehold in the market. A competitor can be bought out or persuaded to merge. Firms may agree to divide markets so that each has a "safe" territory with no competition. Most such barriers created by firms are temporary, ineffective, or both.

If they last very long, these firm-created barriers to entry are likely to invite the scrutiny of the Federal Trade Commission or the Antitrust Division of the Department of Justice, a subject discussed in Chapter 16. Most of the lasting artificial barriers to entry are in fact those created by government—licensing, tariffs, subsidies, large government contracts, and franchises. Even the paperwork associated with complying with environmental and safety standards, a heavier fixed-cost burden for a small firm than a large one, is a barrier to entry. Thus, the federal government reduces competition in some industries by creating entry barriers while at the same time trying to increase competition in other industries by enforcing antitrust laws that prohibit erecting some kinds of barriers to entry.

Product Differentiation

The second source of some monopoly power lies in differences in products (or stores or service providers) that make consumers prefer one brand of coffee or shoes or automobile to another. The differences may be real or only perceived. Coffees differ in flavor and aroma; some buyers will pay a premium for their favorite, while others just want a morning dose of caffeine and don't much care about anything but price. Many adults have identified a few brands of shoes that seem to adapt well to their feet and give them comfortable service, and are likely to be loyal to that brand even if it costs more—up to a point. Autos differ in appearance, comfort, reliability, availability of parts and service, and many other characteristics, so that a Mercedes can cost far more than a Chevrolet and still attract buyers.

Customer loyalty is particularly important in retail sales and services. Hairdressers, restaurants, pet shops, banks, newspapers, radio stations, travel agents, and all of the other firms that supply consumers with their daily goods and services want to develop a repeat clientele. If customers experience satisfactory price, quality, and service, they are likely to make a habit of patronizing that establishment without carefully searching out alternatives. Such loyalty is fragile, however; market power based on customer loyalty is more fragile than power deriving from less changeable sources.

In retailing and personal services, location is often the most important single kind of product differentiation. If the location is convenient, in a high-traffic area, with easy access from highways, the firm has a significant advantage over rivals in less favored locations.

Firms try to create and maintain product differentiation through advertising, a topic to be explored more thoroughly in the next chapter. The important point is that the existence of customer loyalty to a brand, a firm, or a location can be a substantial barrier to the entry of new firms and give the existing firm somewhat more monopoly power than it might otherwise have.

WHAT IS MONOPOLISTIC COMPETITION?

Between pure competition and monopoly lie a whole array of firms with different degrees of monopoly power. As we move from pure competition to monopoly, the barriers to entry grow higher and the number of firms becomes smaller. In some cases product differentiation increases, but that is less important than barriers to entry. Of the two models developed to describe these in-between market structures, the one closer to perfect competition is monopolistic competition.

An industry is monopolistically competitive if it consists of a large number of relatively small firms, low barriers to entry, and differentiated products. Some of these small firms may enjoy a degree of local monopoly in small towns—the only travel agent or barber in town. That monopoly power, however, is usually constrained by the existence of larger nearby towns with competing suppliers.

Because barriers to entry are low and there are many suppliers, the firm faces a highly elastic (almost flat) demand curve. Because there are no substantial fixed costs or economies of scale, both the short-run and the long-run cost curves are U-shaped and reach their minimum level (lowest average cost) at a fairly low level of output. Recall from Chapter 8 that this type of cost situation means that there is room for many firms in the industry. Figure 12-1 on the next page shows the monopolistically competitive firm's cost curves, demand curve, and marginal revenue curve. Panel (a) shows the short-run situation, and Panel (b) shows long-run equilibrium.

In the short-run this firm will make the same production decision as the pure competitor or the monopolist—to produce that output for which marginal revenue equals marginal cost, or Q_1. The price charged is determined from the demand curve to be P_1. This firm is making a profit shown by the shaded area. However, profits are a signal for entry, and since entry barriers are low, new firms will enter the industry. As they enter, they will take customers away from established firms, and demand and

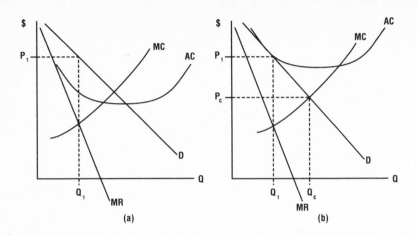

FIG. 12-1 *A Model of Monopolistic Competition*

marginal revenue for those firms will shift down and to the left as their market share declines.[1] This process will continue until the typical firm in this industry is making only the normal profits reflected in the average cost curve. This occurs when the demand curve has fallen to the point where it is tangent to the average cost curve at the profit-maximizing level of output (the one for which MC = MR). Panel (b) shows the firm in long-run equilibrium with no long-run profit or loss.

This firm's market power is fairly modest. It can raise prices without losing all its sales, but its prospects for persistent economic profits are very small. If it continues to develop new and better products, it can stay a jump ahead of the competition, but that gap is so small that the incentive to invest in developing new and better products is rather small. Typically, the new and better products, especially those that are technologically sophisticated or go through lengthy development periods, are developed by manufacturers in oligopolistic industries, leaving the marketing to the smaller, less innovative, monopolistically competitive retailers and wholesalers.

How does the monopolistically competitive market structure compare to perfect competition? Note that the firm is producing less and charging more than a perfectly competitive firm in the long run, because its output and price lie above and to the left of the minimum point on the average cost curve. A purely competitive firm would be producing at P_c, Q_c in Panel (b) of Figure 12-1. There is some loss of efficiency in comparison to perfect competition. Offsetting that drawback of monopolistic competition, however, is a gain in variety—color, size, quality, style, location, service—that is of value to consumers. Monopolistically competitive firms tend to arise and thrive in situations where these forms of nonprice competition are important to their customers. A bushel of wheat is a bushel of wheat, but a pair of jeans is definitely not just a pair of jeans in the eyes of the buyer.

Monopolistic competition is the dominant market structure in retailing and in personal services. Most consumers' daily purchases are made from firms whose market structure is monopolistically competitive. Most new firms are in this type of market structure. Thus, monopolistic competition is a particularly important market model for consumers, small businesses, and would-be entrepreneurs. While it does not give the same results as the purely competitive model, it offers some other advantages. Nonprice competition, which is characteristic of both this market structure and some oligopolies, ensures that consumers will be offered variety in styles, colors, locations, quality, and service as well as in price. A wider range of choices for consumers may be worth the sacrifice of a slightly higher price and smaller quantity than the competitive solution.

No one—no firm, no government agency, no trade organization—chooses the market structure for an industry. The market structure is largely determined by the characteristics of the product or service: how broad a market it reaches, how local the suppliers need to be, how technologically complex the product is, and how costs behave as output expands. It is, however, helpful for the business manager or entrepreneur to use these models to identify what market structure his or her firm belongs to, because that will explain a great deal about the price and output decisions and the behavior of competing firms.

WHAT IS OLIGOPOLY?

Oligopoly covers the widest range on the spectrum. If an industry has more than one firm—even only two or three—it is an oligopoly. If an industry has a large number of firms, but two or three of them are large and the rest of them are very small, it is still an oligopoly. Oligopoly is defined as an industrial structure in which the number of firms is small enough so that firms must take account of the likely reaction of their rivals in making decisions.

If Firm A raises or lowers its price, restyles its model, or opens at a new location, how will its rivals react? Will they follow suit? If Ford raises prices and other auto sellers do likewise, it will not lose very much in the way of sales, because the prices of close substitutes (other cars) have also risen. If Ford offers a rebate and the other firms jump on the bandwagon, Ford's sales will not increase as much as it had hoped, because the prices of close substitutes have fallen also. If K Mart opens a new store in Centerville and Wal-Mart does too, K Mart's projected sales will fall short of expectations. If IBM offers high-speed coprocessors on its microcomputers and Apple doesn't follow suit, IBM has a good chance of increasing its market share.

Oligopoly covers a variety of conditions, but typically oligopoly has high barriers to entry. Often the barriers to entry are related to optimum plant size (economies of scale). In order to fully exploit economies of scale, given the size of the market, it may be that there is only room for a small number of firms. Local retail and service oligopolies are very common. The market in a typical medium-size town can only support a limited number of fast-food restaurants, bookstores, hardware stores, accountants, and optometrists. However, unless the community is very isolated, the power of local oligopolies is limited—how limited depends on the time and expense buyers would incur to seek out goods and services in a nearby community.

While monopolistic competition's defining characteristic is product differentiation, an oligopoly may produce either a differentiated or a homogeneous product. Steel and oil refining are both oligopolies with homogeneous products, while home appliances, aircraft, and autos are highly differentiated. It is high barriers to entry that provide the defining characteristic of oligopoly.

Unlike the other three market structures, oligopoly has no single model to describe the behavior of its firms. Various models have been developed to describe what seem to be characteristic behavior patterns of oligopolistic industries. For instance, economist Paul Sweezy developed a model called the kinked demand curve to describe reluctance to change prices in oligopoly. Later evidence suggests that prices are in fact fairly flexible in oligopoly, although price changes often take the form of experimentation first. That is, firms use rebates, discounts, and promotions to measure the degree of responsiveness before, or instead of, making changes in list prices. Other researchers have tried to use game theory models, developed by mathematicians to describe choices of strategy in chess and other games, to describe the behavior of oligopoly firms.

One fairly simple model is used to describe the special case of a very small number of equal-sized firms. Consider a monopolist who owns four portable hamburger carts in a town that is one mile square. Where should he put his carts (assuming that customers are spread evenly throughout the town?) If he divides the town into four squares, as indicated in Figure 12-2, then one cart should be approximately in the center of each square, because that way no potential customer is ever more than a quarter mile away from one of the four hamburger carts.

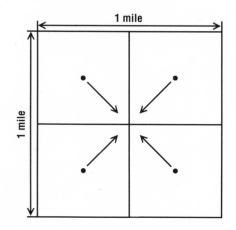

FIG. 12-2 *Convergence in Oligopoly*

Now, suppose he decides that four carts is too much to manage, so he sells three and keeps the fourth. What will happen? Over time, the four sellers will migrate toward the center of the square. Each seller can count on all the customers out toward the fringes of his or her square, because even if that seller moves toward the center, that cart is still the closest to customers farther away from the center. By moving toward the center, each seller hopes to move closer than a competitor to some of the other customers. If one cart does so, it will gain sales. If all four do so, they will wind up clustered around the center, and the folks out at the edge of the square may switch to hot dogs.

There are two lessons in this story. One is that an oligopoly with very few firms will see them all cluster toward a safe, middle-of-the-road strategy. Witness TV networks, political parties, and aircraft manufacturers. The second lesson is that such behavior creates an opportunity around the fringes, if the market can support another firm, for some producer whose location or style or price or quality or service is significantly different. If a TV network or a political party can see a large enough potential market on the fringe—high culture or mud wrestling, far right or far left—then the oligopoly may expand to accommodate one or two more firms to serve the tails of the distribution in taste or location or price. As American auto producers and their Japanese competitors/partners cater to the middle of the market, they leave space for the Hyundais and Yugos at one end of the market, the Mercedes and Jaguars at the other.

Oligopolies sometimes evolve to or from monopolistic competition. The U.S. auto industry was originally monopolistically competitive, but introduction of capital-intensive methods of manufacturing limited the number of firms the market could support. Failures, mergers and takeovers gradually reduced the market to four firms, then three. In more recent years, there were initially many microcomputer manufacturers, all with their own operating systems and their own noninterchangeable software, before the shakeout reduced the number of dominant firms and dominant technologies to IBM (and its clones) and Apple. On the other hand, an oligopoly that starts out with one or two firms because of a hot new product, a patent, control over raw materials, or other barriers to entry may become more competitive once the initial advantage is lost. Deregulation led to more intense competition among airlines in the 1980s, although shakeouts, mergers, and acquisitions finally moved the industry back toward oligopoly by the end of the decade.

IMPERFECT COMPETITION AND THE ROLE OF GOVERNMENT

If pure competition is so efficient, and monopolistic competition is quite acceptable, what can government do to encourage the same benefits from industries that are oligopolistic or monopolistic? There is no way that the government can force such industries as airlines, steel, telephone service, or autos to fit in the same mold as fast food, travel agents, dry cleaning, or shoe stores.

Basically, there are three strategies: break them up, make them behave, or leave them alone. Breaking them up was a popular strategy for some time under the antitrust laws—prohibiting mergers and forcing firms to divest themselves of some of their operations if they appeared to have too much monopoly power. Making them behave is a strategy pursued in two ways: first, by the penalties under the antitrust laws for unfair competition (see Chapter 16), and second, by regulating certain oligopolies as well as natural monopolies in order to expand output, lower prices, and improve services. As you will see in later chapters, this strategy has had mixed results. Leaving them alone, primarily through deregulation, has been the dominant strategy for the 1980s, also with mixed results. Finally, government can also create monopoly power through licenses, tariffs, franchises, and other exclusive privileges that favor one or a few firms over others.

CHAPTER PERSPECTIVE

The introduction of two intermediate market structures, oligopoly and monopolistic competition, provides more realistic models that correspond more closely to the firms with which you may interact every day. If there are barriers to entry, then there is monopoly power. If products are differentiated, there is monopoly power. The defining characteristics of monopolistic competition are differentiated products and many small firms. High barriers to entry and a small number of firms define oligopoly.

Monopolistically competitive firms produce a somewhat smaller output at a somewhat higher price than the purely competitive firm, although they do offer variety in style, quality, location, service, price, and other attributes that are beneficial to consumers. Oligopolists are very sensitive to the decisions made by competing firms and thus may be cautious about change. Government can discourage anticompetitive behavior through the antitrust laws, through regulation, or by trying to dismantle barriers to entry created by government.

FOOTNOTE

1 *New entrants may compete for some of the same resources and also drive up costs, further squeezing profits. For example, a new fast-food restaurant is competing for a limited supply of short-order cooks, driving up their wages in a given area. For simplicity, however, we focus on the reduced demand for Firm A's product as some of its customers shift to Firm B.*

Product Differentiation, Advertising, and Price Discrimination

INTRODUCTION AND MAIN POINTS

The past three chapters have described four prototypical market structures—pure competition, monopoly, monopolistic competition, and oligopoly. Most of the firms with which you are familiar probably lie in one of the last two categories. They enjoy a little monopoly power, and they would like to keep that power, maybe even increase it, and use that power to enhance their present and future net incomes. This chapter discusses how firms try to create some degree of monopoly power through product differentiation and advertising, and how market power is exercised in a particular way—price discrimination—to increase the firm's profits.

After studying the material in this chapter:

▬ You will be able to evaluate the role of product differentiation and advertising in creating market power for firms.

▬ You will understand the various types of price discrimination.

▬ You will know how to explain how price discrimination can be used to increase a firm's profits.

▬ You will be able to identify who gains and who loses from price discrimination, and under what circumstances government should intervene in price discrimination.

DIFFERENTIATED PRODUCTS: JUST A LITTLE MONOPOLY

Product differentiation usually provides a moderate degree of monopoly power. By convincing buyers that other products are imperfect substitutes for yours, product differentiation puts a little slope to the demand curve, or makes the existing slope even steeper. Recall that the fewer good substitutes there are for a product, the less elastic the demand curve will be. If the demand curve is less elastic, a seller can raise the price and lose a relatively small amount of sales.

Product differentiation can also be a barrier to entry, another source of monopoly power. If an established brand, or a few established brands, have built a loyal customer following, it is difficult for a newcomer to find a niche in the market. Coke and Pepsi dominate soft drinks; Gerber owns most of the baby food market; Green Giant and Birdseye are the names that come immediately to mind in frozen vegetables. One of the purposes of advertising is to help to establish and reinforce brand loyalty, making it more difficult for new firms to compete.

Buyers form habits because habits are useful. If customers have had satisfactory experiences with a particular brand, they are likely to make repeat purchases rather than risk experimenting with another brand or to try a new supermarket that may not have the brands they want. Habits means fewer decisions to make and fewer risks to take. Thus, buyers establish habits to simplify the shopping process. Advertising helps firms to take advantage of this tendency of consumers to develop shopping habits, because brand names and store names are easy habits to acquire and remember. Buyers with a habit for your product are buyers with inelastic demand, unlikely to switch unless a very large price difference or a powerful marketing strategy captures their attention.

Are Consumer Tastes Given or Created?

Economists take tastes as given in drawing their demand curves. "Tastes and preferences" was listed as one of the ceteris paribus conditions for the demand curve; a change in those tastes and preferences could shift the demand curve. Economists do not inquire into the psychological foundations of how tastes are acquired and why they change; in general, they leave that question to the people in marketing. Marketing is an applied business discipline. One important area of market research is to examine how advertising influences tastes and preferences. Scholars in this field also work to develop techniques that help firms discover consumers' preferences. Economists' interest is largely confined to marketing's effect on demand elasticity and on market structure and barriers to entry.

One of the great unresolved controversies among economists is whether advertising performs a useful function from the standpoint of society, i.e., does it make the market system work better in satisfying consumer wants? Critics of the market system, particularly John Kenneth Galbraith and Vance Packard, have argued that most tastes and even wants are created through advertising and other means. Power, prestige, social acceptance, popularity, and even sex appeal are sold through advertising in the form of powerful and expensive cars, costly perfume and jewelry, and designer clothing. Other wants, they argue, receive less attention because they are not promoted through advertising—better education, highways, or outdoor recreation, most of which are provided through the public sector.

Defenders of advertising argue that wants are not created; rather, the means of satisfying existing wants are brought to the attention of consumers through advertising. Advertising helps the consumer to find the product and to be aware of its important attributes—quality, style, safety, durability, and price. Thus, they would argue that advertising serves the useful social purpose of providing information to consumers, and that advertising's close relative, market research, serves the equally useful social purpose of providing feedback from buyers to sellers about what the buyer is looking for. In addition, products have many attributes besides price, but some of them—especially those like durability and safety—are difficult for the buyer to evaluate. Advertising, packaging, and salespersons can convey that information.

There is truth in both views. Some advertising is informative and helpful. The labor market works much more efficiently because of the help-wanted ads. Grocery shoppers scan the food ads for coupons and specials before doing their shopping, and these ads ensure that there will be considerable price competition among sellers. Advertising by lawyers, just recently authorized, has increased price competition in legal services. Other ads, however, seem to create wants or greatly amplify existing wants, or to sell products on the basis of attributes they do not possess. Clearly, advertising can work to increase price competition and nonprice competition in some products and some markets, but it can also work to create a little more monopoly power through habit and brand loyalty in other markets.

Advertising, Cost Curves, and Price

Advertising is a cost to the firm. In the short run it is usually a fixed cost, because it is independent of the number of units of output being produced and sold. Thus, it will shift the average cost curve upward. In a monopolistically competitive industry, in the long run, this shift in the cost curve from AC_1 to AC_2 (Figure 13-1), taken by itself, would mean that the long-run equilibrium price would be higher. In addition, the effect of advertising should be to make demand less elastic (D_1 to D_2) if buyers acquire a habit or brand loyalty for this product. This steeper demand curve, in the long run, will be tangent to the average cost curve at a point to the left of the original equilibrium, so quantity will be still smaller and price higher (P_3). Thus, advertising appears to raise prices and lead to restrictions in output.

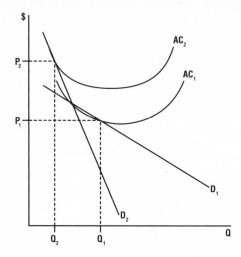

FIG. 13-1 *Advertising, Price, and Output in Monopolistic Competition*

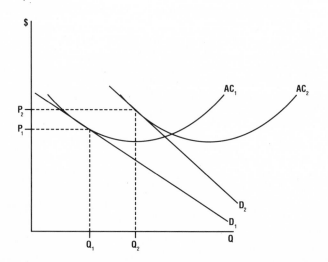

FIG. 13-2 *Advertising Results in Larger Quantity*

the firm to charge successive prices of $8, $6, $4 for the three cassette tapes, instead of charging $4 for all three. The firm has captured the $4 of consumer surplus for the first cassette tape that would normally have gone to the consumer. The firm's extra revenue from price discrimination, over and above what it would have received otherwise, is represented by the shaded area in Figure 13-3(a). A really clever firm with a good grasp on the slope of its demand curve would have priced cassette tapes at $8 for one, $14 for two, and $18 for three, thus capturing more of the consumer surplus (adding the area marked X to its extra revenues). At least, however, it captured some of the surplus with creative price discrimination.

The tuna fish case is similar, as illustrated. The buyer pays 59 cents for the first can and 41 cents for the second can. Without price discrimination the average buyer would buy two cans instead of one only if the price was 41 cents. The first can is worth more than the second to the buyer. Instead of charging 41 cents for each can in order to sell two cans, the seller is able to charge 59 cents for the first can and 41 cents for the second through price discrimination. Again, the shaded area represents extra revenue to the firm over and above the revenue that would be received from ordinary pricing policies.

Second-Degree Price Discrimination

Even more common is second-degree price discrimination, where different prices are charged to different buyers on the basis of differences in elasticity of demand. Notice that in the list of examples above, two involve particular groups of individuals (senior citizens and students) and two others involve time (matinee vs. evening, short vs. long trips). In order to practice second-degree price discrimination, it is necessary to separate the customers and to prevent resale.

The general principle in second-degree price discrimination is to raise prices in the market where demand is inelastic (so loss of sales will be small), and reduce prices in the market where demand is elastic (so that a small cut in price will generate a large increase in sales volume). Recall from Chapter 5 that an increase in price when demand is inelastic will increase total revenue, and a decrease in price when demand is elastic will increase total revenue.

Figure 13-4 illustrates a hypothetical case of separated markets for haircuts. To the left is the inelastic demand for the average middle-class customer, who is always in a hurry and is more concerned about a quick appointment than the cost. To the right is the relatively elastic demand for haircuts by senior citizens and students, who have more time and less income and will shop around or postpone a haircut if the price is too high. The markets can be separated by requiring a drivers' license, student ID, or other proof of age or status in order to qualify for a discount.

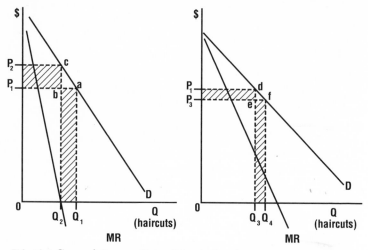

FIG. 13-4 *Second Degree Price Discrimination*

Before price discrimination, all customers had been paying the same price, P_1. Marginal revenue, however, is higher in the elastic market on the right than the inelastic market on the left. An increase in price in the inelastic market to P_2 will mean a loss of revenue of the shaded area Q_1Q_2ab because of a fall in quantity, and a gain in revenue of the shaded area P_1P_2cb because of the increase in price. The second rectangle is larger, so total revenue has increased. In the elastic market price is reduced to P_3. There is a loss of revenue because of the fall in price of shaded area P_2P_3de, and an increase in revenue of Q_3Q_4ef because of the larger quantity. The second rectangle is larger, so once again total revenue has risen. Even if the volume of sales did not increase—if, in effect, sales were "transferred" from the inelastic to the elastic market—total revenue would still increase.

Price discrimination takes two common forms, identifiable groups and time. Sometimes the two merge. For example, the lower airline fares for longer stays and higher fares for quick returns reflect an attempt to separate tourists (elastic demand) from business travelers (inelastic demand). In other cases, different rates reflect different degrees of substitutability. Bowling and movies are cheaper in the afternoon, when there are more good substitute uses of time—working, attending classes, lying out in the sun. In the evening, demand is less elastic because there are fewer good substitutes and the price is higher. Restaurants offer discounts on Mondays because traffic is slow—working parents are more willing to come home and cook early in the week, and less likely to have plans for an evening out than later in the week, and especially on weekends.

Time-of-day pricing is also used to reduce the amount of fixed plant and equipment required. Peak load pricing is commonly used to discourage commuter train travel and use of electricity and telephone services during the higher demand periods. Those whose demand is inelastic will choose the high rate periods to commute, use electricity, and make phone calls, while those who are price-sensitive and flexible will work around the peak periods. In doing so they help to reduce the cost of providing additional capacity and thus increase the profits (or reduce the losses) of train, electric, or telephone service.

A broader form of price discrimination in time has to do with seasonal goods, particularly clothing, yard equipment, beach toys, and Christmas products. Early birds and postseason shoppers are the most price-conscious (elastic) buyers and get the benefit of pre- and postseason sales, while regular in-season buyers pay the "full" price.

Price discrimination is a useful tool in almost any business firm, taking different forms in different kinds of business activity. As long as customers can be segregated easily, it is possible to increase profits without increasing output or sales simply by finding creative ways to charge different prices to different buyers on the basis of their demand elasticities.

Price discrimination is also used, especially in geographically separated markets, to prevent rival firms from getting a toehold in a market. For example, suppose that Firm A has an established monopoly in the sale of peanuts in all of the southeast, and a rival firm tries to get established in the North Carolina market. Firm A can cut its price in North Carolina (where demand is elastic because there are good substitutes available), but keep the price the same in other markets where the competitor is not selling. This tactic makes it difficult for a competing firm to establish a beachhead and sell at a price that makes even a normal profit. Because this type of price discrimination is aimed at creating or maintaining a monopoly, however, it is a violation of the antitrust laws (see Chapter 16).

International Price Discrimination

When price discrimination occurs across national boundaries, it is called dumping. Dumping specifically means that the price in the importing country is lower than in the home country. U.S. firms that think foreign competitors are engaging in dumping, or international price discrimination, can appeal to the International Trade Commission to take action against the foreign firm.

Sometimes dumping is a temporary action to dispose of a surplus, and sometimes it is deliberately undertaken to wipe out a rival in the foreign market. Often, particularly in the case of Japan, dumping reflects the fact that the foreign (especially U.S.) market has more elastic demand than the home market. Because of tight controls on imports and a reluctance to purchase foreign products, the Japanese market has had a very inelastic demand, and Japanese consumers have paid high prices for most goods. In the U.S., however, Japanese products must compete with U.S. products and products of other nations in a very open, competitive market where many substitutes are available. Demand is very price elastic. Consequently, Japanese products often sell for less in the U.S. than in Japan.

If an American competitor can prove that foreign-made products are selling for less in the U.S. than in the home country, after taking into account any cost differences in serving the two markets that might justify the price difference, then the ITC may agree to impose compensating tariffs to correct for price discrimination. Dumping is a form of price discrimination that particularly comes under attack because it is usually practiced by countries that can export freely to the U.S. but restrict imports into their own countries. It is such import restrictions that create the differences in elasticity of demand in the first place.

Who Benefits from Price Discrimination?

Firms engage in *lawful* price discrimination to increase profits in several ways. First, they can generate more revenue out of the same volume of sales if they can separate elastic and inelastic buyers through second-degree price discrimination. Second, they can increase the volume of sales if they can capture consumer surplus through first-degree price discrimination, or if they can increase sales to elastic buyers without cutting the price charged in the inelastic market in second-degree price discrimination. Finally, firms may increase profits by reducing costs if they can use price discrimination to spread customers more evenly, reducing peak demand and thus peak capacity needs.

Some buyers can also benefit from price discrimination, particularly second-degree price discrimination, if they belong to a favored group or if they are flexible about time of day, length of stay, or other factors used to distinguish elastic from inelastic customers. Second-degree price discrimination rewards those who are informed, alert, and flexible and penalizes those who are ignorant, indifferent, inflexible, or sometimes too affluent to care. Since anything that increases buyer awareness and responsiveness makes markets work more efficiently, it can be argued that price discrimination encourages and rewards better-informed consumers.

Losers from price discrimination are harder to identify. Because business firms are likely to incur most of the penalty on such pricing mechanisms as time-of-day rates for electricity and telephone, and higher rates for short-trip business flights, these prices are built indirectly into the costs of other products that we buy. Competing firms are losers if they are victims of geographic price discrimination or international price discrimination, although some remedies are available to them through the antitrust laws and antidumping codes. First-degree price discrimination does extract some consumer surplus, but the buyer is free to accept or reject the offer or to seek out a competing supplier, and usually the seller does not effectively capture all of the consumer surplus.

CHAPTER PERSPECTIVE

Product differentiation creates a little monopoly power. Shopping habits, brand loyalty, and preferences for particular products make a firm's demand less elastic because other products become less satisfactory substitutes for its goods. Brand loyalty is also a barrier to entry, because it makes it difficult for a new product or brand name to gain a foothold and for new firms to wean customers away from established firms or brand names.

Economists assume that consumer tastes and preferences are a given, but in fact these tastes are conveyed to producers through market research and are in turn influenced by advertising. Along with creating habits and brand loyalty and desires for certain products, advertising also supplies useful information about prices, product characteristics, product availability, and opportunities of various kinds for consumers and workers. Advertising raises the firm's costs and makes demand less elastic, so it tends to raise price and reduce quantity. However, if advertising is effective at increasing demand, it may actually increase quantity with little or no effect on price. Thus, there is no consensus on the net benefits or costs of advertising from the standpoint of consumers.

Price discrimination means charging different prices for different units of the same product. Sometimes the firm can practice first-degree price discrimination—charging the same buyer different prices for successive units and capturing some of the buyer's consumer surplus. More common is second-degree price discrimination, which separates buyers by some criterion, such as age, geographical location, time of day, and length of trip. Criteria are chosen that successfully separate buyers into those with more elastic demand and those with less elastic demand. The seller can then raise the price in the inelastic market and reduce it in the elastic market, increasing total profit. Time-of-day pricing increases profits by reducing the firm's need for peak-load capacity. In general, firms and groups with elastic demand benefit from price discrimination, while those with inelastic demand pay higher prices because of price discrimination.

Price discrimination used as a deliberate barrier to entry is a violation of the antitrust laws, and international price discrimination is a violation of antidumping codes. Firms injured by such forms of price discrimination can seek remedies from the federal government.

Firms as Neighbors: External Effects

INTRODUCTION AND MAIN POINTS

Until now, we have treated the firm and the buyer as independent individuals, interacting impersonally in markets. When transactions took place, they were private matters between buyer and seller. In fact, for many economic activities this view is unrealistic. Many transactions have spillover effects on third parties, who are neither buyers nor sellers but neighbors who incur costs or receive benefits from other people's economic activities. These spillover effects are called *externalities*. Externalities can be positive, conferring benefits on innocent bystanders, or they can be negative, inflicting costs on unsuspecting third parties. If such spillovers exist, an economic transaction ceases to be a matter of purely private interest between buyer and seller, and becomes a matter with some degree of public interest as well. For example, virtually all firms are affected by the environmental regulations and other public policies adopted to deal with spillovers.

After studying the material in this chapter:

■ You will know how to identify the effects of positive and negative externalities—at least arising from production and consumption activities—on market price and quantity.

■ You will be able to describe situations in which private solutions to externality problems can be negotiated successfully.

■ You will be able to describe and evaluate the various forms of government intervention to correct externalities.

■ You will understand the risks as well as the benefits of having the government intervene to correct externalities.

WHEN FIRMS PRODUCE TOO MUCH: NEGATIVE EXTERNALITIES

When the production (or consumption) of a good creates harmful spillovers on third parties, in the absence of intervention by government the firm will normally produce too much and charge too little for the good. Firms that cause air or water pollution, health hazards, noise, or other burdens on their neighbors are using a resource for which they are not required to pay the full cost. They are using the air, water, or ground as a trash dump and are not charged for the costs they create. Because such costs are held to an artificially low level, the firm's marginal cost curves (and therefore supply curves) will be below and to the right of where they would be if the firm had to pay all its costs, including the costs inflicted on third parties.

Economists regard externality problems as a matter of poorly defined property rights. The reason that problems of negative externalities most often arise in air or water quality is that property rights to air have rarely been defined at all, and property rights to water have generally been specified in terms of quantity rather than of quality.

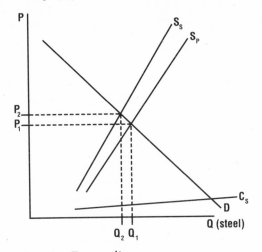

FIG. 14-1 *A Negative Externality*

Figure 14-1 illustrates a negative externality, air pollution caused by steel production. The supply curve labeled S_p represents the sum of the marginal cost curves of the firms in the steel industry, based on their private costs—labor, raw materials, electricity, equipment, etc. On the basis of private supply and demand, without taking negative externalities into consideration, the price will be P_1 and the quantity produced and sold will be Q_1. However, in the process of producing steel, this firm discharges pollutants into the atmosphere. Some of the effects of those pollutants on third parties—people who are neither producers nor buyers of steel—can be measured. It is possible to estimate the increase in respiratory illnesses, for instance, or the damage to house paint so that houses have to be repainted more frequently. Other effects are more subtle, particularly if they result from the combination of this industry's pollutants with others. For example, air pollution from steel production may be one of many factors contributing to the greenhouse effect—the warming of the earth's atmosphere that is resulting in gradual but inexorable changes in both climate and weather.

Assume that these effects can be measured and related to the level of steel output, so that it is possible to determine how such additional cost is imposed on third parties for various levels of steel production. These effects are captured in a social marginal cost curve, C_s in Figure 14-1. Adding these costs to the existing private marginal cost curve (vertically adding the social costs and private costs for each unit of output) results in the "social supply curve" S_s, which reflects both the private and social marginal costs of production. This supply curve intersects the demand curve at price P_2 and quantity Q_2. When all costs are considered, the socially optimal level of steel output is lower and the price is higher.

In most circumstances the market, left to itself, will only reflect private costs and benefits and will not take account of costs imposed on third parties. Consequently, the market outcome is less efficient, or less socially desirable, than the price and quantity that would result if firms had to pay all the costs of production, including the cost of externalities. Imposing such costs on the production process that created them is called "internalizing externalities." In a few cases there are ways to internalize externalities that do not involve the government, but in most cases government intervention is needed to try to bring about the socially optimal price and output.

Note that the goal is *not* zero pollution. Everyone can tolerate a little pollution, and most people are willing to trade off some pollution in exchange for more goods and services. At the socially optimal level of output, Q_2, there is still some pollution, but less than before.

What Is the Best Way to Regulate?
Most firms are subject to some kinds of environmental regulations. Consider a gas station, which is subject to a tax on its

product to discourage consumption; to safety regulations governing the storage of combustible products and the disposal of waste products such as used engine oil; and to laws that protect its employees from various kinds of health and safety risks. These represent some of the tools the government can use to make the supply curve in a polluting industry more closely reflect all costs, including negative externalities. One tool is to regulate the amount of pollutants emitted. A second tool is to tax effluents. A third tool is to create markets in pollution rights. While these three methods are not exhaustive, they do illustrate the principal approaches to reducing pollution and negative externalities.

Regulation forces the firm to reduce pollutants. The regulation may specify the technology to be used—scrubbers, chemical treatment, or other methods. Increasingly, the method of regulation has shifted away from specifying technology toward defining a permitted amount of effluent. This method allows firms to seek out the least costly technology to achieve that result. In either case, complying with regulations has two effects on the level of pollution. First, it reduces pollution directly. Second, and more important from the economist's perspective, it raises the firm's production costs. Higher costs reduce the firm's profit-maximizing level of output (and the pollution associated with producing that output), thus leading the firm to raise its prices, so that at least part of the cost of pollution now falls on consumers of the products responsible for causing the pollution.

A second method is to tax pollution, with a tax or fee for each unit of effluent emitted. This solution is more appealing to economists because it simply ensures that the costs of pollution are reflected in the price, allowing producers and consumers of the product to make choices based on the prices they face. The appropriate tax per unit is measured by the vertical distance between the private and social supply curves in Figure 14-1. Here, the costs of pollution per unit of output rise as output expands, so the appropriate tax should increase with the level of pollution as well.

This tax solution has only had limited use because it is politically unpopular. Environmentalists have labeled pollution taxes or effluent charges "a license to pollute." In fact, the effects of such taxes are very similar to those of regulation; faced with an effluent charge, the firm can either pay the fees or find ways to reduce its emissions in order to reduce the charge.

A third approach is to create pollution "rights," a solution developed first in air quality in California. A desired level of air quality (or water quality) is established, and the pollution "czar" or agency in charge creates enough emission rights for particular types of pollutants—sulfur dioxide, for example—in order to maintain the desired level of environmental quality. Usually these rights are assigned to existing firms that emit the particular pollutant. New firms that emit that pollutant and that wish to locate in the area, or existing firms wishing to expand their production levels, must purchase pollution rights from other firms. Newcomers may buy out other firms in order to acquire their pollution rights or to assist them in reducing their emissions, thus creating some "excess pollution capacity" that can then be exploited by the new or expanding firm. Private markets develop in which pollution rights are bought and sold. Since the desired result is air quality or water quality, rather than controlling the emissions from specific firms or the output of particular industries, this approach makes good sense for certain situations. However, its use has been limited thus far.

Problems of Regulating Negative Externalities

The principal difficulty in regulating negative externalities is measuring the social cost or damage done. Firms whose production processes create externalities understandably want to minimize the value of damages, while environmentalists or neighbors may exaggerate the harm. The problem is further compounded by how long it takes to see the harmful effects. Some costs are immediate and obvious—effects on adjacent land values from hazardous waste sites or jetport noise, for example. Other forms of pollution have long-term health effects that are difficult to detect and measure in the short term. Some pollutants are tolerable in small doses, while others are intolerable even in minimal amounts. Each year brings new discoveries of environmental hazards, such as radon in houses and the effects of pesticide residue on farm workers in the late 1980s.

The regulatory approach must be designed carefully to allow firms to seek out new technology and adapt their particular situation and product to the needs of environmental quality in their own ways. The last decade has seen increased openness to approaches that concentrate on results rather than on methods of limiting pollution, allowing firms to seek the least-cost methods of achieving the desired goal.

Regulation itself creates additional costs. Regulations must be administered, creating a bureaucracy to design rules and carry them out and a paperwork burden on the firms that must document their compliance. These costs add even further to the firm's expenses, so that its prices may go from below optimum to above optimum while output shrinks below the intended target level. In each case the benefits of the output must be weighed against the current and future estimates of costs to third parties from the associated pollution. No matter what approach is used, optimal environmental regulation is extremely difficult to design and implement.

Private Solutions

In some cases it is possible for the parties involved to negotiate a solution without direct government intervention, usually when only a small number of claimants is involved. Suppose a factory is discharging chemicals into a small lake that it shares with two other property owners. The other two owners would like to use the lake for swimming, but the chemicals make this impossible. Since the chemicals are sharply diluted after leaving the lake and cause no measurable harm to downstream users, the problem is confined to three parties, all adjacent landowners. In this case it is possible to negotiate an agreement. The issue is one of property rights to the lake, which are not clearly defined. If the property right to determine the use of the lake belongs to the factory, then the other two landowners can only get their way if they can persuade (or, more likely, pay) the factory owners to reduce their effluents, perhaps by treatment or by storage and disposal elsewhere. If the property rights belong equally to all three landowners, then the other two can vote for no effluent, and the factory must purchase from them the right to use the lake for disposal, or else cease discharging chemicals into the lake.

When property rights are not clearly defined, the right often is appropriated by the first user. If the other landowners were there first, the factory will probably have to bribe or persuade them to grant effluent rights. If the factory was there first, the other landowners are more likely to have to pay for the privilege of converting the use of the lake from a waste dump to a swimming hole.

More often such cases wind up in court. However, in the case of small but temporary externalities—loud parties at your neighbors' house, smoke from your neighbor's barbecue grill—private solutions can be negotiated with less cost and less acrimony than are likely to result from government intervention.

WHEN FIRMS PRODUCE TOO LITTLE: POSITIVE EXTERNALITIES

A second type of externality problem results from positive spillover benefits associated with the consumption or production of a particular good. When Louis receives a good education, he benefits, his family benefits, his community benefits. Most of the benefits accrue to Louis, but the community has a more informed citizen, a more productive worker, a person less likely to wind up dependent on the community for support through welfare and food stamps. There are social benefits, or spillovers, from Louis's education.

The XYZ Corporation has flowers on its front lawn. They were planted for the personal enjoyment of the owner, but they create spillover benefits for everyone that passes by. Since XYZ cannot charge for their benefits, the owner will decide how much effort to put into her yard based on her own personal cost and benefit calculations, ignoring the value of the spillovers.

Rod gets a flu shot for his own benefit, but in the process he reduces the probability that everyone he works with will catch the flu this year. Rod, however, does not take these spillover benefits into account in deciding whether to get a flu shot.

Farmer Brown sprays her farm for mosquitos in order to keep the livestock from being bitten on warm summer nights. In the process she creates spillover benefits for her neighbors, who also are less bothered by mosquitos.

An electric power company dams a river for hydropower purposes. Spillover benefits to adjacent landowners include flood control and recreational opportunities. Unless the power company owns all the land around the lake, some of the benefits spill over to others.

All of these are examples of positive externalities, or spillover benefits from private consumption or production activities. If the individual makes a decision about how much to produce or consume without taking positive spillovers into account, the result is likely to be too little of a good thing! Yet the market often fails to provide a way for these secondary gainers to signal and to pay for the benefits they receive, so the producer of positive externalities produces too little.

Subsidies to Expand Output and Consumption

Figure 14-2 illustrates the supply and demand for technical education, which is assumed to have spillover benefits to society. The supply curve reflects increasing marginal costs. The demand curve, labeled D_p, shows private demand for such education, based on personal benefits. The spillover benefits to society from each person educated are shown on D_s. Recall that the price on the demand curve is a measure of value or benefit to the user. For each person educated, just add the private benefits on D_p to the social benefits on D_s to obtain the total benefits, shown as the kinked, heavy line D_t. For example, the education of the tenth person creates private benefits of $1000 and social benefits of $150 for a total value of $1150.

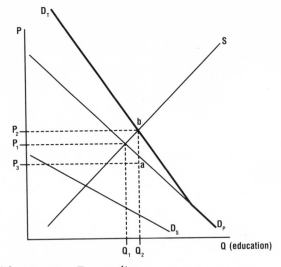

FIG. 14-2 *A Positive Externality*

If the market is left to itself, equilibrium will occur where private demand intersects private supply at P_1, Q_1. The social optimum occurs when all demand—private plus spillover—is taken into account in determining the output level, which occurs at P_2, Q_2. At the higher price, however, fewer individuals, not more, would invest in technical education. If society wants those extra units of education to be produced and consumed, a subsidy must be offered. The subsidy must be sufficient to reduce the price of Q_2 units of output to the demand price of P_3 in order to induce people to purchase more education. Thus, the optimum subsidy is the vertical distance between the supply and demand curves, or ab.

Positive externalities offer justification for many types of subsidies, particularly in education. In higher education suppliers often combine price discrimination with subsidizing goods and services that have positive externalities. A pricing pattern that combines financial aid for poor students, scholarships for bright students, work-study opportunities for hard-working students, and full price for the rest, provides a subsidy to students with more elastic demand while charging the others the full price. Governments subsidize the purchase of nutritious food for selected groups with the WIC (Women, Infants, and Children) program and the food stamp programs because better health in these groups benefits everyone. Both governments and private individuals subsidize the arts because they perceive cultural benefits to others from developing a taste and a clientele for such programs.

To whom should the subsidy be paid, the seller or the buyer? From the perspective of the outcome—more output, lower price paid by consumers—it shouldn't matter. In a competitive market a subsidy to sellers will reduce their costs, and competitive forces ensure that lower prices will result. The government can and does subsidize producers in order to reduce the cost of education, health care, day care, senior citizen programs, and many other goods and services in order to expand consumption. If the subsidy is paid to buyers—education vouchers, food stamps, coupons valid for free shots at clinics, etc.—then they will purchase more, driving up the price received by the seller to P_2 in Figure 14-2 but reducing the net price (net of subsidy) paid by the buyer to P_3. Often the subsidy is paid to the buyer in order to expand the range of choice or to ensure the desired result when the sellers' side of the market is not highly competitive.

Private Solutions

Positive externalities, like negative externalities, sometimes lend themselves to private solutions, particularly when the number of participants is small. In small communities there is more likely to be public support for parks, arts programs, beautification efforts, and other activities with positive spillover benefits. Much of the support for the performing arts comes from such private subsidies. Often firms that are large employers in small towns choose to subsidize such programs because they can capture some of the benefits—attractive, cultured communities make it easier to attract and retain high-quality workers. As communities get larger, however (or firms get smaller), there is a tendency to look for a free ride. Potential contributors are aware that their individual contributions are so small a part of the total that the outcome does not depend on their participation; in addition, their individual benefits are relatively small. If the outcome will occur—the show will go on, the park will get new benches, the trees will be planted—with or without the participation of X, what incentive does X have to contribute? X becomes a *free rider*. Free rider, an old union term for nonunion workers who enjoy the protection of the union contract, is a term that has been borrowed by economists to describe this type of behavior.

Free riding is more difficult in small groups, small communities, or small companies. The anonymity of a large city not only means that X's marginal contribution has a negligible effect on the outcome; it also means that X can fail to contribute and not suffer any social consequences for that behavior. In a large city some other method must be found to make the less willing to contribute their fair share. The usual method is to tax. Thus, where there is a free rider problem affecting a good that is considered desirable or necessary, some role for government is inevitable. The market has no easy solution to positive externalities involving large numbers of individuals.

For certain goods, the benefits consist almost entirely of spillovers. There is no identifiable primary buyer because everyone within a given area shares equally in the consumption, with or without a contribution. It may be more costly to exclude nonpayers than it is worth. The number of such goods is not large, but there are familiar examples, such as national defense and lighthouses. Such goods, called *public goods*, are discussed in greater detail in Chapter 16.

CHAPTER PERSPECTIVE

The production or consumption of certain goods and services can have effects on third parties (households or firms) who are neither buyers nor sellers of those goods. When there are negative externalities, too much of the good or service will be produced and consumed at too low a price. The goal of regulators in this case is to reduce production (and with it the negative externalities, most often air or water pollution) by driving up the price.

There are several ways to achieve such goals. The government may specify the technology to be used, or it may tax emissions or effluents, or it may issue limited property rights to pollute and allow them to be bought and sold among firms. Any one of these methods will achieve the desired result, but the effects are very different. The last two solutions leave more discretion for producers to find the best way to reduce emissions, or even the best firm to ask to reduce emissions. All of these solutions create political difficulties of various kinds having to do with the distribution of costs and benefits of regulatory activities.

If the numbers of producers and/or consumers involved is small, a private solution may be feasible. Whichever party appears to have the property right to use the air, land, or water in a particular way can negotiate with the competing party, letting the market decide which use has the highest priority.

If the production or consumption of a particular good results in beneficial spillovers, then the private market solution will result in too little output at too low a price. Both output and price must be increased, but in order to ensure that the additional output is sold, there must be a subsidy equal to the vertical distance between the private supply curve and private demand curve at the socially optimal output level. Private solutions may be feasible if the number of parties involved is small, but once the number of buyers and/or sellers gets large, a free rider problem is likely to develop. In these cases only government intervention can push the market in the direction of the socially desirable output level.

The Firm in the International Marketplace

INTRODUCTION AND MAIN POINTS

American firms operate in an increasingly open and competitive world marketplace. Many of their competitors, suppliers, and customers are in other countries. Many firms, both domestic and foreign, are multinationals, with headquarters in one country and affiliates, subsidiaries, or joint ventures in other countries. In order to carry out transactions across national lines, American firms must learn to deal with foreign exchange markets, tariffs and customs procedures, and other national regulations that affect trade across national borders.[1] Much of what economists have observed about trade between buyers and sellers in different countries also applies to trade between different regions of the same country, separated not by different currencies and different governments, but by distance and lack of information.

After studying the material in this chapter:

▬ You will be able to explain the concept of comparative advantage, the basis for U.S. policy in international trade.

▬ You will see how tariffs and quotas work, and who gains and who loses from restrictions on free trade.

▬ You will understand how changes in the international price of the U.S. dollar affect American export- and import-competing industries.

▬ You will be able to explain why a firm might choose to produce abroad rather than at home.

INTERNATIONAL COMPETITION AND DOMESTIC FIRMS

Some producers face a great deal of competition within their own country. Many other firms produce the same or similar products, and the firm in that situation has relatively little market power. Foreign competition just adds to the existing challenge of finding and keeping a niche in a highly contested marketplace. Other firms, primarily those in monopolistic competition or oligopolistic industries, have relatively little domestic competition. Their market power may be held in check primarily by actual or potential foreign competition.

In the United States, the government's policy has long been one of promoting competition in the interests of consumer welfare and productive efficiency. Thus, foreign competition is usually regarded as a good thing. U.S. trade policy has been relatively free since 1934, encouraging imports by lowering trade barriers and encouraging other countries to lower barriers to U.S. exports. This positive attitude toward foreign competition is not always widely shared by trading partners, however. Differences in attitudes toward foreign competition have been a major source of friction between the U.S. and Japan and between the U.S. and the European Economic Community.

Who Produces What—Comparative Advantage and Other Explanations

The basis for a free trade policy was laid out in Adam Smith's 1776 *Wealth of Nations*, then developed and expounded by British economists (particularly David Ricardo) throughout the 19th century. They offered two arguments for free trade. The primary argument was the theory of comparative advantage. The second argument was based on the benefits for consumers of having foreign competitors to challenge domestic monopoly power. A third, closely related argument emerged in the 20th century based on economies of scale.

The comparative advantage argument has received the most attention. Comparative advantage rests on the fairly simple idea that different countries—or different individuals—often have different opportunity costs for producing the same goods or services. For example, Fred may be much faster at welding than at typing, because of natural ability or acquired skills. Dora may be faster at typing than at welding, for the same reasons. Fred can produce more welding per day than Dora, so his labor costs per welding job will be lower. Dora, likewise, can produce more typed pages than Fred per day—perhaps 100 pages to Fred's 25 pages. If both received an hourly wage of $5.00, her labor cost per page would be only 5 cents, while Fred's would be 20 cents. If Fred concentrates on what he does well—welding—while Dora types full speed, there will be more output than if each person tried to do some of each task.

What applies to individuals also applies to countries. If countries, especially small countries, limit themselves to a few products that they are particularly efficient at making, instead of trying to produce a little of everything, they can trade for other products and enjoy more total consumption.

This argument, called absolute advantage, is widely accepted. A more difficult problem arises when one worker is better at both activities. Suppose that Dora can not only type more pages than Fred, but she can also weld more pipes in a day. Ricardo analyzed this situation and discovered that even if one person, or country, is better at both products, there is still a gain from specialization and trade. If Dora is better at both, there will still be one activity in which her margin of superiority is greater. She should specialize in that product or service, because that is where her comparative advantage lies; by the same token, Fred should specialize in that product or service in which his disadvantage is less, because that is where his comparative advantage lies.

Figure 15-1 illustrates a simple model of comparative advantage for two countries producing two products, bread and wine.[2] The following points lie on the respective production possibilities curves of Countries A and B:

Country A		Country B	
Bread	Wine	Bread	Wine
0	100	0	75
5	90	5	70
10	80	10	65
15	70	15	60
20	60	20	55
25	50	25	50
30	40	30	45
35	**30**	35	40
40	20	**40**	**35**
45	10	45	30
50	0	50	25
		55	20
		60	15
		65	10
		70	5
		75	0

Before trade, Country A is producing 35 units of bread and 30 of wine for its own consumption, and Country B is producing 40 of bread, 35 of wine (points X and X′ on their respective production possibilities curves). The question posed by the theory of comparative advantage is the following: Is it possible to change how much each country produces of each product so that more total output is produced with no increase in resources, and then engage in trade so that each country can consume more of at least one product and no less of the other? If the answer to both parts of this question is yes, then specialization and trade offers the same benefit as more resources or better technology. It allows a country to move beyond its present production possibilities limitation to a higher level of consumption.

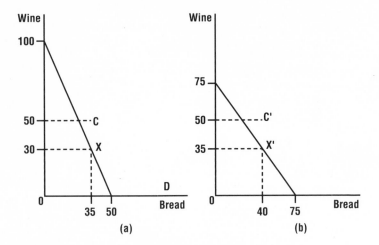

FIG. 15-1 *Specialization Based on Comparative Advantage*

The theory of comparative advantage says that each country should specialize in that product in which its opportunity cost is lower. A's opportunity cost for bread in terms of wine forgone is given by the schedule above, or by the slope of the production possibilities curve in Figure 15-1. Each extra loaf of bread means giving up production of two units of wine. For B, the opportunity cost is 1 for 1.[3] B's bread is cheaper than A's in terms of wine forgone, but this means that A's wine is cheaper than B's in terms of bread forgone (1/2 bread vs. 1 bread). A should specialize in wine and B in bread; A will produce 100 units of wine and B will produce 75 units of bread (points Y and Y' on their production possibilities curves).

Note that at this point "world" output has risen. Before specialization, total wine production was 65 (A produced 30 and B produced 35) and total bread production was 75 (A produced 35 and B produced 40). Specialization has increased wine production by 35 units with no reduction in bread production. If these two countries can agree on a rate at which to trade these goods—such as 1.5 units of wine per loaf of bread—both can consume more of one or both products because there is more available.

Points C and C′ in Figure 15-1 show how much bread and wine each country can consume in a good trade environment. At C Country A is consuming 50 units of wine and 35 of bread, for a gain of 20 wine. Country B is consuming 50 units of wine and 40 of bread, for a gain of 25 wine. Other combinations are also possible. The point is that real output increases and consumers enjoy more real goods and services when specialization takes place on the basis of comparative advantage.

Twentieth-century economists have tried to identify what the sources of comparative advantage are. One important source of differences in opportunity costs, on which comparative advantage is based, is resource endowments. One country may be rich in capital, a second in labor, a third in land, while in each case the other two broad groups of resources are in short supply. It would make sense for the first country to be highly specialized in producing those products that use large amounts of capital and relatively less labor and land, the second to specialize in labor-intensive products, and the third in land-intensive (usually agricultural) production. We would expect that those resources that are abundant in a given country will be relatively cheap, while scarce resources are relatively expensive. Land, for example, is expensive in Japan because it is relatively scarce, while land is still relatively cheap in most parts of the U.S. Thus, the U.S. has a clear competitive advantage over Japan in land-intensive agricultural products.

Differences in resources available (including access to different technology) results in different opportunity costs for producing particular goods. If markets are open and competitive within and between countries, and if exchange rates are set at appropriate levels, the prices of tradeable goods will reflect these differences in opportunity costs. Responding to these price signals, each nation will produce and export goods for which its opportunity costs are lowest and import those goods in which its opportunity costs are higher.

Competition and Economies of Scale

The other two benefits of trade, in addition to increased output from specialization, are competition and economies of scale. As was mentioned earlier, many industries are monopolistically competitive or oligopolistic within the country. In the absence of foreign competition, the firms in such industries would produce less output, charge higher prices, and often enjoy persistent profits because barriers to entry would prevent rivals from entering the industry. Foreign competition fills an important gap, forcing these firms to be efficient, price-competitive, and attuned to the needs and concerns of consumers. Foreign competition can convert a domestic monopoly into an international oligopoly, or a domestic oligopoly into an international industry that is more nearly monopolistically competitive. Americans have seen the important role played by foreign competition in many industries, particularly steel and automobiles, in making the domestic industry more responsive to the needs of its customers.

Economies of scale are a second benefit from international trade. Industries that enjoy substantial economies of scale must serve a large market in order to attain the minimum average cost. If they are limited to serving the domestic market, the industry will be likely to have only one or just a few firms. In small countries even a single firm may not be able to generate enough sales to get to the most efficient output level, where average costs are at a minimum. Serving a world market allows firms to achieve economies of scale while at the same time ensuring some competition for firms that would otherwise be operating in conditions of monopoly or oligopoly.

Other Explanations of Trade Patterns

A significant part of the patterns of trade between countries can be explained by comparative advantage, supplemented by the development of economies of scale. A nation may begin with a very small comparative advantage (a slight price edge.) If that nation uses that slight price advantage to increase market share, and if the product involved is one in which there are economies of scale, the expansion in output will mean that average costs will fall.[4] The nation's cost advantage thus becomes larger, and its comparative advantage is strengthened. This explains the long-term dominance of the U.S. in such industries as trucks, aircraft, and mainframe computers, all with significant economies of scale. A small difference in cost in industries with scale economies is enough to launch a long-term comparative advantage.

Other (complementary) explanations of the pattern of trade have also been offered. Raymond Vernon of Harvard University was the first to point to the product cycle as an additional explanation of trading patterns in some types of products. When a product is new, it is produced in (and exported by) the country where it was first developed. As that nation's producers continue to experiment with, develop, and standardize the product, they will continue to export. Once the technology is known and the product is standardized, however, other countries are likely to jump in and try to develop its production, first for the home market and eventually for exports. Over time the production of the newly standardized product will migrate to those countries whose resource endowment is best suited for that product, enabling them to produce at least cost. The classic instance of this pattern is the transistor in the 1950s and early 1960s, which was an American invention. Once it was standardized, however, its production quickly shifted to Japan, which at that time had an abundance of low-cost, semiskilled labor.

Swedish economist Stassan Linder points out yet another determinant of trading patterns. He observes that the bulk of trade takes place between the developed, industrial countries, whose resource endowments are similar, rather than between nations at different stages of development, whose resources are very different. Linder argues that production of certain goods develops in response to home demand. As producers develop and refine the product and start looking for other market opportunities, they begin to export. Markets for such products are most likely to be found in countries with similar tastes based on similar income levels. Thus, home demand provides the original "inspiration," and the product will be exported after it has been developed and perfected at home.

A final contributing factor to trade patterns is the transportation requirements of the product. Does the factory need to be located near inputs that are costly to transport (a resource-oriented product)? Does production need to be located close to the market because the product is fragile, perishable, or in need of service support (market-oriented)? Or can the factory be anywhere (footloose) because transportation requirements are relatively unimportant? Resource-oriented plants will be located near the raw materials. Market-oriented production will be scattered among many countries. It is only the footloose industries where it is meaningful to examine the other, nontransport-related explanations of comparative advantage.

Tariffs, Quotas, and Commercial Policy

Firms that must compete with foreign producers often seek protection and assistance from the government. Sometimes such protection is justified because of anticompetitive behavior on the part of the foreign producer. The foreign competitor may be engaging in international price discrimination, or dumping, to drive out competitors and dominate the market.[5] American firms have at various times complained of dumping in a number of products ranging from Japanese cars and TVs to plastic mattress handles from Canada and chickens exported to third countries by the European Economic Community.

Other reasons for seeking protection include strategic importance of the industry for national defense (trucks), a domestic firm in competition with an international cartel (domestic oil and OPEC), or handicaps experienced by the domestic producer because of public policy decisions (occupational safety, minimum wage, or environmental regulations, for example) that are not shared by the foreign competitor.[6]

Some of these reasons are legitimate, some are semilegitimate, and others are largely emotional. The basic reason that a firm seeks protection from foreign competitors is to increase its monopoly position, so that it can raise its price and still enjoy a large sales volume based on increased market share. These gains to the import-competing firm are financed by consumers, who pay higher prices and enjoy less of the product. Thus, the effect of protection is to transfer income or "utility" from consumers of imported goods to producers (owners and workers) of import-competing goods.

The primary tools of protection are tariffs and quotas. A tariff is a tax on imported goods. A quota is a physical limitation on the number of units of a good that can be imported during a year. The effects are quite similar. Figure 15-2 analyzes the impact of a tariff on television sets. S_d represents the domestic supply curve, and D is the domestic demand curve. For simplicity, assume that the importing country is small relative to the world market, so that its citizens can buy all the foreign television sets they like at the going price of $250.[7]

Before the tariff, the price of a television set (17″ screen, color, remote control) was $250. Domestic producers were producing 1,000 sets a month, and consumers were buying 2,500 sets a month; thus, 1,500 sets were being imported each month. Now domestic TV producers persuade the government to impose a tariff of $50 per set on imported television sets. The price paid by consumers rises to $300. Domestic producers are better able to compete at this price; their output rises to 1,200 sets a month. Consumers, faced with higher prices, cut back their purchases to 2,000 sets a month. Imports fall from 1,500 a month to 800 a month. Domestic producers have gained, while foreign producers and domestic consumers have lost. A third loser, not shown on this diagram, is likely to be domestic firms that export other products, because other countries are likely to retaliate with tariffs of their own.

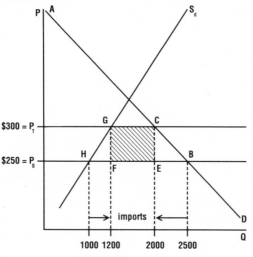

FIG. 15-2 *Effects of a Tariff*

Using the concept of consumer surplus developed in Chapter 4, it is possible to measure the loss to consumers and to see where it went. Triangle ABP_0 measures the original consumer surplus before the tariff.[8] The tariff shrinks consumer surplus to triangle ACPT. The loss of consumer surplus is measured by the quadrilateral P_0PTCB. Part of that loss to consumers, who are now consuming fewer units at a higher price, goes to the government in tariff revenue. Tariff revenue is equal to the volume of imports multiplied by the tariff $PT - P_0$, or rectangle CEFG, which is known as the revenue effect. Another part of that loss became producer surplus in the amount of quadrilateral P_0PTGH (called the protective effect). Producer surplus measures the earnings over and above the sum of marginal costs of production, which goes to benefit the owners and workers in the protected industry in the form of higher wages and/or profits. When protection was given to the auto industry in the early 1980s, the immediate result was a wage hike and larger bonuses to upper management!

A third part of the loss to consumers goes to pay for the increasing marginal cost of shifting purchases away from more efficient foreign suppliers to less efficient domestic firms. This effect is measured by triangle FGH (the efficiency effect). Finally, there is a component of consumer surplus that is lost (not transferred to anyone), measured by triangle BCE. This is called the deadweight loss.

The model leads to rather negative conclusions about tariffs. Similar models with similar conclusions can be developed for quotas. In fact, economists are generally more critical of quotas, because the revenue that goes to the government in a tariff model is converted to monopoly profits for importing firms under a quota. The reason for the negative conclusion is that trade policy is always examined from the perspective of the consumer (who is the loser from tariffs and quotas); in addition, the primary unstated goal is short-run efficiency, which is served by using the least-cost (foreign) supplier. Different assumptions or different priorities—the perspective of the producer, or a longer run viewpoint—can sometimes support different conclusions. Japan, for example, stresses production and long-term market share rather than consumption and short-run efficiency. The result has been rapid growth in output but very slow improvements in the average Japanese household's standard of living.

TRADE AND THE DOLLAR

U.S. trade policy is very much affected by fluctuations in the price of the dollar. As a macroeconomic issue, the determinants of the price of the dollar are largely outside the scope of this book, but it is helpful to look at how those changes affect trade policy. In the early 1980s the price of the dollar rose sharply in terms of most other currencies, largely because foreigners wanted dollars in order to invest in the United States. The rising dollar made U.S. exports more expensive, and imports cheaper. American exporters of trucks, farm machinery, and even agricultural products found it difficult to compete abroad, while import-competing industries such as textiles, shoes, and autos sought protection. Both groups argued that they were no less efficient than they had been before, but they were less able to compete because of developments in financial markets over which they had no control. Between 1985 and 1989 the picture changed as the dollar's value dropped sharply. Exports rose and imports slowed, but the trade deficit remained.

Prior to 1973 the price of the U.S. dollar was set and maintained by the Federal Reserve, as it was in most other countries by their central banks. After a major policy change in 1973, the price of the dollar (and most other major currencies) has been determined by market forces. If foreigners want to invest in the U.S. more than Americans want to invest abroad, the price of the dollar will be bid up. High real interest rates (market interest rates adjusted for expected inflation) in the U.S. in the early 1980s were the primary reason for the inflow of foreign investments. American exporters and import-competing producers suffered losses of sales for reasons quite unrelated to conditions in their particular markets.

Floating exchange rates have offered some important benefits, but they have not provided any stability or predictability to currency prices. Indeed, they have added yet another headache to the already complex problem of selling abroad or competing with imported goods. Firms that are interested in developing foreign markets or that have foreign competition—and that includes most firms—must keep a close eye on the dollar's value because of its effect on their markets.

MULTINATIONAL FIRMS—WHO, WHAT, WHY

The multinational firm, along with floating exchange rates, has complicated the process of international trade considerably in the last few decades. It is much more difficult to distinguish international from domestic trade when goods, finished or partly finished, pass from one branch of a company to another across national boundaries. Employees can emigrate without changing employers. Final goods may have parts of their production process in three or four different countries.

Firms build or buy plants abroad for a number of reasons. Often management is trying to safeguard or acquire a market share that is threatened by tariffs or other trade barriers. Producing inside the tariff wall is one way around that problem. Other firms have patents, processes, brand names, or trade secrets that they are unwilling to license but will make available to their own subsidiaries in other countries. For some products (market-oriented) production near the point of sale is important not only when the product is fragile or perishable but also when it must be adapted to local market requirements. Foreign firms have increasingly opened facilities in the U.S. for access to technology and to be close to a major market.

The growth of multinationals since the 1940s has led to considerable research on the effects of such firms. Do they increase or decrease competition? Do they increase or displace home country exports? Do they benefit the home country or the foreign host?

No definitive answers can be given to these questions. In some cases multinationals provide much-needed competition for sleepy domestic monopolies or oligopolies, shaking up an unresponsive industry. In other cases they destroy local competition or forestall its development. Establishing a foreign subsidiary is likely to displace home country exports (sometimes even resulting in imports!), but often the subsidiary is a defensive action to retain a market that was in danger of being lost otherwise. At least some of the revenue from the foreign subsidiary will accrue to the benefit of the home or parent country where the multinational has its headquarters.

Multinationals have been seen as threats to the sovereignty of small host countries, because such firms often wield more economic power than the host government. Such giant corporations have posed a challenge to the sovereignty of even large countries such as the U.S., which finds it difficult to make its companies' foreign subsidiaries observe U.S. antitrust laws or refrain from sales of certain goods to unfriendly nations.

CHAPTER PERSPECTIVE

Most larger firms, and many smaller ones, are affected by international trade either because they sell abroad or because they compete with producers of imported goods. International trade is considered beneficial to consumers because it increases total output, offers lower prices and greater variety, subjects domestic oligopolies and monopolies to greater competition, and allows firms to attain economies of scale.

The basic argument for free international trade is that specialization and exchange based on comparative advantage will increase total output and allow both trading partners to enjoy a higher standard of living. Each country should produce that product, or those products, in which its opportunity costs are lower.

Comparative advantage is not the only explanation of trade patterns. Sometimes trade patterns reflect the fact that a good is input-oriented or market-oriented because of problems in transporting either raw materials or the finished product. The product cycle explains trade patterns in newly developing products, and the demand similarities among countries at the same level of economic development explain the high volume of trade between industrial, developed countries.

Tariffs and quotas are the main forms of protection. Both benefit import-competing producers at the expense of consumers, foreign producers, and often exporters.

Changes in the exchange rate affect the ability of firms to compete internationally. For example, a high dollar price, due to increased foreign investment, will make exports more expensive and imports cheaper, while a declining dollar benefits both export firms and import-competing firms.

The multinational corporation is a firm with headquarters in one country and one or more subsidiaries or partly owned affiliates in other countries. Multinationals sometimes increase competition and sometimes decrease it. They are likely to reduce home country exports, but often those exports were likely to disappear anyway. Multinationals pose problems of asserting sovereignty for both small host countries and large parent countries whose multinationals' subsidiaries do not always conform to the operating rules of the parent country.

FOOTNOTES

1 *Like most countries, the U.S. offers technical assistance to firms in identifying export markets and working through the complex maze of regulations governing international sales. Regional trade offices under the U.S. Department of Commerce are located in most major cities.*

2 *By limiting output to two products, it is possible to illustrate comparative advantage with production possibilities curves. The insights of this model remain valid in a multicountry, multiproduct model, as the writings of 20th-century economists have demonstrated.*

3 *A quick way to compute opportunity cost is given by the end points. If A produces only wine, it is giving up the 50 units of bread it could produce. Each unit of wine costs 1/2 a bread (100/50), or each bread costs 2 wine. For B, producing 75 wine means giving up production of 75 bread. Since both production possibilities curves are straight line, the cost of one product in terms of the other forgone is constant. Each extra wine costs 1/2 a bread for A, and 1 bread for B.*

4 *If you have forgotten the meaning of this term, you may want to refer back to Chapter 7.*

5 *Dumping and other forms of price discrimination were discussed in Chapter 13.*

6 *Some nations, particularly small and less developed ones, seek to attract industry by becoming environmental "havens," imposing less stringent rules on air and water pollution, dumping, etc. They are willing to levy those costs on their citizens and their environment in order to create job opportunities. The domestic firm finds it difficult to compete with a foreign producer that can "buy the environment" as a productive resource at a much lower price.*

7 *If this assumption of a small country is relaxed, the conclusions are similar, but the diagram is more complex.*

8 *Recall that consumer surplus measures the difference between what consumers paid in total for a particular quantity of a good and what the value of that quantity was to consumers. The difference arises because all consumers buy at the price of the last or marginal units, but prior units are worth more to them.*

The Government, the Firm, and the Market

INTRODUCTION AND MAIN POINTS

Over the course of the last 15 chapters it has become increasingly apparent that the government plays a significant role even in a supposedly capitalistic economy. The government collects taxes, offers subsidies, produces public goods, changes the distribution of income, defines and protects property rights, corrects externalities, regulates monopolies, and in general fills in the spaces that the market leaves blank and corrects some of the excesses of unbridled free enterprise. State and local government provide infrastructure and amenities such as roads, schools, parks, and sewers, and guarantee access to many services to all citizens, not just those who can afford to pay.

While the private sector is often critical of the actions of government, most business firms would agree that at least some of these actions of government are appropriate and desirable. However, they may also point out that in the process of correcting for market failure, governments can create a few new kinds of failure of their own.

After studying the material in this chapter:

■ You will understand the role of the government in creating and protecting property rights in a market system.

■ You will see the rationale for, and the costs of, various types of government regulation of business.

■ You will know how to evaluate the advantages and drawbacks of the various types of federal, state, and local taxes imposed on business firms.

■ You will be able to identify the ways in which government fails in its efforts to "improve on" the workings of the market.

GOVERNMENT AS CREATOR AND PROTECTOR OF FIRMS: PROPERTY RIGHTS

The most basic function of government in a private enterprise economy is to define and enforce property rights. Without government, brute force would determine who "owned" certain assets—land, raw materials, buildings, equipment—and disputes over property rights would be resolved by the same means. Incentives to produce, to save, to invest, and to accumulate property would be very weak in the absence of any assurance that one's ownership of assets and the fruits of one's labors would be safeguarded. Contracts could not be entered into with any assurance that they would be enforceable. Governments offer such assurances, with police and courts to enforce contracts and ownership rights.

Governments can also create new property rights, or take old ones away. The U.S. federal government took away the right to hold gold from its citizens in 1934, a right not restored until 40 years later. The copyright and patent procedures create exclusive rights to the use of inventions, compositions, and works of literature. With the invention of television, the government created exclusive franchise rights to certain segments of the airwaves that were granted to individuals and corporations. The regulatory agencies of government—the Federal Aviation Authority (FAA), Food and Drug Administration (FDA), Securities and Exchange Commission (SEC), and similar agencies—are constantly defining, redefining, and restricting property rights. A go-ahead from the FDA to market a new drug creates a property right that can make a big difference to a pharmaceutical manufacturer, who pays dearly in research and testing for this right. Individuals acquire a property right with a motor vehicle license or a driver's license, subject to restrictions on the condition of the vehicle, the speed at which it is operated, and other enforceable limits on property rights.

Many of the property rights that government defines and enforces relate to one party's actions infringing on the property rights of others. Zoning, for example, both protects you from what your neighbors may want to do with their property and limits your right to inflict undesirable property uses on them. Zoning is an important policy issue for retail and service firms because it limits where they can locate and how they can use their property. Environmental regulations, and occupational health and safety regulations, have put further limits on the perceived property rights of firms to use the air and water as a dump for refuse, or to expose their employees to potentially hazardous working conditions.

No area of public policy is as diverse or as fraught with controversy as the definition and enforcement of property rights. Billions of dollars in lobbying efforts are poured into obtaining offshore oil drilling rights or the right to harvest timber on federal lands, renewing a TV station's license, getting new drugs approved, and resisting proposed limitations on the right to own or purchase firearms. Every business firm is at once grateful for the assurance of protection of property rights—such as security of person and property against theft and vandalism, enforcement of contracts—and resentful of some of the limitations on property rights that governments impose at all levels.

COSTS AND BENEFITS OF REGULATION

Governments, particularly the federal government, engage in two kinds of regulation. The older type of regulation was aimed primarily at reducing or controlling monopoly power by regulating natural monopolies or public utilities and by enforcing the antitrust laws. The newer type, or the so-called social regulations developed over the last 25 years. Social regulations is a loose term that covers correcting externalities and regulations intended to safeguard safety and health. Air quality standards, mandatory seat belts, earplugs and safety helmets on construction sites, cleaning cotton dust out of the air in cotton mills, and restrictions on dumping toxic wastes all fall into this category. Most, but not all, social regulation is related to the establishment and enforcement of property rights that define who has what rights to use an asset and to what restrictions those rights are subject.

Monopoly and Competition

Unlike many other developed, industrial countries, including Japan and West Germany, the U.S. has chosen to actively promote competition and discourage concentration, cooperation, collusion, or mergers among firms in the same industry for almost a century. This policy has rarely gone so far as to say bigness is inherently bad, but it has come close. "Natural monopolies"—firms such as electric and natural gas producers, as you recall from Chapter 11, that can only achieve economies of scale if they are the sole firm in the market—are generally regulated, most often at the state government level.

Other monopolies that do not fit this category of natural monopoly are carefully scrutinized to see how they came by their monopoly power. The Sherman Act in 1890 made monopolizing illegal, with the term monopolizing defined as acts undertaken to create a monopoly. Further legislation such as the Clayton Act (1914) and the Robinson-Patman Act (1932) spelled out what kinds of actions would be considered as monopolizing. Strict enforcement of the antitrust laws would mean few, if any, unregulated monopolies, and fewer oligopolies, or at least oligopolies with larger numbers of competing firms than would otherwise exist.

One of the most unusual pro-competitive steps ever taken by the U.S. government was to end the Alcoa monopoly in U.S. aluminum by creating two rival government-owned firms during World War II, both of which were subsequently sold to private buyers to compete with Alcoa. More common remedies for lack of competition, or threatened lack of competition, are to forbid mergers and order divestiture of certain subsidiaries, as in the case of Ma Bell and the Baby Bells (regional operating companies formerly owned by AT&T).

Antitrust policy balances the traditional microeconomic emphasis on the benefits of competition to the consumer with the recognition that pure competition is hardly the best or even a feasible market structure for most industries. Antitrust policy has been criticized for depriving the economy of the benefits of larger firms and interfirm cooperation, especially in such areas as research and development and presenting a common front in dealing with international cartels.[1] One critic described antitrust policy as encouraging competition and punishing the winners. Other critics also point out that antitrust enforcement is highly political; Justice Departments vary greatly from one administration to another both in terms of intensity of effort and in the criteria for selection of cases.

Firms find ways to become large without running afoul of the antitrust laws. The frenzy of mergers, acquisitions, and divestitures of subsidiaries that produce products unrelated to the parent company's main product line (conglomerates) in the last two decades is one result of the antitrust laws, which focus on competition in a particular industry but do not attack market power that is based on a small market share in each of a large number of industries. Critics, again, blame antitrust policy for some of the undesirable results of the conglomerate mergers of the last two decades; they argue that these firms would be more efficient if the antitrust laws would allow them to become that large and power-ful by concentrating resources and management talent in a par-ticular industry rather than spreading those resources thinly over a whole array of unrelated enterprises.

While antitrust policy has been combatting certain kinds of bigness, other actions of government have tended to promote concentration and monopoly. Government licensing and franchises, as well as patents and copyrights, create monopolies. Government procurement practices favor large firms at the expense of small ones. Government paperwork to comply with tax laws, safety and health regulations, and other laws are far more burdensome on small firms than large ones. All these actions of government tend to favor larger firms. Offsetting these pro-concentration efforts has been a weak and relatively ineffec-tive effort to encourage the development and growth of small business through the Small Business Administration. This agency makes loans to new small businesses and supports Small Business Development Centers affiliated with colleges through-out the country to provide technical assistance to fledgling entre-preneurs. On balance, however—putting together antitrust, paperwork, procurement, licenses, franchises, small business development, and other policies—the overall public policy direc-tion has been to encourage larger firms rather than smaller ones.

The role that government plays in restraining monopoly and promoting competition is thus not very clear. Observers across the political spectrum question not only the effectiveness of antimonopoly policies, but even whether they are desirable at all, or whether they cost the economy valuable benefits to be derived from bigness, longevity of firms, and interfirm cooperation.

Externalities

Recall from Chapter 14 that a significant form of market failure that seems to call for government intervention is the existence of externalities, both positive and negative. The range of remedies is broad. Often the remedy for negative externalities takes the form of direct regulation, specifying either inputs to be used or out-puts, such as the fuel efficiency of the auto firm's fleet, or the number of units of sulfur dioxide to be emitted into the atmosphere. Positive externalities have resulted in public produc-tion, as in highways, airports, and public education; or subsidies, as in health care and higher education. In recent years, governments at all levels have experimented more with market based solutions such as taxes, subsidies, and establishment of property rights to the use of common property such as air and water.

Safety and Health

Safety and health includes a broad range of regulatory activity that not only involves workplace safety but also protecting consumers from unsafe products. In general, the government is intervening where information is costly to acquire or technically difficult for the lay person to understand and interpret, so that consumers or workers may be unaware of the risks they face from working in certain conditions (for example, with asbestos in the ceiling, or noise that over time can impair their hearing). In some cases, the government's role is limited to providing information about the risks and allowing the consumer or worker to make that decision with full information. This solution is expressed in hazardous warnings on cigarettes and contents labeling on most household products, such as food, household pesticides, and cleaning products. In other cases, where the risks are unknown or long-term in nature, the government may restrict the product (for example, limiting drugs to prescription by a physician) or prohibit its use altogether, which has been done for many drugs and chemicals.

Requiring that products incorporate safety features or that certain workplace hazards be eliminated is yet another approach to safety and health. Power tools generally have safeguards required by law, although in a society where lawsuits are common, firms increasingly have a financial incentive to take such precautions on their own. Requiring safety glasses or earplugs where there are risks to eyes or hearing are typical government-mandated workplace safety rules that carry fines when they are violated.

The market will in most cases eventually weed out unsafe or hazardous products and conditions, but that offers small comfort to those who suffer illness, injury, or death in the process of generating that information to the market. Thus, the government intervenes to reduce the cost of providing information about risk. Such information is a public good—it can be consumed by everyone, whether they pay or not—and the market is therefore not likely to provide enough information. Firms may benefit also. With lower product liability risk, their insurance premiums are lower. Since safety features are not highly visible, many firms would prefer that they be mandated by government so that their sales of safe products will not be undermined by the flashy or low price appeal of a product that is really more dangerous or risky.

It is difficult to draw the line between appropriate and inappropriate safety and health regulations, or to count the costs of such regulations. In addition to the costs of drafting and implementing such regulations, and firms' compliance costs, there are less visible costs. While the Food and Drug Administration may have saved many lives by preventing unsafe drugs from reaching the market, they have also allowed needless pain, suffering, and deaths from the slow process of approving ultimately beneficial drugs. When the government requires safety features on cars that drive up their price, some consumers are priced out of the market and wind up driving older, much less safe cars than they might have been able to afford with less regulation. To the extent that workplace safety raises labor costs, output and jobs are lost. There is no easy way to compare the costs and benefits of safety and health regulations.

TAXES AND BUSINESS FIRMS

While some taxes are imposed in order to correct negative externalities, or to discourage consumption, most taxes serve the simple and direct purpose of raising revenue to finance government expenditures. Some taxes are legally imposed on the household or consumer, while others are the legal liability of the corporation. The person or firm that is legally liable for the tax, however, may not be the same one that bears most of the burden of the tax in the form of lower income received or higher prices paid.[2] Taxes are a broad and complex subject; we will limit our attention here to some of the major tax issues facing all business firms.[3]

There are two major federal taxes with legal incidence on the firm: the employer's share of the Social Security tax and the corporate income tax. Unemployment insurance taxes and various excises are lesser federal taxes that are also the legal obligation of the firm. At the state and local level, firms pay property taxes and corporate income taxes, and may pay sales taxes on some or all of what they buy. Some of the burden of retail sales taxes may also fall on the firm, both in states where the legal liability is on the seller and in states where the legal liability is on the buyer. Finally, a business license fee, which is similar to a tax and is often tied to the firm's revenues, is an important local revenue source in many cities and a substantial cost for some firms, especially retailers and small service establishments.

If a firm is able to pass the cost of a tax on to its customers, the tax is said to be *shifted*. The incidence of the tax is then said to lie on whoever actually bears the burden of the tax. Taxes can be shifted to suppliers (including workers) as well as to customers. The firm's ability to shift a tax depends on its degree of market power, i.e., how inelastic its demand curve is, or how inelastic the supply curves are that it faces as a buyer of inputs.

Figure 16-1 illustrates the effects of a sales tax in two different situations. In panel (a) the firm faces a highly elastic demand curve. When the increase in cost in the form of a sales or excise tax is added to the firm's marginal cost (supply) curve, the supply curve shifts to S_2. The tax per unit is the vertical distance between the two supply curves. The price paid by the buyer rises slightly, to P_2. The price received by the seller after paying the tax, however, falls to P_3. As you can see, most of the burden of the tax falls on the seller. In panel (b), the demand curve is much less elastic, and the burden of the tax falls much more heavily on the buyer, i.e., more of the tax is shifted forward to the buyer.

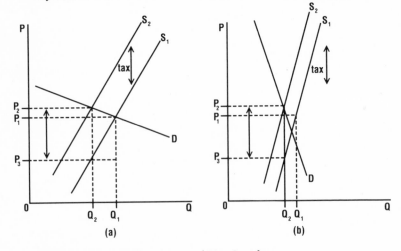

FIG. 16-1 *Demand Elasticity and Tax Incidence*

In general, sales taxes are the easiest to shift, especially if they fall on all sellers. Sales taxes are more likely to burden the seller if they are local taxes that buyers can easily escape by shopping in the next town or the next county. Corporate income or profits taxes are harder to shift, although some of the burden may fall on the employees in the form of lower wages. Most of this tax, however, is paid by the owners or stockholders. Property taxes are usually the most difficult tax for firms to shift, because the firm can only avoid paying them if it relocates.

Regardless of the type of tax, it is important to note that firms do not pay taxes. People pay taxes. The correct question about who pays taxes for which firms are liable is whether those taxes fall primarily on the firm's customers in the form of higher prices, the firm's employees in the form of lower net wages, or the firm's owners in the form of reduced dividends or profits. In most cases, some of the burden will fall on each group.

A PUBLIC CHOICE VIEW OF GOVERNMENT FAILURE

In the 1970s and 1980s a group of economists with an interest in how government decisions were made began exploring the workings of government from an economic perspective. In particular, they were critical of the "market failure" school of thought that had offered such an extensive agenda of government intervention in order to improve on the workings of the marketplace. According to public-choice economists, it is true that the market can fail, but so can government; and there is no reason to expect that government regulations designed to correct market failure will make society better off.

These critics point to the complex decision process in government, where voters must select candidates based on a whole array of positions and issues, but often cannot obtain enough information to make an intelligent decision. Information is costly for the voter to obtain, and since individual voters have so little impact on the outcome, the benefit from obtaining good information is low. Thus, voters are likely to be "rationally ignorant"— ignorant because the benefits of being informed are less than the costs. Without the constraint of observant voters, politicians will behave differently than they would in a more closely watched, competitive political environment.

In the legislative arena where decisions are made, logrolling, vote-trading, and other political tactics may result in less satisfactory results than society would expect from the unregulated market. In particular, public-choice economists point to the power and influence of special-interest groups engaged in rent-seeking behavior. *Rent-seeking* refers to actions of private individuals to persuade government to enact legislation that will give them some degree of monopoly power, enabling them to earn a return on their resources that is greater than it would have been without government help. The role of such special-interest groups has attracted considerable attention in the last few decades, because politicians depend on their support in election campaigns. Awarding exclusive franchises, setting standards that help limit the number of competitors, enacting special tax breaks for certain industries, authorizing tariffs and quotas, and increasing farm price supports are examples of the results of rent-seeking by special-interest groups.

The central lesson of public choice is caution. It is true that the market's results are often less than perfectly satisfactory, but there is no guarantee that government intervention will be better. In fact, it may be worse; in some cases, the harm done by market failure may be less than the harm that would be done by the most likely form of government intervention. There are no hard-and-fast rules to determine when to tolerate market failure and when to intervene, but certainly the lesson of public choice has been to look carefully before opting for a governmental solution.

CHAPTER PERSPECTIVE

In a market economic system, the primary role of government is to define and enforce property rights. Since a market system has no way to create and define such rights, it depends on an outside source to determine who owns what resources and to set rules that prevent one person from infringing on the rights of another to use those resources in particular ways.

A second role of government in a market system is to correct various forms of market failure. One form of market failure is the existence of monopoly power, which is addressed in the United States with a combination of regulation of natural monopoly, such as public utilities, and antitrust laws. A second form of market failure consists of externalities, which were discussed at length in Chapter 14. A third form of market failure lies in hazards to safety and health because of imperfect information. The government may limit its protection in such cases to labels and hazard warnings, or it may actually specify product safety features and workplace safety requirements. When government provides such protection, it also limits the range of consumer choice and may keep workers from getting risky jobs they are willing to take or consumers from obtaining products they would like to consume even with full knowledge of the risks.

In order to finance their activities, governments collect taxes. Some of these taxes are legally assessed on the owners of business firms. Among major taxes directly affecting business firms are corporate income taxes, sales taxes, Social Security taxes, and property taxes. Even if the firm is legally liable for the tax, the actual burden or incidence of the tax is often shared by the firm's owners, its workers, and its customers in varying proportions.

Public choice is a relatively new area of economic theory that examines the decision-making process in government and has concluded that, in many cases, attempts to correct for market failure will result in government failure. Thus, caution is in order. The political decision making process is dominated by voter ignorance, logrolling, vote-trading, and rent-seeking by special interest groups. Under such circumstances, it is sometimes more feasible to tolerate market failure than to risk the potential government failures that may come about in attempting to "improve on" the market.

FOOTNOTES

1 *An international cartel consists of two or more firms from different countries that work together to set prices, control markets, and eliminate competition. Thus, cartels acquire and share the benefits of a monopoly. The two best known cartels of this century are the OPEC oil cartel and the deBeers diamond cartel.*

2 *The study of who actually bears the burden of a tax is called incidence theory.*

3 *Another volume in this series, Accounting and Taxation, addresses tax issues facing firms in more detail.*

Labor Markets

INTRODUCTION AND MAIN POINTS

Firms operate in the market to sell their products or services. They also operate as buyers on the other side of the market, the resource markets in which firms purchase the services of the factors of production. Capital markets, one of the major resource markets, were examined in detail in an earlier chapter. Probably the most important resource market for nearly all firms, in terms of the number of dollars expended, is the labor market.

After studying the material in this chapter:

▬ You will know the factors that determine the wages paid to various types and amounts of labor.

▬ You will be able to explain why different workers earn different wages, and the role of discrimination in the labor market.

▬ You will have a better understanding of how labor markets work both under competitive conditions and with imperfect competition.

▬ You will know how resource markets affect the distribution of income.

THE MARKET FOR LABOR

The market for labor is similar to the product markets. There is a downward-sloping demand curve and an upward-sloping supply curve resulting in an equilibrium in price (wage) and quantity (worker-hours). The demand curve slopes downward for some of the same reasons that product demand curves do so. If labor becomes cheaper relative to other inputs (especially capital), the firm will substitute labor for capital; if labor becomes more expensive relative to capital, the firm will substitute capital for labor. The supply curve slopes upward because it takes a higher wage to attract more workers into the market. Additional workers, or additional hours from present workers, have higher and higher opportunity costs in terms of these workers' alternative uses of time. They can be lured from housekeeping, leisure, or other jobs only by higher wages.

These reasons are adequate to explain the appearance of resource supply and demand curves. However, on the demand side there is an important difference between product demand and resource demand, including specifically labor demand. Buyers demand goods and services for their intrinsic value, utility, or satisfaction. Firms demand labor only because there is final demand for the products and services that labor produces. The demand for labor is a *derived demand*; that is, it is derived from the demand for the product of labor. The explanation of this relationship draws on the production function developed in Chapter 6, combined with the demand and marginal revenue curves for the product.

Labor Demand and Marginal Product

Recall that the total product function in Chapter 6 looked like panel (a) of Figure 17-1, and the marginal product curve looked like panel (b). Marginal product is the extra product produced by one additional unit of labor—an extra worker, or an extra worker-hour. The marginal product (MP) of a worker is an important consideration in the decision to hire. How much will this worker add to the firm's output? Is he or she worth what the employer has to pay? In order to answer this question, the manager needs to consider not only how much extra output this worker will produce, but how much that output will sell for.

If the firm is a pure competitor, selling as much as it likes at the going market price, then the answer is simple. Multiply the worker's marginal product by the product price to obtain the *value of marginal product* (VMP). Figure 17-2 shows a VMP curve for production workers in a steel plant. VMP curve V_c, like the marginal product curve in Figure 17-1, is a downward sloping straight line, but instead of having workers on the horizontal axis and units of output on the vertical axis, it has workers on the horizontal axis and dollar values on the vertical axis. These dollar values measure what the extra worker adds to the firm's revenues, or what they are "worth" to the firm. The firm is willing to pay the worker up to or equal to the value of what the worker adds to the firm's output. The value of marginal product not only represents the worker's addition to the firm's revenues; it is also equal to the maximum wage that the firm is willing to pay for each extra worker. In other words, the value of marginal product curve is the firm's demand curve for labor.

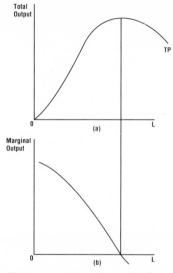

FIG. 17-1 *Total and Marginal Product of Labor*

If the firm is not a pure competitor, then as output expands, it must cut the price of its product in order to sell more units, because it faces a downward sloping demand curve. VMP is still equal to marginal product multiplied by product price to obtain a demand curve for labor, but now MP is multiplied by a declining product price instead of a constant price. The result is a VMP curve such as V_0 that is much steeper for firms that are not pure competitors.[1]

Table 17-1 shows the total product, marginal product, demand, and VMP for two firms, one in pure competition, one an oligopolist. The first three columns correspond to Figure 17-1; they simply show the relationship between the number of workers and the firm's total and marginal product, as we discussed in an earlier chapter. The last four columns show the demand curve for a pure competitor and an oligopolist. For the pure competitor, the price is given at $15, so VMP is simply $15 times marginal product. For the oligopolist, price falls as output expands, so the VMP column is the change in total revenue, which declines as both output and price fall. In each case, the number of units of labor plotted against the VMP schedule will result in a straight line demand curve, as shown in Figure 17-2. Note that the oligopolist's demand curve is much steeper than the pure competitor's.

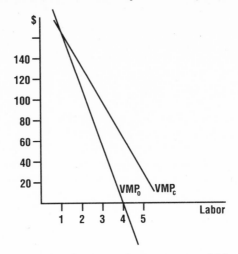

FIG. 17-2 *Labor Demand in Pure Competition and Monopoly*

Table 17-1
Value of Marginal Product and Demand for Labor

Units of Labor	Total Product	Marginal Product	Pure Competition Price	VMP	Price	Oligopoly Total Revenue	VMP
1	10	10	$15	$150	$20	$200	$200
2	18	8	$15	$120	$18	$324	$124
3	24	6	$15	$ 90	$16	$384	$ 60
4	28	4	$15	$ 60	$14	$392	$ 8
5	30	2	$15	$ 30	$12	$360	$ 32

Supply of Labor

The market supply of labor is generally expected to slope upward. For the competitive firm, however, which is a relatively small purchaser of labor services, the supply curve is horizontal. This firm can purchase all the labor it requires of a particular type or skill level (machinists, word processors, clerks, engineers, accountants) at the going wage, which is determined in the market by the sum of all the demands of various firms and the total supply of workers. A firm that represents a large share of the market for a particular type of labor, however, will face an upward sloping supply curve for labor. It can only induce more workers of that type to be supplied—to give up leisure, recreation, or other kinds of work—by offering a higher wage.

For the market, or the large firm, the supply curve of labor slopes upward for several reasons. First, in order to attract some workers away from leisure, housework, school, or other nonmarket activities, it may be necessary to offer a higher wage to match the opportunity cost of their alternative use of time. Second, a higher wage may result from a bidding war for a given quantity of workers.

Consider the market for unskilled labor. Some workers may be enticed into the market at the minimum wage (or would work for even less), but many potential workers value their alternative use of time at higher than the minimum wage. If employers of unskilled labor require more workers than are available at the minimum wage, they must offer higher wages in order to attract students, housewives, retired persons and other potential workers from their present pursuits. Housewives with small children, in particular, have high opportunity costs for market work because of child care expenses. In order to induce present workers to put in more hours (even overtime!) it may be necessary to offer a higher wage. In order to keep workers once they have acquired some skills and experience and are more attractive to other employers, it will be necessary to offer higher wages. Otherwise the firm expends a substantial amount of resources on training for minimum wage workers who are then bid away by competing employers.

The second reason that the curve slopes upward, for both unskilled and specialized labor, is that firms and occupations must bid workers away from other firms and other occupations. The teaching profession lost many of its most skilled members in the 1970s and 1980s. Teachers' salaries have risen substantially as school districts have tried to recruit teachers from other districts as well as to attract new workers away from other occupations. Other occupations still in high demand with rising wages are accountants and marketers, although the glamorous professions of computer science, engineering, medicine, and law appear to have peaked in terms of wages.

Shifts in the Labor Market

Figure 17-3 shows the market for machinists. The typical firm, a pure competitor, is shown in panel (a). This firm hires a small number of machinists for its operation at a wage determined by the sum of all workers and firms in this market, shown in panel (b). The market wage, W_e, is determined by the interaction of supply and demand. The small firm in panel (a) takes that wage as given and elects to hire five machinists at that wage, because the demand curve reflects the value of marginal product (VMP_1), and VMP for the fifth machinist is equal to the wage, W_e. The first four machinists add more to the firm's output than to its costs, and the last one adds just as much to output as to costs. A sixth machinist would not be hired because her VMP would be less than the going wage.

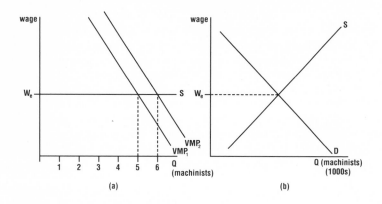

FIG. 17-3 *Labor Supply and Demand*

If this firm finds that demand for its product has increased, or that technological change has made machinists more productive, its demand curve would shift to VMP_2 and the sixth machinist would be hired. A higher product price makes the output of the sixth machinist more valuable. An improvement in technology will increase the marginal product (MP) of the sixth machinist. Either of these events will shift the firm's demand curve to the right—from VMP_1 to VMP_2.

The supply curve facing the firm can shift either upward or downward due to factors beyond the control of the individual firm. Market demand for machinists might increase, as in Figure 17-4, from D_1 to D_2, driving up the market price, perhaps because of expansion in another industry—more defense contracts, for example. This particular firm, whose demand curve has not shifted, would respond by hiring fewer machinists. Most likely, one of its machinists would be attracted away to another firm by a better offer, and the firm would have to increase the wages of the remaining machinists in order to keep them from leaving also. Alternatively, the supply of machinists might increase due to a training program at a nearby technical center, expanding the number of machinists available. The wage would fall and the firm would respond by hiring more machinists at the lower wage.[2]

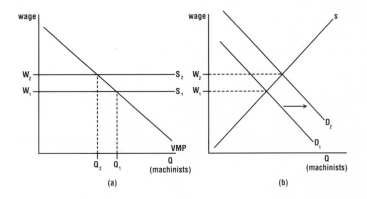

FIG. 17-4 *Shift in Market Labor Demand*

IMPERFECT COMPETITION IN THE LABOR MARKET

Thus far, we have assumed that the labor market itself is perfectly competitive on the side of the sellers, even though some of the firms buying labor services may operate in the product markets where they sell under conditions of imperfect competition on the buyers' side. That is, there are many firms hiring labor, and many workers, all very similar. No one worker can affect the market price of labor—even his or her particular kind of labor—by choosing to work more, or less, or not at all. Firms, likewise, take the going wage as a given and respond to it by deciding how many workers to hire.

In some labor markets, perfect competition or close to perfect competition is the rule. Unskilled labor is largely interchangeable, and so are many unskilled or entry level jobs. Beyond that level, however, jobs are highly differentiated in terms of the skills required and the rewards, both monetary and nonmonetary, that they offer. Workers, likewise, are quite different from each other. In these circumstances, there is likely to be imperfect competition among sellers as well as buyers of labor.

Most labor markets are monopolistically competitive on both sides of the market, because every job and every worker is a little different from every other one. Secretarial jobs may require similar skills and duties, but secretaries have strong preferences in the kinds of bosses they work for, and vice versa. A job as a retail clerk in a nice department store may not pay much more than clerking in a discount store or a convenience store, but working conditions and clientele are very different. As workers and jobs move up the skill ladder, such differences become even more pronounced.

The Buyer's Side—Monopsony

When there is imperfect competition among firms—only one buyer or only a few buyers of labor in a particular town, or a particular worker skill—then there is said to be *monopsony* (one buyer) or *oligopsony* (very few buyers). Monopsony buyers in the labor market are rare, even more today than in earlier times, when company towns in textiles, coal, and other products gave the hiring firm considerable market power. The company town is largely a thing of the past. However, oligopsony—a limited number of labor markets for a particular geographic market or a particular type of skill—is not as rare, and monopsonistic competition (a large number of differentiated buyers of labor services) is the rule rather than the exception in labor markets. The model represented in Figure 17-5 is one of pure monopsony—a sole buyer. This model represents the opposite end of the spectrum from Figures 17-3 and 17-4, which represented a purely competitive buyer of labor services. The outcome in terms of wages and workers hired in markets where monopsonistic competition or oligopsony prevails will lie somewhere between these two extremes.

Because the monopsonist is the sole buyer of labor in a particular market or of a particular type, this firm faces an upward sloping supply curve of labor.[3] It cannot hire all the workers it wants to at the going wage. Suppose that you were the sole employer of carpenters in a given area. Initially, you may be able to hire several at a given wage, but more carpenters will be costly. Your carpenters may have to work overtime, or carpenters may have to be attracted in from other counties or states, or people not really trained as carpenters will have to be hastily trained and attracted away from other jobs. As you try to expand your purchase of carpentry services, you drive up the price.

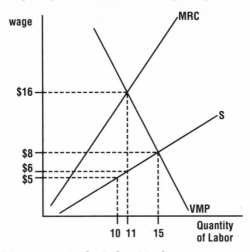

FIG. 17-5 *Monopsony in the Labor Market*

Recall that when the firm's demand curve sloped downward, its marginal revenue curve sloped downward even more steeply. A similar situation faces the monopsonistic buyer. The supply curve slopes upward, but the firm's *marginal resource cost* slopes upward even more steeply. Why? Because the firm must increase the wages of present workers when it hires new workers at a higher wage. It cannot pay the newest, least experienced worker $6 an hour when the present employees are only receiving $5 an hour. Thus, when this firm increases its labor force from 10 workers to 11, it must pay the 11th worker $6 an hour, but it must pay the other 10 workers an extra $1 per hour as well. Marginal resource cost is not the $6 for the extra worker-hour, but $6 plus $10 in extra hourly wages for the old workers, or $16!

The monopsonist, like the monopolist, makes profit maximizing decisions at the margin—that is, by weighing each decision in terms of what it adds to revenues vs. what it adds to costs. The decision to hire an extra worker is made by comparing what that worker adds to revenue to what that worker adds to cost. In this case, the 11th worker is hired, because at that quantity of workers, VMP is equal to marginal resource cost. Note, however, that if this firm was a perfect competitor, its marginal resource cost curve would not be so steep. When the competitive firm chooses the quantity of workers, it sets VMP equal to the wage, which is the same as its marginal resource cost; it hires 15 workers instead of 11, and pays an hourly wage of $8 instead of $6. Thus, monopsonistic firms hire fewer workers at lower wages than firms buying labor in more competitive markets.

Pure monopsony is rare. Imperfect competition in labor markets, however, is not. Sometimes imperfect competition in labor markets results from worker immobility, or imperfect information about job opportunities and wages. Other times it results from government restrictions, limiting the number of airlines, TV stations, or banks in a particular area and thus creating monopsony buyers for the specialized skills required in those industries. One of the most powerful government-promoted monopsonies has been in professional sports, where a combination of exemption from antitrust laws, exclusive franchises, and player drafts has limited the number of alternative employers that professional athletes can work for.

The Seller's Side—Human Capital and Rents
Every seller of labor tries to create a little monopoly power by acquiring and marketing unique skills, talents, abilities and experiences that will enable him or her to command a higher price than the nearest substitute. This collection of acquired attributes is called *human capital*, because the process of acquiring these skills is much like the process of accumulating financial or physical capital. In order to acquire human capital, individuals must forego present consumption and devote scarce resources of time and money to acquiring skills through education and training. They will undertake this sacrifice only if they expect to earn a return on their investment in the form of a higher wage than they would otherwise have earned. Instead of investing in stocks, bonds, a fast food franchise, or real estate, they have invested in themselves. Thus, part of their earnings should be wages to labor, but part of it should represent a return to invested capital.

In the process of acquiring human capital, workers also acquire a little monopoly power. There are fewer college graduates than high school graduates, fewer trained machinists than gas station attendants, fewer doctors and lawyers than people with general liberal arts or business or education degrees. The rarer one's skills and training are in relation to demand, the more monopoly power one possesses. The same models that apply to monopolistically competitive, oligopolistic, and monopolistic sellers of products and services also apply to the sellers of labor services under the same conditions. The quantity sold will be smaller and the price (wage) will be higher than in perfect competition.

Some human capital is inherited or inborn—athletic skills, intelligence, musical talent. In most cases further investment is required to develop that skill or talent into marketable human capital. Thus, the return to any particular worker with some degree of uniqueness is a mixture of simple wages, return to capital, and monopoly "profits"—or rents, as they are usually known in the labor market.

Rent (a concept explored more thoroughly in Chapter 19) is any payment to a factor of production in excess of its opportunity cost or next best alternative. If Jack Smith can earn $150,000 a year playing in the NBA and his next best alternative, given his skills and training, is working as a high school coach at $22,000 a year, then $128,000 of his income is economic rent—earnings in excess of his opportunity cost. It does not matter how much of that rent is a return on his investment in his basketball skills and how much simply reflects his monopoly position as the best slam-dunker in the business. All of the return above the value of his next best alternative is defined as economic rent.

Labor Market Discrimination

Some workers, particularly blacks, Hispanics, and women, appear to earn substantially less than equally qualified white males in the same or similar jobs. This information is widely interpreted as evidence of discrimination. Before looking at comparative data and concluding that discrimination is rampant, however, there are a few cautions. One of the slogans of the women's movement throughout the 1970s and 1980s was "59 cents"—women earn 59% of what men earn. This figure has risen somewhat, but is still less than 70%. There are some sound reasons other than discrimination that can explain about two-thirds of the difference. On average, women have less experience than men, and have elected to enter a narrower range of occupations than men. As women gain more experience, the differential should narrow. Women have also historically been concentrated in a fairly narrow range of occupations—"women's jobs" including teaching, nursing, and secretarial jobs. As women have entered in larger numbers into nontraditional occupations, such as business and engineering, the pay differential has also started to drop. There does remain an earnings difference, however, which is not explained by experience or job choice. These same points are valid in explaining the earnings of black and Hispanic workers as well.

When certain occupations are closed to a minority group on the basis of race or sex, the supply of labor in that occupation is restricted, and the supply of labor in "permitted" or "approved" occupations is larger than it otherwise would be. This situation is depicted in Figure 17-6, where panel (a) represents the labor market in the restricted occupation and panel (b) the labor market in the permitted occupation. S_u represents what the labor supply would be in each market in the absence of labor market segmentation, and S_a represents the actual supply with segregated markets. Clearly the wage is higher in the restricted occupation and lower in the permitted occupation than it would be in free and open markets with no discrimination.

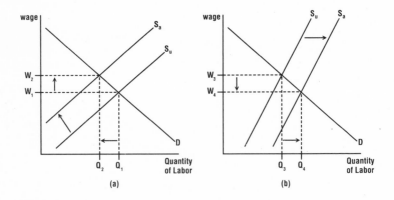

FIG. 17-6 *Labor Market Discrimination*

In a "perfect" market—one where information was abundant and cheap, and changing jobs or workers was costless—such discrimination could not persist. Some bright entrepreneur would hire only blacks, Hispanics and women at the going lower rate and undersell his or her competitors. As the market for "cheaper" non-white, non-male workers expanded in response to the bargain rates, the wages of these workers would rise and the differential would disappear. Thus, the existence and persistence of discrimination suggests that labor markets function somewhat less than perfectly.

LABOR MARKETS AND THE DISTRIBUTION OF INCOME

Wages and salaries are the largest single component of households' income—about two-thirds of total income generated in the U.S. economy, or more than twice the combined value of rent, interest, profits, and the net income of proprietorships. Thus, what happens in labor markets goes a long way to determine who gets what share of total output, and how equal or unequal the distribution of income will be. Much of the rest of income distribution is determined by ownership of financial and physical productive assets, which generate income in the form of rent, interest, dividends, and profits.

The income distribution that results from the market is highly unequal. Even after taxes and transfer payments, which modify the distribution to some extent, it remains highly unequal. In the 1980s, about 5% of income went to the poorest 20% of the population, while more than 40% of income went to the top 20% of income earners. These relative shares have changed very little in the last 40 years. One of the most persistent criticisms of a market system is that it allows great poverty to coexist with great wealth, and results in substantial inequality in the distribution of goods and services. While some people take comfort in observing equally severe inequality in some Communist countries, such as the Soviet Union, the fact remains that income distribution in the U.S. is noticeably less equal than in some other advanced nations, particularly in Western Europe.

CHAPTER PERSPECTIVE

The demand for labor is determined by the value of its marginal product, while the supply reflects increasing opportunity costs. The supply of labor facing a competitive firm is horizontal, and the firm selects a labor quantity by setting the wage equal to the value of marginal product. Labor demand can shift because of changes in worker productivity or changes in the demand for the product that the worker is hired to produce.

Imperfect competition can exist on either side of the labor market. Imperfect competition on the buyer's side is called monopsony. A monopsonistic buyer of labor will hire fewer workers and pay a lower wage than a competitive firm in the same situation. Imperfect competition on the seller's side is similar to monopoly in the sale of goods and services. A monopoly seller of labor will charge a higher price (wage) and offer fewer hours than a competitive seller.

Workers attempt to accumulate human capital in the form of specialized skills, training and experience in order to differentiate themselves and acquire monopoly power in the labor market. Some workers possess special and unique skills so that their wage is much higher than their next best alternative. The difference is called economic rent.

Discrimination in the labor market results in lower earnings for those who are excluded from certain occupations. Discrimination implies that labor markets are not working efficiently.

Labor markets play a major role in determining the distribution of income. In spite of taxes and transfer payments, the distribution of income in the United States is still highly unequal.

FOOTNOTES

1 *Technically, the marginal revenue multiplied by quantity of output for the oligopolist is called marginal revenue product rather than value of marginal product.*

2 *In practice, during times when prices are rising slightly to moderately—2-5% inflation a year—real wages can be allowed to fall simply by increasing them more slowly than the rate of inflation. A little inflation can ease relative wage adjustments by not forcing an actual reduction in the money or nominal wage.*

3 *If the firm, as is likely, is also a monopolist or oligopolist on the seller side of the market, its demand curve for labor will slope downward more steeply than a more competitive firm, because it must reduce the price to sell the extra units of output that extra labor produces.*

Unions, Government, and the Labor Market

INTRODUCTION AND MAIN POINTS

The labor market is complicated not only by elements of monopsony on the buyers' side, and product differentiation on the sellers' side, but also by the presence of two important additional players in the market, unions and government. Unions organize workers to reduce the degree of competition among sellers of labor services. Governments intervene in the labor market in numerous ways, including supervising union elections, setting minimum wages and regulating working conditions. Governments themselves are major employers, and often find themselves negotiating with public employee unions.

After studying the material in this chapter:
— You will be able to describe the role and purpose of labor unions.
— You will know how to explain the advantages and drawbacks of minimum wage laws, plant closing restrictions, and right-to-work laws.
— You will understand the impact and the problems associated with public employee unions.
— You will recognize the many ways in which government affects the workings of labor markets.

WHAT DO UNIONS DO?

Unions are organizations of workers whose purpose is to negotiate collectively with employers in order to improve the economic welfare of their members. That is an American definition of unions, in the tradition of "business unionism" successfully pioneered by Samuel Gompers in the nineteenth century. In Europe and elsewhere, unions often have a political agenda as well. While American unions have had some involvement in politics, supporting candidates and legislation that reflect their interests, their primary issues are bread and butter ones, and they tend to be much less radical and much less anti-capitalist than unions in many other countries.

Exclusive Unions

There are basically two types of unions, the exclusive unions originally organized in the American Federation of Labor (AFL) and the inclusive or industrial unions originally united into the Congress of Industrial Organizations (CIO). The two groups merged in 1955 to form the AFL-CIO, in which both types of unions coexist and sometimes overlap.

Exclusive unions were formed in the skilled trades, such as carpentry, plumbing, and electrical workers. Admission to the union was restricted in order to control the supply of workers. It was not enough to have acquired the necessary skills. One needed a sponsor to join the union, and sponsors were hard to come by without friends or relatives in the union. By restricting the supply of a particular skill, these workers could command a higher price. Unions negotiated contracts with employers that limited hiring to union members, in order to enforce the supply restrictions and keep the wage high. The building trades and professional theatre (later television), all using a variety of skilled crafts, lent themselves to the development of craft unions along the exclusive union model. While exclusive unions have some interest in other labor issues, such as child labor, the minimum wage, and immigration, they tend to be less political because these issues have less direct impact on their wages and working condition than they do with inclusive unions.

Inclusive Unions

Inclusive unions, such as the United Auto Workers (UAW), the United Mine Workers, or the steelworkers, tend to be organized along industry lines rather than craft or trade lines. All the workers in a particular industry, regardless of their particular skill or job title, are welcome in the same union. These unions are inclusive in the sense that they include everyone in the industry that is not management, from floor sweeper to skilled machinist, in the same union. However, the term inclusive refers specifically to the fact that unions of this type are not very interested in restricting their numbers. In fact, their power derives from the large numbers of workers for whom they can speak, and from the power to strike. Since few workers, including the unemployed, are willing to cross a union picket line during a strike, management can be forced to agree to union wage demands in order to continue production. By organizing an inclusive union, perfectly competitive sellers of labor are converted into a monopoly supplier of labor, the union, with much more bargaining power.

Inclusive unions, like exclusive unions, are interested in improving the wages and working conditions of their members, but they approach these goals in a different way. One way is to increase demand for labor, particularly union labor. A second way is to restrict the overall size of the labor force rather than the supply of workers to a particular industry or trade.

Figure 18-1 illustrates exclusive and inclusive unions. In panel (a), the exclusive union raises wages by restricting supply, reducing it from S_n to S_u and raising the wage from W_N to W_u. In panel (b), the inclusive union raises wages by increasing the demand for labor from D_N to D_u, while holding supply fixed through broad effects on aggregate labor supply. As a result, the wage rises from W_N to W_u. However, in the first panel the number of workers has declined (from Q_N to Q_u), while in the second panel the number of workers has increased (again, from Q_N to Q_u).

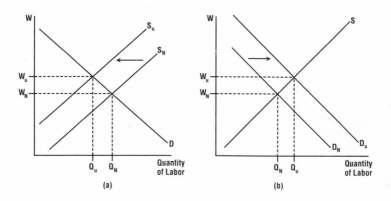

FIG. 18-1 *Exclusive and Inclusive Unions*

Inclusive unions try to increase worker demand by promoting demand for the final product, working together with management. The "Crafted with Pride in the USA" and "Look for the union label" campaigns are good examples of this policy. Inclusive unions often work closely with management to restrict imports in order to expand sales of the domestic product and thus increase demand for labor. These unions also try to encourage substitution of labor for capital through work rules (such as featherbedding) in order to increase labor demand.

At the same time, inclusive unions try to restrict the overall supply of labor in a variety of ways. Unions are generally opposed to liberal immigration laws or to allowing children to work. They support early and generous retirement programs and are generally inclined to think that women's place is in the home, not the workplace. All of these policies would restrict the labor force participation rate and thus the total labor supply, raising wages for those who work.

It is possible for inclusive unions and exclusive unions to cooperate in the AFL-CIO because two of the three strategies are complementary. Expanding labor demand and restricting overall labor supply benefit both inclusive and exclusive unions. Exclusive unions pursue the additional policy of restricting their own numbers, while inclusive unions do not.

CURRENT LABOR CONTROVERSIES
The labor controversies of the 1980s and 1990s are not new or different. These issues have been around for four or five decades and will persist well into the next century. Five broad labor issues are of particular importance and are likely to continue to be at the forefront of public debate; the minimum wage, plant closings, right-to-work laws, public employee unionism, and labor market discrimination.

Raising the Minimum Wage
Raising the minimum wage was an annual issue in Congress throughout the 1980s, but it remained at the $3.35 level set in 1979 for the next ten years.[1] As prices continued to rise, the purchasing power of the minimum wage continued to fall, and fewer and fewer workers, even in entry level, unskilled jobs, were working at that wage. There is no reason not to expect the level of the minimum wage, or even whether there should be any minimum wage at all, to continue to spark controversy in the foreseeable future.

Opponents of a minimum wage, or of an increase in the minimum wage, argue that it reduces the number of entry level jobs. There are some tasks that are not worth paying very much for—stock clerks, floorsweepers, and babysitters, for example. These jobs would be eliminated at a higher minimum wage. Yet, for some workers, such jobs are the only point of entry into the job market. A large share of workers at the minimum wage are not supporting families, or even themselves. Many are teenagers getting some work experience while living at home. Their opportunity to gain experience and move up the work ladder would be impaired by a higher minimum wage. Furthermore, a higher minimum wage pushes up wages all the way up the skill ladder, driving up prices. Thus, critics argue, a higher minimum wage could be responsible for both greater unemployment and more inflation. Finally, they argue, some of the employers of unskilled labor face heavy foreign competition from countries with no minimum wage and very low wages. A higher minimum wage would drive up costs and prices for these firms and make it even more difficult for them to compete.

Advocates of the minimum wage, or an increase in the minimum wage, argue that most markets have some degree of imperfection, and the minimum wage offers some protection and bargaining power to the least organized, most competitive segment of the labor force. They point out that the primary argument against it—higher unemployment among unskilled workers—is based on the existence of highly competitive markets on the buying side, which do not exist in reality. In fact, they argue, there is a degree of monopsony power in most labor markets, and in many cases a higher minimum wage will not result in more unemployment—in fact, it may result in less unemployment!

To visualize these two arguments, consider Figure 18-2. Panel (a) represents the traditional argument that a higher minimum wage reduces the number of jobs, although it does benefit those who remain employed. OL_1 workers keep their jobs at the higher minimum wage W_m, while L_1L_2 workers lose their jobs, and L_2L_3 are attracted into the market by the higher wage and unable to find work. Thus, even critics of the minimum wage would agree that some group of workers benefit from the minimum wage. Depending on elasticity of supply and demand for labor, these gains may even outweigh the losses to the second group who lose their jobs.

In panel (b), the firm has monopsony power, so it determines employment by setting VMP equal to marginal resource cost. Before the minimum wage, the wage was equal to W_1 and there were L_1 workers employed. Now the minimum wage of W_M is imposed. Up to the minimum wage, the firm now faces a horizontal supply curve of labor, on which supply is equal to marginal resource cost. Firms can hire any number of workers up to L_3 at the minimum wage. Beyond that level of worker use, the firm would face the same supply curve and marginal resource cost curve as before. As a result of the minimum wage, this firm is paying a higher wage (W_M) but employing more workers (L_2 instead of L_1). Critics argue that this case would be uncommon, but it does describe a situation where the minimum wage is unequivocally beneficial.

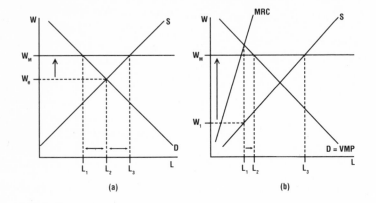

FIG. 18-2 *Two Views of the Minimum Wage*

Clearly there is no simple "right" answer on the issue of the minimum wage. Its impact will be different in different industries, different occupations, and different parts of the country. Its effects depend on the elasticity of supply and demand for labor and the degree of competition on the buyers' side of the unskilled labor market.

Right-to-Work Laws

Right-to-work laws are laws passed by individual states, under authorization in the 1947 Taft-Hartley Act, to outlaw the union shop. A union shop is a plant or firm in which the union contract requires that all new nonmanagement employees must become members of the union within 30 days of hiring. The union shop strengthens the bargaining power of unions. From a union perspective, workers who benefit from union negotiations in their wages and working conditions without belonging to the union or paying dues are "free riders"—the same term used for those who do not contribute to the cost of a public good. A union is a public good, whose successes benefit members and nonmembers alike.

In right-to-work states, a union shop is not permitted to be part of a contract between a union and the employer. Twenty states presently have such a law, most of them in the south and southwest. These laws have been used to attract industry away from states where union shops are permitted. In general, business firms have favored right-to-work laws, while unions have lobbied hard against them, because such laws shift the uneasy balance of power between unions and the firms with whom they deal.

Plant Closings

Plant closing legislation is a convenient but misleading name for a variety of legislation specifying what firms are required to do when they close a plant. Some of this legislation has been enacted at the state level; after several years of consideration by Congress, a bill addressing plant closings was passed and signed into law by President Reagan in 1988. The focus of most of the controversy revolves around the amount of notice that must be given to employees, in order to allow them to search for alternative employment.

With exemptions for small firms and for emergency situations, the new federal law requires that firms planning to close a plant give their employees 60 days notice. (Such a requirement has been the law for many years in Canada, Japan, and most of the nations of Western Europe.) Proponents of the 1988 law argued that this requirement will reduce the hardship on employees by giving them more lead time to locate other employment. Critics argue that it is costly to firms, who lose some of their best workers before the actual shutdown takes place, and see more workers taking vacations, sick time, and other benefits in anticipation of the end—all of which can seriously reduce production. Like right-to-work laws, this law has been a battleground between lobbyists for union groups and business organizations. Experience in the 1990s should determine whether advocates or critics of this law were correct in their predictions.

225

Public Employee Unions

Governments—federal, state, and local—are major employers in the U.S. About 15 percent of the U.S. labor force is employed by government. A number of these workers are represented by unions. In some states these unions have the right to strike, while in other states (and with the federal government), they do not have that right. Often public employees provide vital services for which the risk or cost of interruption is a serious public concern—air traffic controllers, police, fire protection, public school teachers, and others.

In some situations the government is a monopsony buyer of services. It is the only market for military employees, and local and state government are the major employers of people who want to provide law enforcement services, although there are some private jobs in providing protection and security. Thus, with some monopsony power on the buyer's side of the market, a case could be made for the value of a union in creating some counterbalancing market power on the sellers' side. However, the public sector is somewhat different from the private sector, in that there is less pressure to resist wage demands in the public sector. There is no profit-or-loss test, and it is often possible to raise taxes to accommodate public employees, especially when employee salaries are a relatively modest part of the total budget. Public employees are also voters, often very active, organized and informed voters, and can put pressure on their employer at the ballot box. For this reason, some critics of public employee unions would like to put more restrictions on their bargaining rights, especially their right to strike.

Equal Opportunity, Affirmative Action, and Comparable Worth

A final, important issue in the labor market is that of discrimination, especially on the basis of race or sex. Legislation in the 1960s made it illegal to discriminate, but put the burden of proof on the person who was rejected to prove discrimination. Affirmative action, an experiment largely confined to the 1970s, required firms doing business with the federal government to come up with a specific plan to increase opportunities for women and minorities. Both of these strategies have had some limited effectiveness in breaking down barriers to opportunities in professions and industries that had discriminated in the past.

In the 1980s, the most recent attempt to reduce perceived labor market discrimination, particularly against women, took the form of comparable worth legislation. Such legislation would require that some agency or commission attempt to measure the "value" of an occupation in terms of skills and training required and other factors, and determine what constitutes jobs of equal worth in order to insist on equal pay. Comparable worth is an indirect attack on race and sex discrimination in the labor market. To date, objections from many quarters of the labor market have kept such legislation from being enacted at the federal level.

GOVERNMENT AND LABOR MARKETS

As these five issues suggest, governments at all levels have played and continue to play an important role in labor markets. The minimum wage is federally legislated. Plant closing laws, right-to-work laws, and comparable worth all require legislative action. In addition, governments play other important roles in the labor market. Landmark legislation in the 1930s and 1940s defined the rights and obligations of unions. Government regulation plays an important role in workplace safety and other working conditions. Finally, governments are themselves major employers, and their wages, working conditions, and discriminatory or non-discriminatory practices spill over to the private market.

Government and Unions

Unions had a long fight for recognition that culminated in the Norris-LaGuardia Act (1932) and the Wagner Act (1935) that guaranteed workers the legal right to organize and bargain collectively, and forbade certain union-busting activities practiced by business firms. The result of this legislation was a rapid increase in unionization of the U.S. labor force. After World War II, anti-union reaction led to the passage of the Taft-Hartley Act in 1947, which placed restrictions on unions and authorized state right-to-work laws.

The National Labor Relations Board is a federal agency, created in 1935, that oversees union elections and takes actions against firms engaging in illegal anti-union tactics. Thus, the federal government plays an important role in making sure that both unions and business firms play according to a defined set of labor relations rules.

Government Regulation in Labor Markets

One of the most important government regulations in the labor market is the minimum wage. The federal government also regulates hours, overtime, and safety conditions through a variety of laws and agencies. Overtime and pay requirements for excess hours over a specified number are set by the federal government and enforced through the Department of Labor. The Occupational Safety and Health Administration (OSHA) is responsible for regulating workplace safety.

These regulations are somewhat controversial. Free market advocates would argue that the worker should be informed of risks and allowed to decide whether to enter a hazardous occupation. Certainly such regulations increase the costs of production and reduce the number of jobs and the level of output that a society enjoys. There is no easy way to measure the lives saved or injuries avoided against the costs that regulations create in terms of lost jobs and output.

Governments as Employers

Finally, the government is a significant employer. Fifteen percent of the labor force works for the government. In many state capitals, or in small towns with federal or state facilities (hospitals, prisons, military bases) the ratio is much higher; sometimes the state government or a federal installation is effectively a monopsony or oligopsony buyer of many kinds of labor services. In a small town where a government agency is the major employer, the wages of secretaries, janitors, and other workers also employed privately are likely to be determined by the government as the principal employer and spill over to private industry in the area.

If the government pays well, private firms must offer competitive wages and fringe benefits to be able to attract employees. If, as is more likely, the government facility does not pay particularly well, then private firms in the area may enjoy some "bargains" in terms of labor costs that firms in other areas may not. The government is a large enough employer to significantly affect the wage structure, the pattern of fringe benefits, the degree of discrimination, and other factors that describe labor market conditions. Often it has the opportunity to have a greater impact on the labor market by example than by legislation affecting private employers.

CHAPTER PERSPECTIVE

Unions are organizations of employees that bargain on behalf of their members for better wages and working conditions. Exclusive unions operate primarily by limiting supply, restricting entry into the union. Inclusive unions try to improve their members' welfare by increasing demand for labor and also by restricting the supply of labor in general rather than to a particular occupation.

Raising the minimum wage is a perennial labor issue. Critics argue that it reduces jobs, increases inflation, and makes some American firms less able to compete in world markets. Proponents argue that beneficiaries may exceed losers, and that in some cases a higher minimum wage would actually increase employments as well as wages.

Right-to-work laws forbid a union shop contract and make it more difficult to develop a strong union base in states with such laws. Plant closing legislation requires firms that are closing plants to give adequate notice to their employees in order to permit them to seek work elsewhere. Public employee unions represent workers employed by federal, state, and local governments, and are often not permitted to strike.

Legislation in the 1960s and 1970s attempted to reduce labor market discrimination through equal employment opportunities and affirmative action. In the 1980s, a further attempt at reducing discrimination, primarily sex discrimination, proposed that the government determine the comparable worth of various occupations and require that workers be paid accordingly. This proposal has met sharp criticism from some quarters as excessive interference in the workings of markets.

Governments play many important roles in labor markets, as overseers of union-business firm relations, as regulators of hours and working conditions, and as major employers. In many markets, the government as a major employer sets the local standard for the private sector for wages, fringe benefits, and working conditions.

FOOTNOTE

1 *Legislation passed in 1989 provided for modest increases in the minimum wage in 1990 and 1991.*

Enterprise, Profit, Land, and Rent

INTRODUCTION AND MAIN POINTS

The last two chapters have explored the workings of labor markets, and an earlier chapter looked at capital and capital markets. There are two other important factors of production: enterprise, which earns profits, and land (including raw materials, climate, rainfall, and other gifts of nature), which earns rent. These two factors of production and their earnings are the subject of this chapter.

The role of the entrepreneur is a central one in a market economic system, because the entrepreneur takes risks and develops new products and methods of production. These are the dynamic activities that keep a market system changing, growing, and responsive to changing forces around it. Successes are rewarded with profits, and failures are penalized by losses.

The role of land and natural resources is often of great importance in determining what products a nation will produce, export, and import. Natural resources have been an important foundation for U.S. development. They are, however, neither a guarantee nor a requirement for economic success. Japan has demonstrated that ample natural resources are far less critical to successful economic development than enterprise, while countries like Brazil and Mexico offer convincing evidence that natural resources alone are not enough to succeed.

After studying the material in this chapter:

▬ You will understand the role of the entrepreneur and the function of profit in a market system.

▬ You will see how to distinguish between invention and innovation, normal profit and economic profit.

▬ You will be able to explain the advantages and disadvantages of taxing normal profits and economic profits.

▬ You will be able to explain what determines the amount of rent, or the price paid for the use of land.

THE ROLE OF THE ENTREPRENEUR IN A MARKET SYSTEM

The market system assumes that there will be entrepreneurs. A capitalistic system would stagnate without those persons of vision and imagination, who have an eye to profit and an ear to the public's tastes and desires, who can take a new idea and identify and exploit its commercial possibilities, and who can also organize, manage, and supervise the production process. Some of these latter functions can be carried out by highly paid and highly skilled managerial employees, as they usually are in larger firms. Except for very small firms, part or all of the management role of the entrepreneur is usually delegated. Two basic functions of the entrepreneur, however, cannot be shifted to skilled management. These functions are innovation and risk-taking.

Invention and Innovation

The process of developing new ideas and making them commercially feasible is really a two-stage process, consisting of invention followed by innovation. The first stage, invention, is the new idea—the better mousetrap, the new chemical compound, the restyled car, the brand new electronic product like compact discs and high resolution TV. Sometimes these new ideas emerge from the lone inventor, a Steve Jobs in his garage developing Apple computers, the modern-day Thomas Edisons. They may also emerge from the company's own research division in larger companies, although the inventions from this source are more likely to be refinements of existing products or concepts. Inventions may develop from external research at universities or private research groups, or as by-products of other scientific activities— Teflon as a by-product of the space program, for example.

Invention is not an entrepreneurial role; in fact, no one is really certain how to make invention happen. It is the task of the entrepreneur to seek out such inventions, identify their commercial potential, organize the production process, and get the new or improved product on the market. This series of steps is called innovation. The first wave of entrepreneurs makes a profit with an innovation, and other entrepreneurs follow in their wake, lured by the signal of profit. The second wave of entrepreneurs produces similar products, expanding the range of consumer choice with minor variations and increasing competition in the market until the original profits are largely eliminated.

Risk and Profit

The second role of the entrepreneur, in addition to innovation, is to take risks. The risk undertaken is that one will guess wrong on a product or market, lose one's capital, go bankrupt, and have to start over. Entrepreneurs take risks in order to earn profits, which are the reward for risk-taking. Unlike wages for labor, interest on capital, or rent on land, there is no close relationship between the amount of risk undertaken and the profits that result. Sometimes losses result, other times very small profits. But it is only those who are willing to assume risks that earn any profit at all.

In modern capitalistic economies, the role of the entrepreneur has become diffused. A large part of profits go to stockholders as a reward for taking the risk of ownership. Capital lent to the firm in the form of bonds or other loans is promised a specific interest return as long as the firm does not go bankrupt. Common stockholders have no similar dividend guaranteed. If the firm does well, their dividends will be large and the value of their shares will rise; if the firm does poorly, their dividends will be small or nonexistent and the value of their ownership shares will fall. A firm may have no real entrepreneur in both the innovating and risk-taking senses, just innovating managers and risk-taking stockholders. That is, the stockholders take the risks while the top management is responsible for the innovating role of the entrepreneur. When top management includes some major stockholders, these people may combine both entrepreneurial functions to some degree.

THE FUNCTION OF PROFIT

The purpose of profit is twofold. It is a reward to enterprise, to risk-taking and innovation, in order to encourage more of both. It is also a signal to the second tier of entrepreneurs to follow the leaders into more lucrative ventures. A certain normal amount of profit is built into the cost functions discussed earlier. Profits in excess of that amount are economic profits.

Normal Profits

Normal profits are a cost. They are the normal return to the innovating-organizing-risk taking functions of enterprise, just enough to pay the opportunity cost of the next best use of those entrepreneurial resources. Normal profits will neither attract new firms into the industry nor be so low as to drive entrepreneurs out of the industry. Normal profits will vary from industry to industry, depending on other (nonmonetary) attractions of that industry and the amount of risk and other entrepreneurial effort required to earn that profit. In equilibrium, the representative firm is earning normal profit and only normal profit—no more, no less.

Economic Profits as Signals

Economic profits are any profits in excess of the normal level. These profits indicate high demand and opportunity for capital owners to reallocate their resources and for entrepreneurs to follow a path pioneered by someone else in exploiting a newly discovered market opportunity—a new product, a new group of buyers, a new taste or fad, a new location. If barriers to entry do not prevent risk-takers and innovators (entrepreneurs) from responding to the signal, new firms will enter the market, shifting the market supply to the right, competing for scarce resources so as to drive cost curves up, reducing price, and eliminating the economic profits that attracted them in the first place. Having fulfilled their signalling function of expanding supply, economic profits disappear. Only if barriers to entry exist can economic profits persist.

It is easy to confuse economic profits with rent. Economic profits are the result of an increase in demand and/or a reduction in costs that signals other firms to enter the market or expand output. Economic rents are earnings in excess of opportunity costs, as we discussed earlier. In the absence of barriers to entry, economic profits will serve their purpose and disappear. Rents, however, can persist. A firm or resource earns rents because it possesses some unique advantage—a personable owner, a great chef, a prime location, control over a particularly important input. Even if the average or representative firm in the industry ceases to earn economic profits, some firms may continue to earn what appears to be more than normal profits but is actually economic rent.

For most purposes, society treats rents and persistent monopoly profits the same way, because they are very similar in their origin and effects. They derive from special circumstances, and they serve no useful purpose of bringing about expansion of output or rewarding risk-taking and innovation.

Taxing Profits

The federal government taxes corporate net income, or profits. So do a majority of state governments, and a handful of local governments. During the "energy crisis" of the 1970s, there was a "windfall profits tax" on the excess profits of domestic oil-producing firms that resulted from the increase in the price of oil because of actions of OPEC, the international oil cartel. How and why do governments tax profits, and what effects do these taxes have?

The principal tax on corporate profits is the federal corporate income tax (at different rates from those paid by individuals), and the principal tax on the profits of proprietorships is the federal personal income tax.[1] Corporate profits take the form of net income of corporations after all expenses have been paid, and it is this net income that is subject to the federal tax. Corporate net income corresponds roughly to the economist's concept of normal plus economic profit.

This profit, or net corporate income, is used to pay taxes, to pay dividends to stockholders, and to retain and reinvest in the corporation. When stockholders receive dividends, on which corporate income taxes have already been paid, they are taxed again as personal income. When the corporation retains earnings and reinvests them in the firm, the value of the firm's assets grow and, if the stock market is at all efficient, the value of the stockholders' shares will increase. If the stockholder sells the shares, the increase in value is subject to personal income taxes at the capital gains rate. Sometimes capital gains receive more favorable tax rates. Currently, they are taxed at the same rate as ordinary income.

Thus, while all corporate profits are eventually subject to taxation twice, the second part of the tax (the personal income tax on the owners or stockholders) is deferred when income is retained by the corporation. Retained earnings are only subject to tax when they affect the value of the stock and the stock is then sold, creating a taxable capital gain. Thus, the tax system favors retaining corporate net earnings over paying dividends.

The treatment of corporate net income for tax purposes continues to be a source of controversy. Business lobbyists point to the unfairness of double taxation, while their opponents point to all of the special provisions in the tax law that are available to reduce tax burdens on corporations but not individuals, and the generally lower rates on corporate net income. Each revision of the tax code raises the question of appropriate treatment of corporate profits anew.

LAND AND LAND RENTS

The last factor of production is land—raw land (improvements, such as dikes, buildings, clearing timber, and draining swamps are classed as capital), forests, rivers, rainfall, climate, soil quality, minerals, and all kinds of raw materials. The original ownership of most land and land rights is shrouded in history; in the U.S., much of it goes back to treaties made and broken with the original inhabitants, royal charters, homesteading arrangements, and a patchwork of other methods of allocating land among competing claimants. Water rights belong to the riparian (waterfront) owner or the owner above the groundwater in the east, but are established by prior appropriations in western states. Owners have found that their title to land does not extend in many cases to mineral rights, timber rights, or water rights. The Federal government leases rights to harvest timber, oil, and other resources on federal land, including offshore drilling rights. In terms of determining ownership and defining property rights, land is the most complex of the four types of productive resources. In this section we will focus primarily on land in the narrow sense—acreage, location, soil quality, and scenic beauty. Raw materials and other aspects of land are sufficiently similar to the commodities discussed in earlier chapters that they do not require separate treatment.

Rent and Land Prices

The price paid for the use of land is termed rent. If the land is rented by a tenant farmer, then explicit rent is paid. If the land is used by the owner, then one of the owner's costs of operation is implicit rent, an opportunity cost that should be subtracted in order to correctly determine profit.

Recall that the term "economic rent" was used in Chapter 17 to describe the earnings of a worker in excess of his or her next best alternative. The excess earnings resulted from some unique quality the worker possessed—acting talent, athletic ability, etc. This rent payment was the difference between the actual payment and the amount needed to call the resource forth. The term originated with land because no payment is necessary to call land forth. Land is just there. The purpose of land rent, and indeed of all economic rent, is to decide who gets to use the resource.

Figure 19-1 illustrates the allocation of a fixed stock of land among competing users. The opportunity cost of the land is zero, because there is a fixed stock that will be there at any price.

However, the demand curve intersects this fixed stock at a positive price. If land were given away, the quantity demanded would exceed the quantity supplied by amount AB. Competition for land through bidding would drive the price up to rent R_1, at which price the market is cleared. The sole function of rent is to allocate a scarce resource among competing users. The second function of price, to call forth an increase in quantity supplied, does not work in this case because there is no more land to come forth.

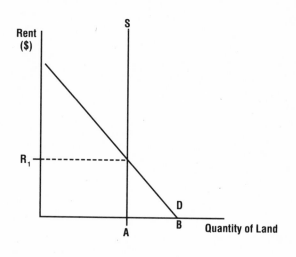

FIG. 19-1 *Land Rent*

Land is not a uniform commodity. It varies in many characteristics. For farming, soil quality and rainfall are important. For other purposes, location—near cities, near major highways, or near recreation areas—is the most important characteristic. The price a piece of land commands depends on what attributes it possesses. The least desirable land will command a low rent, and the most desirable land—downtown Manhattan, beachfront, or along an interstate—will command proportionally higher prices because more buyers are interested in owning those pieces of real estate. Competition for the most desirable land will drive up the price. As the most desirable land—the closest to the city or highway, the easiest to build on, or the best soil quality—is put to use, buyers will move on the less desirable land, which will command a lower price. As population increases with a fixed stock of land, the prices of all grades of land will increase together, but in the same hierarchy of relative prices.

Capitalization and Land Prices

The price of a unit of land is the present value of its expected future stream of income or services. This is the same method that is used to value most income-producing assets. Those future services may be highly subjective, or they may be easily translated into dollars of farm crops, revenue from a high traffic downtown store location, or a higher price that a house can command because of the choice residential location. If something happens to change that expected future income stream, the impact will be felt in the current selling price of the land. That is, changes in property taxes, access to highways, value of water or mineral rights, zoning classification, or other important rights attached to a unit of property will be incorporated into its price.

Consider a parcel of land with a present value of $10,000. This value reflects the expected future net revenues from the best available use of that land, discounted at the market interest rate. Now suppose that the local property tax rate increases and, as a result, the property taxes on this parcel rise sharply. What will happen to its price? The projected net revenue in each subsequent year will be less because of the higher taxes. At the same interest rate, its present value and its selling price will fall, perhaps to $9,500. The increased property tax has been capitalized, i.e., incorporated into the current market value of the property. The burden of the increased tax falls entirely on the owner at the time the property tax was raised, because if that person keeps the property, he or she must pay the higher taxes; if it is sold, that person receives a lower price. The next owner must pay the higher taxes, but is compensated by a lower purchase price.

The same principle applies to all kinds of changes that affect the expected future income from a parcel of land. The costs or benefits of rezoning, the noise from a newly located airport or smell from a sewage treatment facility that suddenly appears in your backyard, all accrue to those who owned the property at the time the decision was announced. The next owner buys the property at a higher or lower price with the zoning, airport noise, or sewage smell as part of the package.

Choosing a Location

Understanding capitalization is helpful in making locational decisions, which are one of the most common uses of the cost-benefit calculations described in several earlier chapters. If the market is functioning efficiently, the relative advantages and drawbacks of various locations are reflected in their relative prices. Does this mean that it does not matter which location you select? Not necessarily. The price of the land may not reflect all of the potential uses, just the most likely ones or the ones that have come to the seller's attention.[2]

If you have decided that a particular location will be a high traffic spot for a souvenir shop, you may be willing to pay a higher price for that lot than someone looking for a site for a fast food franchise or a shoe repair shop. Your present value will be higher, and your rival bidders may settle for a lower traffic, lower priced location. The market will allocate the site to the most profitable use. If a piece of land seems artificially cheap, it might be worth checking on what hidden drawbacks—easements, rights of way, trains running by in the middle of the night—that have been capitalized into its price.

It is not possible to make a good site decision without fitting the site into the total picture of the firm's operations. If you have a good grasp of projected operating costs and revenues at that site, then you can discount the expected net revenues for some reasonable time horizon, estimate the resale value of the land at the end of that time, and determine whether its present value to you is equal to or greater than the asking price. You will need to compare this site with other sites offering different locational advantages and drawbacks and therefore different projected net revenues before making a decision. Finally, to complete the cost-benefit analysis of alternative sites, it is necessary to figure in all the other, non-quantitative considerations—whether managers or workers will have to relocate or face long commuting times, how customer loyalty will be affected, and other concerns.

CHAPTER PERSPECTIVE

The entrepreneur plays a central role in a market system as the innovator and risk taker. Inventions can be generated in a variety of ways, but it is the entrepreneur's task to make those inventions commercially feasible. Entrepreneurs innovate and take risks in hope of making profits, which are the reward for these two functions. Normal profit is a part of costs and covers the opportunity cost of keeping entrepreneurial resources in this firm instead of elsewhere. Economic profits are profits in excess of this normal level and serve as a signal to enter the industry and expand production.

Corporate profits are subject to federal corporate income taxes as well as state and even local corporate income taxes in many states. Corporate profits are taxed twice, once to the corporation and again to the owners when they receive dividend income or when they receive capital gains on the sale of their stock. Proprietors' net income, which includes their profits, is subject to ordinary personal income taxes.

Land includes all natural resources and earns rent, which in the broad sense means any payment to a factor of production in excess of the amount necessary to call it forth. Different prices for different units of land reflect the advantages and drawbacks of these different units. For farm land, such factors as soil quality, fertility, and rainfall are important. For other uses, location is the most important factor. The selling price of a unit of land reflects the present value of the expected future net earnings, discounted at the market rate of interest. If any of the attributes of a unit of land change—taxes, zoning, adjacent uses—the value of expected future net income from that land will also change and be reflected in its price. Thus, when such changes occur, all the costs or benefits accrue to the present owner of the land.

FOOTNOTES

1 *This brief discussion cannot possibly do justice to the complexities of these two taxes. We will limit our discussion to the economic effects of these taxes. The reader may want to look in another volume in this series for a more detailed treatment of taxation of corporations and proprietorships.*

2 *One of the best examples of different perception occurred in some older cities early in the process of "gentrification"—reclaiming older, rundown buildings for middle and upper income housing with extensive remodelling. The seller saw a run-down building in a deteriorating neighborhood; the early buyers saw the potential of an old, well-constructed building.*

Keeping Up: A Guide to Economic Information

INTRODUCTION AND MAIN POINTS

Economics is a discipline that continues to grow, develop, and change in response to new ideas and new challenges. While the theory in this book will stand you in good stead in analyzing most microeconomic problems, what you have learned is only the tip of the iceberg. An economically literate person needs to keep abreast of new economic developments of interest in his or her business or occupation. Individuals must also keep abreast of public policy issues that concern everyone as citizens as well as affecting them personally in their roles as buyers, workers, and entrepreneurs.

Economic tools and knowledge, like all capital, will decay with lack of use. Reading regularly from a good mix of books, magazines, and other sources will help you keep your economics human capital ready for use. This chapter is basically an annotated bibliography to assist you in continuing your economic education.

WHAT DOES A BUSINESS MANAGER NEED TO KNOW?

This question is a favorite of college students. What do I need to know? How will this course, or this knowledge, help me in my chosen career or in daily life? After they graduate and start working, they will discover—as readers of this book may already know—that everything you learn and know is useful sometime, somewhere, often when you least expect it to be needed.

A business manager needs to know some basic economic principles in order to more fully appreciate interactions with customers, suppliers, and employees. What are their motives? What incentives are they responding to, and what kinds of incentives do I need to offer? What are their costs and benefits in this situation? What constraints do they face? Managers also need to know, or even anticipate, changes in the environment in which they work—market conditions such as labor availability, interest rates, and price level changes, as well as government-created conditions such as tax laws and environmental regulations. Keeping up with the business press will keep you alert to what is going on. Feeding that information into what you have already learned will help you to use that information to understand how such changes affect you and how you should respond.

A lifelong economics reading habit should include several newspapers or periodicals on a regular basis and at least one book a month on economics or business topics. This steady diet should keep you abreast and provide ample raw material for practicing your economics skills.

EXPANDING YOUR BASE: TEXTBOOKS

Before you embark on your reading program, you may want to expand your command of the basic tools of managerial economics, and perhaps expand those skills to include some macroeconomics (aggregate economics and public policy). If you would like to shore up basic skills, there are a variety of principles textbooks designed for both the one semester and the two semester market that should be suitable. Here are a few of them.

One-semester books:

Gordon, Sanford D., and George G. Dawson, *Introductory Economics*, 6th edition, Lexington, MA: D.C. Heath and Company, 1987.

Hailstones, Thomas, *Basic Economics*, 8th edition, Cincinnati, OH: Southwestern Publishing, 1988.

Mabry, Rodney H., and Holley H. Ulbrich, *Introduction to Economic Principles*, New York: McGraw Hill, 1989.

Reynolds, Lloyd, *The American Economy in Perspective*, 2nd edition, New York: McGraw Hill, 1987.

Two-semester books:

Amacher, Ryan C., and Holley H. Ulbrich, *Principles of Economics*, 4th edition: Cincinnati, OH: Southwestern Publishing Co., 1989.

Baumol, William J., and Blinder, Alan S., *Economics: Principles and Policy*, 4th ed., San Diego: Harcourt Brace Jovanovich, 1988.

Byrns, Ralph, and Gerald Stone, *Principles of Economics*, 5th edition: Glenview, IL: Scott Foresman, 1989.

If you feel like you would like to move to a more sophisticated level, there are a number of textbooks written for intermediate microeconomic theory that would be a logical next step. Here are a few of the more popular titles:

Browning, Edgar K., and Jacquelene M. Browning, *Microeconomic Theory and Applications*, 3rd ed. Boston: Little, Brown and Co, 1989.

Lindsay, Cotton Mather, *Applied Price Theory*, 2nd ed. New York: Dryden Press, 1988.

Leftwich, Richard H., and Ross Eckert, *The Price System and Resource Allocation*, 10th edition. Homewood, IL: Dryden Press, 1988.

These books, or similar ones, are available at college bookstores or in many libraries. It would probably be a good idea to add one or more of them to your permanent collection.

KEEPING UP WITH EVENTS: PERIODICALS

The best newspaper for business and economics news is *The Wall Street Journal* in the United States. *The New York Times* also has good financial coverage. Weekly magazines include *Business Week*, *Forbes*, and (from the United Kingdom, with a global view) *The Economist*.

Other, less frequent periodicals of interest in both economics and business include:

Challenge: The Magazine of Economic Affairs. This bimonthly magazine is designed for a popular audience and looks at current public policy issues.

Harvard Business Review, Inc., Fortune and *Forbes*, all monthly, cover a variety of business and economic issues in a lively and timely manner.

The *Reviews* (or in Chicago, *Perspectives*) of the 12 regional Federal Reserve banks mix rather technical articles with public policy discussions and descriptions of economic conditions in their respective regions.

The Conference Board publishes monthly business indicators in its *Statistical Bulletin* as well as periodic research reports.

Major universities in most states often publish a monthly or quarterly review that focuses on state and regional business and economic concerns. Check your library or call the business school at your state university.

Articles of personal financial interest can be found monthly in *Changing Times* and *Money*.

The U.S. Department of Labor publishes the *Monthly Labor Review*, which is a good source for labor statistics, price indexes, and articles on labor markets and labor issues. The U.S. Commerce Department publishes (also monthly) the *Survey of Current Business*, with a variety of business data and some brief articles. This periodical tends to focus on the national picture, but there is some data on particular industries.

The National Association of Business Economists issues a quarterly, *Business Economics*, that is quite appropriate for a business audience.

In addition to general interest articles in economics and business, the book reviews and ads in some of these periodicals will keep you informed of new and interesting titles in economics and business that you may want to read.

GENERAL INTEREST READING LIST

Good books in economics and business are hard to find. The business/economics shelf in most popular bookstores is small, hidden, and full of titles on investing in real estate, get-rich-quick schemes, and similar titles. More serious and substantive books call for a detective, or at least a starter reading list. We offer a short list of titles in several areas: collections of readings, the popular economic press, and economic novels.

The following titles are collections of readings of current interest. Most are designed as supplementary reading for college students, but they should appeal to a much broader audience. These collections, or similar ones, are available at many college bookstores or from the publisher.

Annual Editions: Economics, Guilford, CT: Dushkin Publishing Group, Inc., annual collection of readings on current economic issues.

Adams, John (ed), *The Contemporary International Economy: A Reader*, 3rd edition. New York: St. Martin's Press, 1987. Although designed for a college audience, this collection of readings on international issues is accessible and interesting to the general interest reader with a minimal economics background.

Carson, Robert B., *Economic Issues Today: Alternative Approaches*, 4th ed. New York: St. Martin's Press, 1986. This unusual collection of readings looks at current macro and micro issues—poverty, unemployment, monopoly, etc.—from conservative, liberal, and radical perspectives.

North, Douglass C., and Roger LeRoy Miller, *The Economics of Public Issues*, 7th ed. New York: Harper and Row, 1987;

and Miller, Roger LeRoy and Daniel K. Benjamin, *The Economics of Macro Issues*, St. Paul, MN: West Publishing Co., 1989. This matched set is also a popular college supplement; short essays on economic questions stressing current events and current applications.

Swartz, Thomas and Frank Bonello, *Taking Sides: Clashing Views on Controversial Economic Issues*, 4th ed. Guilford, CT: Dushkin Publishing Group, 1988. This collection of reprints pairs pro and con views on plant closings, right-to-work laws, poverty, discrimination, and a variety of other issues.

The next group of books represents the "popular press" in economics—recognized good economists and good writers across the political spectrum. All of these writers know how to make economics accessible and interesting to the general reading public. Each of them has a point of view, a range of interests, and a style of presentation that makes them uniquely appealing. Most of these names will be familiar, and most of these books are available at good bookstores and libraries.

Blinder, Alan S., *Hard Heads, Soft Hearts: Tough-Minded Economics for a Just Society*, Reading, MA; Addison-Wesley, 1988. A recent work arguing that economic policy must be both efficient (hard heads) and compassionate (soft hearts), with applications to macroeconomics and to international trade policy.

Boulding, Kenneth, *Economics as a Science*, New York: McGraw Hill, 1970. This out-of-print classic may be available at the library. Boulding is one of the most philosophical of twentieth century economists, and that approach is reflected in this collection of essays. Boulding is also the author of *Human Betterment*, Beverly Hills: Sage Publications, 1985. In this book, he makes a case for economists using normative (evaluative) analysis where values are clearly spelled out, rather than pretending to a scientific objectivity that does not really stand up to scrutiny.

Friedman, Milton, *Capitalism and Freedom*, Chicago: The University of Chicago Press, 1981. This classic defense of capitalism is designed for a popular audience. Friedman and his wife Rose are also the authors of *Free to Choose*, New York: Harcourt, Brace, Jovanovich, 1980, another conservative classic that makes a lucid and compelling case for using markets to address problems.

Galbraith, John K., *Economics in Perspective*, New York: Houghton Mifflin, 1987. This is the most recent work from the prolific pen of this retired Harvard economist and former Ambassador to India, who is a witty and caustic critic of the American economic system.

Heilbroner, Robert L., *The Nature and Logic of Capitalism*, New York: Norton, 1985. Heilbroner, another excellent writer, takes a critical look at the workings of a market economic system in this book. His most recent work, a collection of essays, is *Behind the Veil of Economics: Essays in the Worldly Philosophy*, New York: Norton, 1988.

Okun, Arthur M., *Equality and Efficiency: The Big Trade-off*, Washington, D.C.: Brookings Institution, 1975. Okun was a Yale economist and chaired the Council of Economic Advisers in the 1960s. This book is another economic classic, addressing a conflict between making markets work well and looking after the "losers" in a market system that is probably the most fundamental issue facing capitalism.

Schelling, Thomas, *Micromotives and Macrobehavior*, New York: W.W. Norton, 1978, and *Choice and Consequence*, Cambridge, MA: Harvard University Press, 1984. Schelling writes nonmathematical game theory, or applications of economic principles to problems of group choice and group decisions—where people sit at concerts, why private solutions to highway congestion don't occur, and other intriguing questions with broad applications to business, economics, and daily life.

Stigler, George, *The Intellectual and the Marketplace*, Cambridge, MA: Harvard University Press, 1984. This University of Chicago Nobel Laureate is a wise and witty observer of the economic scene, as these essays will demonstrate.

Thurow, Lester, *Dangerous Currents: The State of Economics*, New York: Vintage Books, 1984; *The Zero Sum Society*, New York: Penguin Books, 1981; *The Zero Sum Solution*, New York, Simon and Schuster, 1986. The dean of the Sloan School of Management at MIT is a "pundit"—an economist frequently called upon to comment on current affairs by the media. These three books are accessible to the general reader and make some complex issues and topics, such as efficient markets and rational expectations, something that any educated person can comprehend.

If you exhaust this list and are still searching for your favorite economic author, you may want to try one or more of the following. These authors have also written works of general interest, although most are less widely known outside professional economics circles.

Lee, Dwight R. and Richard B. McKenzie, *Regulating Government*, New York: Lexington Books, 1986. Discusses the role of government and the use of constitutions as a way of constraining government.

McKenzie, Richard B., *Fairness of Markets: A Search for Justice in a Free Society*, Lexington, MA: Heath, Lexington Books, 1987. A restatement for the lay person of the conservative positions on such issues as trade policy, minimum wages, and plant closings. McKenzie also has several other popular books out on current economic issues.

Alchian, Armen A., *Economic Forces at Work*, Indianapolis, IN: Liberty Press, 1977. A collection of essays on the economics of information, property rights, cost, and inflation by one of the most influential microeconomists of the twentieth century.

Rhoads, Stephen E., *The Economist's View of the World: Government, Markets, and Public Policy*, New York: Cambridge University Press, 1985. Looks at what economics has contributed to the other social sciences, considers the limitations of economics.

Schultze, Charles L., *The Public Use of Private Interest*, Washington, D.C.: Brookings Institution, 1977. Describes how public policy can harness private self-interest to accomplish societal objectives.

Sowell, Thomas, *Markets and Minorities*, New York: Basic Books, 1981. The nation's best known black economist discusses the reasons why minorities, especially blacks, do and do not succeed in a market system.

The economics novel as an art form is still in the developmental stage, but there are a few good ones that have appeal to the economics-minded general reader:

Jevons, Marshall (pseudonym), *Murder at the Margin* (1978), Glen Ridge, NJ: Thomas Horton and Daughters; and *The Fatal Equilibrium* (1985), Cambridge, MA: MIT Press. Two murder mysteries; the detective, an economics professor, uses economic theory to solve the case. These may be difficult to locate, but are worth the effort.

Pool, John Charles and Ross M. LaRoe, *Default!*, New York: St. Martin's Press, 1988. An international economics spy story, based on the Third World debt crisis.

Erdman, Paul, *The Billion Dollar Sure Thing*, Berkley Books, New York, 1974. A dated but still interesting novel of international financial intrigue. Erdman has several other novels on similar topics.

Finally, no general interest reading list in any social science discipline would be complete without a timeless classic:

Huff, Darrell and Irving Geis, *How to Lie with Statistics*, New York: W.W. Norton, 1954 (copyright renewed, 1982). This classic guide to interpreting and misinterpreting statistics is delightful reading with relevance to almost any field.

SPECIAL TOPICS IN MICROECONOMICS

One of the most popular topics of discussion in political and economic circles of the last decade is the ability of American firms to compete abroad. Numerous books have addressed competitiveness, industrial policy as a way to help our firms compete, the rise of Japan as a trade and industry rival, and related subjects. Here is a sampling of that literature:

Barfield, Claude E. and William A. Schambra, eds., *The Politics of Industrial Policy*, Washington, D.C.: American Enterprise Institute, 1986, offers a good survey of issues on industrial policy, domestic and international.

Prestowitz, Clyde V., Jr., *Trading Places: How We Allowed Japan to Take the Lead*, New York: Basic Books, 1988. This critical and thoughtful look at the consequences of U.S. trade and industrial policy vis-a-vis Japan is written by a former Commerce Department official.

Lawrence, Robert Z., *Can America Compete?*, Washington, D.C.: Brookings Institution, 1984, takes a careful look at myths and facts in the continuing debate over the relative decline of U.S. industry.

Obey, David, and Paul Sarbanes, eds., *The Changing American Economy*. New York: Basil Blackwell, 1986. A collection of readings and suggestions for policy change in the U.S. economy, stressing industrial policy as it is practiced in Europe and Japan.

Reich, Robert, *Tales of a New America*, New York: Times Books, 1986. Reich, the guru of the greening of America, looks at competitiveness and industrial policy.

Spence, A. Michael and Heather A. Hazard, *International Competitiveness*, Cambridge, MA: Ballinger Publishing, 1988, offer a collection of essays on international competition, with varying levels of sophistication. Most are accessible to the general reader.

Other international topics of interest center around the workings of international finance. A few suggested readings in that area:

Aliber, Rober Z., *The International Money Game*, 5th edition. New York: Basic Books, 1984. A well done and diverse reader on international monetary issues.

Pool, John Charles, and Steve Samos, *The ABCs of International Finance*, Lexington, MA: Lexington Books, 1987.

Individuals with an interest in marketing and consumer psychology might find the following books of interest:

Maital, Shlomo, *Minds, Markets, and Money*, New York: Basic Books, 1982. This unusual book blends economics and psychology to explore why people act as they do in working, saving, investing, and other forms of economic behavior.

Scitovsky, Tibor, *The Joyless Economy*, London: Oxford University Press, 1976, offers an interesting merger of economic theory and basic psychology that looks at the whole person and how that affects consumer behavior.

Business history is another fascinating area. Here is a sampler of reading in that area:

Chandler, Alfred D., Jr, *The Visible Hand*, Cambridge, MA: Harvard University Press, 1977, offers an influential history of the rise of modern management and big business, 1850-1920.

Hughes, Jonathan, *The Vital Few*, London: Oxford University Press, 1965, stresses the role of great entrepreneurs in the growth and development of the American economy.

McGraw, Thomas K., *Prophets of Regulation*, Cambridge, MA: Harvard University Press, 1984, is an unusual biographical history of regulation in America.

Owen, David, *The Man Who Invented Saturday Morning*, New York: Villard Books, 1988. This is a delightful collection of short essays on entrepreneurs, successful and unsuccessful business ventures in recent decades; must reading for the entrepreneurial business person.

A closely related book on entrepreneurship is

Herbert, Robert F. and Albert N. Link. *The Entrepreneur*, New York: Praeger Publishers, 1982 offers some good ideas about what it takes to be a successful entrepreneur.

Since business firms must deal with unions and/or labor on a regular basis, you may be interested in labor history and the goals of unions. Here are some possible resources in that area:

Freeman, Richard B. and James Medoff, *What Do Unions Do?*, New York: Basic Books, 1984. Designed for the general reader, this book looks at the purposes and workings of unions.

Hirsch, Barry T. and John T. Addison, *The Economic Analysis of Unions: New Approaches and Evidence*, Boston: Allen & Unwin, 1986. This book is somewhat more technical, looking at the actual experience with unions in the U.S. economy.

Another important area for microeconomics and managerial economics is market structure and public policy toward competition and monopoly. These topics are considered in the following books:

Adams, Walter and James Brock, *The Bigness Complex: Industry, Labor, and the American Economy*, New York: Pantheon, 1986. This book is critical of big firms and their efforts to get help and protection from government.

Asch, Peter, *Industrial Organization and Antitrust Policy*, revised edition, New York: John Wiley and Sons, 1983. A rather standard treatment of public policy toward large firms, designed for a college audience.

Scherer, R.M., *Industrial Market Structure and Economic Performance*, Chicago: Rand McNally, 1980. Also designed for a college audience, this book is a more detailed look at the issues raised in this book concerning monopoly, oligopoly, and monopolistic competition.

If you are curious about the development of economic ideas, some of the best writing in economics traces how economists, ideas, and events interacted to develop modern economic theory. Any of the following will give you an idea of how economic ideas developed in response to the questions facing society over the last 200 years:

Canterbery, E. Ray, *The Making of Economics*, 3rd edition. Belmont, CA: Wadsworth Publishing, 1987.

Breit, William and Roger L. Ransom, *The Academic Scribblers; Economists in Collision*, 2nd ed. Hinsdale, IL: Dryden Press, 1982.

Heilbroner, Robert L., *The Worldly Philosophers*, 6th edition. New York: Simon and Schuster, 1987.

Okior, Loren J., *Galbraith, Harrington, Heilbroner: Economics and Dissent in an Age of Optimism*, Princeton, NJ: Princeton University Press, 1988.

THINK TANKS AND OTHER RESOURCES

Economics is blessed with a full range of "think tanks" to contemplate policy, support policy-related research, and disseminate a variety of ideas. Think tanks range from the Hoover, Cato and Heritage Foundations on the conservative end of the spectrum through American Enterprise Institute and the Brookings Institution in the center to the Urban Institute on the liberal end. Most issue periodical papers, monographs, and books. Brookings puts forth *Economic Choices 19XX* most years, as well as *The Brookings Bulletin* and *Brookings Papers on Economic Activity* (the last two being more technical than the others). The Heritage Foundation offers a series of background papers on various issues as well as a journal, *Policy Review*. The Cato Institute offers *Cato Journal*. While each institute or think tank has a particular philosophical orientation and agenda, they are all useful sources of information and ideas.

CHAPTER PERSPECTIVE

Economics usually receives short shrift in typical mall or chain bookstores, with a shelf or two devoted to the latest get rich quick scheme. It takes a little searching to discover that there is, indeed, a flourishing popular literature in economics, available on order, in college bookstores and larger commercial bookstores, or from larger public libraries.[1] The list in this chapter should contain at least some items to appeal to the tastes and interests of even the fussiest reader. Like any form of literature, a few "favorite authors" will quickly lead you to their other works or related works, and you will be able to expand your reading list on your own. Remember, it is only with regular and continued exposure to good economics literature that you can maintain and expand the economics human capital you have developed by working through this book.

FOOTNOTE

1 *To the authors' knowledge, the only bookstore specializing in business, economics, and political science is Kramer's in Washington, D.C. You may want to check this store out if you are in the D.C. area.*

Index